THE ARCHITECTURE OF LIGHT

THE ARCHITECTURE OF LIGHT

ARCHITECTURAL LIGHTING DESIGN CONCEPTS AND TECHNIQUES

A TEXTBOOK OF PROCEDURES AND PRACTICES FOR THE
ARCHITECT, INTERIOR DESIGNER AND LIGHTING DESIGNER

SAGE RUSSELL

Conceptnine

CONCEPTNINE PRINT MEDIA

Library of Congress Cataloging in Publication Data

Russell, Sage.
The Architecture of Light / by Sage Russell.
p. cm.
Includes index.
ISBN-13: 978-0-9800617-0-3
ISBN-10: 0-9800617-0-9
Library of Congress Control Number: 2007942363
1. Electric lighting. 2. Lighting, Architectural and decorative. I. Title

ARC007010

1.2
10 9 8 7 6 5 4 3 2 1

Special thanks to the lighting designers, design instructors and mentors who have shaped my impression of light and how it affects design.
Most notably:

David DiLaura, for inspiring an unfailing interest in the science of illumination.

Patrick Quigley, the inspiration behind all things choreography related.

Greg Gorman, who taught me that light is responsible for beauty.

Nancy Clanton, a driving force in spreading the word about light and the environment.

Cynthia Burke, my longtime design colleague who gave me every opportunity to shine.

I would also like to extend a special thanks to my editors. Without these dedicated souls, there is no doubt that the content and legibility of this text would have suffered greatly. In the same breath I would like to absolve them of any responsibility for the information provided here. Any errors or erroneous content is purely the fault of the author.

Lastly,
This book is dedicated to my students and clients who indulge my sprawling monologues about design, art, culture, food, travel and everything else.

More teaching and learning resources can be found online at:

WWW.LIGHTINGTEXTBOOK.COM

Contents

Contents (Continued)

The Pitch

Light is truly a designer's medium. It is among the most powerful tools we have to affect change in how we perceive and experience the environment around us. Light belongs as a controllable tool of space design, just as form, scale, and material do. Light translates vision, and it is vision that gives us a major portion of our experiences.

This book delivers a unique type of training: one that makes designing with light an intuitive visual process that can deliver a whole new appreciation for the capabilities of architecture and design. Here one will find a procedure for conjuring ideas and the visual tools for translating those ideas. A designer with this type of understanding will be inspired and equipped to enrich his/her design through the application of light.

This knowledge is for architects, landscape architects, interior designers, planners and lighting designers aspiring to develop intuition and confidence in designing with light. It is these people who are responsible for bringing organization and emotional experience to the environments we interact with every day. The concepts and processes put forth in this book are intended to be immediately useful to any designer who wants to include light as an ally in design.

My goal in assembling this book is to provide information to the people who are poised to make the most of it. Often times, those who have the best chance of applying designed light to maximum effect are deprived of the necessary knowledge. Consequently, lighting decisions often fall by the wayside, and powerful design opportunities are missed.

Regardless of the designer's current familiarity with lighting design, this book will provide the reader with a more meaningful understanding of the role of light in the designed environment. Within these pages, one will find creative procedures and graphic techniques for generating and communicating lighting design concepts. This intuition and tool set will help the designer to make lighting design decisions with confidence and joy. My intention is not to create lighting technical experts, but rather to provide a working familiarity of the power and effect of light.

I hope to empower those with the opportunity to design with light to go forward with confidence, lay claim to light as a design tool, and use it to add impact and meaning to their design.

Sage Russell,
La Jolla, CA
2009

Part I
The Fundamentals of Light

Chapter 1

The Design Mentality

Before we go on to discuss how to apply light in the designed environment, we must look at how we consider design and how we come up with ideas. We must solidify our creative process. As designers, we are idea people. That is our nature; it is what people expect of us and what our clients ask of us. We are in the business of generating ideas. This task seems easy enough as humans are naturally blessed with creative spirit. There is an unfortunate tendency, however, for that spirit to be stifled in some people and nurtured in others. At some point, often childhood, a person is told that perhaps he/she is "just not artistic" or "not a creative person." In all cases, this claim is false. Creativity is human nature. When we call ourselves designers, we are telling the world that we have decided to nurture creativity and dedicate ourselves to the cultivation of ideas.

There are two procedures that are invaluable to anyone pursuing the creative capabilities of his/her mind: the common "brainstorm" and the process of reverse engineering design.

THE BRAINSTORM

Brainstorming is one of the most valuable processes in which an "idea person" can engage. It is the simple process of writing down any and all ideas that come to mind when thinking on a specific topic or challenge. There is one and only one fundamental rule to a brainstorm: *there are no wrong answers in a brainstorm*. This simple rule translates well to creativity and design because there are no wrong answers in design, simply ideas and possibilities that are more appropriate than others. The designer cannot afford to become too attached to one seemingly good idea. In the process of design, ideas are shot down for a myriad of reasons, and the designer must be ready with a head full of other ideas waiting to be expressed.

For a designer, the brainstorm is the freedom to conjure and cultivate any and all ideas that come to mind regarding a specific design challenge. These ideas are a product of that particular designer's background, education, past experiences, values, sources of inspiration, and beliefs about design. These ideas are as individual as the designer, and it is this uniqueness that compels people to seek out designers for ideas and solutions.

The necessary first step of the brainstorm is the process of writing all of these ideas down. Creating a list or diagram of ideas gets them out of one's head and onto paper. Emptying the head creates room for more ideas to germinate and keeps the same ideas from circulating and cluttering the mind. Jotting down these ideas also results in a permanent record of them, so that none will be lost in the dark corridors of the brain.

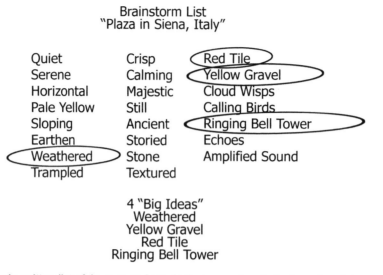

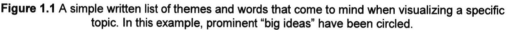

Brainstorm List
"Plaza in Siena, Italy"

Figure 1.1 A simple written list of themes and words that come to mind when visualizing a specific topic. In this example, prominent "big ideas" have been circled.

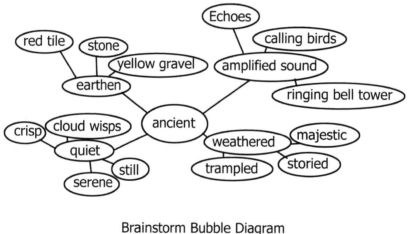

Brainstorm Bubble Diagram
"Plaza in Siena, Italy"

Figure 1.2 A bubble diagram shows the relationship between ideas as they progress.

The products of a brainstorm are proof that we all have great ideas. The dedicated designer is simply more diligent in cultivating ideas, writing them down, communicating them, and keeping track of them. If we don't allow ourselves free reign to conjure ideas, and get them down on paper, the ideas are lost forever, victims of the powerful forces of self censorship and self-criticism. Let it be said that in the land of design, there is no shortage of skeptics and critics to tell us that our ideas are too whimsical, too expensive, too time-consuming, or too unrealistic. If we expect that this refining of ideas will come from outside forces, it becomes very clear that we have no business critiquing them internally. Thus, we go forward, writing down ideas, concepts and solutions as fast as we can think of them, knowing that through the process of developing design, the best ideas will rise to the top.

The reward of this process is the confidence to propose ideas without fear of rejection. When we know that we have a long written list of great ideas, and a brain that can conjure new ones at will, then we are much more productive when engaged with others in the process of refining them. We are neither dismayed nor dejected when our ideas are deemed unsuitable. We see criticism as a challenge, rather than a threat. This welcoming of feedback and "thick skin" is one of the most valuable traits of a skilled designer.

Making a regular habit of Brainstorming develops the creative productivity and flexibility that are the foundation of a designer's confidence and skill.

REVERSE ENGINEERING FROM DESIGN

The process of reverse engineering is exactly as its name indicates. It is a tool of dissecting something to discover what makes it work. Take, for example, a guitar maker who takes apart a beautiful acoustic guitar to identify exactly how that guitar gets its woody, slightly hollow sound. Upon dissection, it is discovered that the sound is the product of a veneer of rare Sumatran Teak wood bonded to the inside. The guitar maker can now incorporate this simple feature in constructing guitars in the future whenever the same sound is desired. How, you may ask, does this anecdote apply to the design mentality? The answer lies in the belief that as designers dealing in the realm of the built environment, we are responsible for designing spaces that compel interaction and elicit emotion. Besides the basic function of the spaces we design, we care most about how people feel and, therefore, how they behave and interact with our design.

We experience designed environments and the natural world around us everyday and thus have the opportunity to reverse engineer design everyday. What we, as designers, can do to make use of this skill is to take the time to identify how we feel in our environment and what is at work to make us feel that way. Dissecting our experiences in this way has three distinct steps:

Step 1: Experience life

Go places, meet people, and put ourselves in as many engaging situations as possible. This act is really a byproduct of life, and it is safe to say that nearly everyone does so simply by leaving the house each day.

Step 2: Assess the emotional effect

This step takes a little more dedication. It is the exercise of taking stock of your feelings or emotional state in a given situation or environment. This skill is the sort we credit poets, artists and philosophers as possessing. Assessing how one feels is not automatic, and there are certainly people who go about their daily lives never stopping to realize how an environment affects them.

Step 3: Identify the mechanisms responsible for the emotional effect

This step takes the time to identify what about the situation or environment is causing the emotional response we are experiencing. It is a mental step in which only a few engage.

An example of this thought process might occur as follows:

Anyone can stand at the edge of a slow moving creek in the woods.

An enlightened person might take the time to realize the sense of peace, calm, tranquility and connection to nature that is present.

It is the designer who takes the time to recognize that these feelings are the product of the shifting breeze rustling in the reeds; the glint and flicker of sunlight on the water surface; and the earthy hues of green, brown and yellows.

With this awareness, when the designer is called upon to create an environment that delivers a feeling of calm, tranquility and peace, he or she knows that earthy tones, natural materials, and a specific quality of light and shade will provide the desired emotional response.

These ingredients do not need to be translated literally, but knowledge of them will bring us one step closer to a design solution possessing depth, context and permanence.

To practice this procedure, we can take any piece of imagery, song, or film and dissect it to figure out why it works. In music, art and film, nothing is done by accident, and each ingredient contributes to a specific effect.

Watch a favorite film or listen to a favorite song. Study these things with the intent of identifying the emotions induced and then identifying the mechanisms responsible for the emotion. What becomes immediately apparent is that light quantity and quality play a dominant role in how we visualize an environment.

After one experiences this art or design with this goal in mind, make a chart on a piece of paper. On the left side of the paper, start a column titled "Emotion and Feeling." Fill this column with the many identifiable feelings associated with the design. On the right side of this paper, start a column titled "Mechanism Responsible." Take the time to identify what specific ingredients were responsible for the emotions and feeling. Is it a perspective or a point of view? Is it a tone or tempo or beat? Is it a specific color, texture, or quality of light? Identifying these ingredients puts the designer on a path to calling on them to create a predictable effect in his/her own design.

Reverse Engineering Design
"The Interogation Room"

Emotion / Feeling	Mechanism Responsible
exposed	mirror wall
nervous	bright light
on edge	buzzing light
being watched	echoes
artificial	hard surfaces
controlled	no furniture
confined	heavy door
threatened	standing men
helpless	cheap materials

Figure 1.4 Dissecting an environment gives one specific ingredients for use later to create a similar emotional experience.

If we can adopt the habit of reverse engineering the world around us, we can quickly hone our skills as creative thinkers and designers. Once we have taken the time to identify the mechanisms that work in an environment to create certain feelings, we can use those mechanisms to create the same effect in our own design. In this manner, the designer builds an ever-growing toolbox of techniques and ingredients that can be put to use to elicit a predictable effect. The designer gains the ability to translate the feelings of an environment into tangible, tactile ingredients that can be injected into any setting.

As we move forward and discuss the specific nuances and effects we can encourage with light, let us keep these two tools as part of our everyday design process. Our techniques for cultivating and expressing lighting design ideas are quite specific, but let us always make use of these fundamental skills. Design starts with the ability to conjure ideas without self censure and the awareness to constantly figure out why our favorite environments work the way they do. If we can incorporate these tools as habits, we will be much better prepared to provide the constant flow of ideas and concepts that people expect of us.

Chapter 2

The Power and Purpose of Light

Because our journey is one of enriching and enhancing our designs with light, we will first take some time to establish why light is such a useful tool in creating emotion and altering our perception of the world around us. There is an indoctrination required so that we move forward with an unfailing faith in the power of light to affect design.

WHY WE STUDY LIGHT

In the built environment, it is safe to say that the majority of our experiences are visual. Sound, smell, and touch certainly play various roles, but the typical person relies on vision to deliver a very large quantity of information.

Vision, by its very nature, is a product of light. It is the result of the creation of light, the reflection of light, and, ultimately, the absorption of light by our visual system. Logic dictates then that if we want to have maximum control of the designed environment, we must become intimate with light and learn to make it our ally in translating design.

Light can quickly and powerfully alter the appearance and emotional effect of our designed spaces. A designer can spend any amount of time refining the layout of a space, the scale of a space, the materials and finishes of a space. However with a few simple strokes, lighting can be added that will truly enhance or utterly destroy the desired effect. A designer may envision a meditation lodge fashioned from bamboo sheathing with natural river rock floor. The lodge may have heavy dark wood furniture and oiled, bronze hardware and accents. Despite the effort and attention to detail, we can change the emotional effect in a heartbeat by installing red strobe lights and a disco ball. An extreme example, to be sure, but the point is valid. If one wants to change the mood of a space, change the lighting. If one wants to change the scale of a space, change the lighting. If one wants to change the color of a space, change the lighting. Once you recognize how many aspects there are to light, you start to understand that it serves as an efficient, effective, and powerful way to accomplish a design goal. With just a basic understanding of the colors, intensities, and textures of light, a designer gains an understanding of which types of light support, and which will detract from a project's design goals.

THE CONTROLLABLE ASPECTS OF LIGHT: BEYOND ON AND OFF

Light is much more than we give it credit for, and it deserves to be treated with the care of any design medium. Just as a designer takes care in making decisions about the nuances and subtleties of color and material, so, too, must he/she take care in making decisions about light. Light can be controlled to a much higher degree than is commonly considered. To make the most of light, we must investigate what we can control about our light. There are a handful of properties that must be addressed in order to make a well-thought-out lighting decision. Every piece of light we add to an environment must be considered in terms of three basic properties: Intensity, Color, and Texture.

Light Intensity: Bright vs. Dark.

Intensity is the most obvious and well understood aspect of light. It is one step beyond simply on or off: is this light dim, or is it bright? We tend to associate low light levels with more relaxed, intimate, personal environments. We translate higher light levels to be more sterile, public, active, and kinetic.

Figure 2.1 Higher light levels (left) translate an exposed, public feeling. Low light levels (right) translate calm and privacy.

Light Color: Warm vs. Cool.

There are a number of ways to alter the color of our light sources both subtly and overtly. Lighting sources can exhibit all manner of different color temperatures, warm or cool, as slight variations of neutral. Our light sources can also be modified to exhibit very saturated, vivid colors. These colors have varying effect on mood, depending on a person's experiences, culture and conditioning. Color and color temperature can determine whether a person feels comfortable enough to linger in an environment or whether he/she is driven away. Color can immediately affect mood and state of mind. Warm lighting colors, yellows and reds, tend to elicit calm, relaxation and a slower pace of action. Cool colors, blues, tend to elicit activity and create a productive pace. Distinctly saturated colors get used in our high-design, themed environment because they create visual interest and a unique experience.

Figure 2.2 Warm Light (left) and cool light (right) should be chosen for the way they reveal the colors and materials in a space, and the mood desired.

Light Texture: Directional vs. Diffuse.

Texture is perhaps the least understood or considered aspect of light. The texture of the light we introduce into a space has a dramatic effect on the overall feeling and function. When we speak of light texture, we are talking about the way that light is delivered from the source. On one end of the spectrum we have soft, even, diffuse light that is the product of luminaires that incorporate diffusers. On the other end of the spectrum we have the harsh, directional light that is the product of luminaires that utilize precision reflectors and lenses that deliver light in a specific direction. Think of an average glowing globe (diffuse) versus a directed spot light (directional).

Figure 2.3 Strongly colored light grabs our attention and transports us away from the ordinary, neutral environments we are used to.

The significant differences between the two textures manifest in the shadows and the shapes of light created by these sources.

Diffuse sources produce light that overlaps to fill in shadows and has ill-defined borders as the light sprawls from the source. *Directional* sources create distinct shapes of light with clear boundaries. Use of directional light results in harsh shadows and contrast as that light is either delivered or blocked completely by an object.

Figure 2.4 Diffuse light (left) reduces shadows and encourages long term visual comfort.
Directional light (right) creates contrast and visual interest.

Once we expand our thinking to recognize these three properties, we start to get a glimpse of the depth of decision-making that is required to ensure that the light we are adding to a space is working toward our design goals.

When we refer back to the notion that designers are in charge of encouraging emotion, we can begin to see that for every emotion that can be described, there is a corresponding *light intensity*, *light color*, and *light texture* that successfully encourages that emotion. When we want to create relaxed, calm, soothing environments, we implement lower light levels, warmer light colors, and more diffuse sources. When we are designing more kinetic, active, productive spaces, we apply higher light levels, cooler light, and more directional sources. Much of what we will be adding to our knowledge of light revolves around articulating lighting decisions like these to encourage deeper thought about the light we add. In this manner, we utilize light to its fullest potential in our design.

MAKING LIGHTING DECISIONS THROUGHOUT THE DESIGN PROCESS

An articulate approach to making lighting decisions is most effective when applied within the frame work of one of our favorite maxims: "Make lighting design decisions at every step of the design process." Far too often, architects and designers design in the dark. They often embark on a path of design, design, design, and once the space is completely "designed," it is then "lit up."

The thought process that is implemented in this text is nearly the opposite. A designer should look for every opportunity to think about how light should be used in a design. Light can certainly be "applied" to an already-designed space, but the result will never reach the level of greatness that is possible when light is *integrated* into a project every step of the way. For design to transition to greatness, lighting has to be considered at each significant design juncture. The great design projects that we admire come from all realms of taste and style, but the one thing they share is thoughtful lighting integration.

For every design decision, there is a lighting decision to be made that can either support or erode the design. The more comfortable a designer becomes with light, the more likely that designer is to automatically consider light in the decision-making process. For every form decision, scale decision, material decision and color decision, there is a complementary lighting decision. If these lighting decisions are made through the design process, the result is a depth of design that cannot be obtained by simply pouring light onto a completely designed project.

HOW HUMANS USE LIGHT

To warm ourselves up to the notion of the importance of light, it is useful to account for some of the ways human beings react and respond to light. Once we recognize how we use light in our daily lives, we can start to produce very sophisticated effects through our lighting decisions. Because of our long-standing relationship with light, it has the power to affect our subconscious in ways that no other medium can. It this subconscious relationship that provides our most powerful lighting tools. When we consider how long humankind has spent experiencing light, we can begin to appreciate all of the ways that light is utilized beyond simply "seeing."

It is important to recognize that for the vast majority of our history here on earth we, as humans, have grown accustomed to the sun as our primary source of light. In all of its incarnations; sunrise, sunset, high-noon, shaded and diffused, the sun is responsible for most of our responses to light. This relationship explains why we rely on the light quality in our environment to inform so many of our behavioral cues.

Light as Mood

We rely on light both consciously and subconsciously to tell us the level of activity and the type of mood we should carry into a space. These effects likely relate back to light qualities that we associate with different times of day, as well as light qualities of different seasons. As discussed earlier, we all have an innate understanding of the types of light conducive to activity and excitement, as well as light that encourages calm and relaxation. These light qualities can be extended to encourage moods of sadness and depression or happiness and joy. Humans rely on light to inform them of the time of day and consequently, the mood and activities that should follow. Light quality may remind us of seasons that call for celebration or seasons that call for work and diligence. There is extensive study of how specific wavelengths (colors) of light affect our well-being and how light deficiencies negatively affect our physiology. All of these topics become critical when implementing modern electric light sources and making use of daylight.

Light as Instruction

Through experience and conditioning, humans have also developed movement and location responses that we derive directly from light. We use light to instruct us where to go, what areas to move toward and what paths to follow. We read the angle and intensity of sunlight to tell us where we are geographically. Designers can increase light levels to define areas that people belong in and subsequently leave dark those areas in-which people do not belong. Colors of light can be used as cues to stop or proceed. Flashing light can be used to grab attention or warn people away. These effects all rely on the controllable aspects of light discussed earlier. To make use of these powerful responses, the designer must also consider specific shapes, specific patterns, and specific movements of light.

ATTRACTION TO LIGHT: PHOTOTROPISM

The most powerful human response to light is the most simple: it is the fundamental *attraction* that humans have toward light and lighted spaces. Just like moths to a flame, we drift towards areas of brightness. This unconscious desire is significant because it is instinctual. It differs from our response to many other elements of design that are a product of taste, trend or favor. We are told that the human affinity for light is a mechanism of survival. This instinct has a name: we call it *Phototropism* (Latin for Light-attracted). This very simple response means that at the most fundamental level of design, by simply putting light in the right place, we can help direct people's path of experience and encourage their interaction with the space. Many of the lighting effects we will employ rely on this one simple premise of human behavior.

Image courtesy of Erco   www.erco.com

Figure 2.5 When put to use correctly, lighted surfaces serve to make way-finding intuitive.

In order to appreciate the effectiveness of using light to attract people and guide their experience, it is helpful to investigate why humans may have developed this type of response. On a very basic level, it is about vision. The human visual system is very finely tuned for translating light in the environment. As the saying goes, a picture is worth a thousand words. It is safe to say that seeing is one of the fastest ways to learn about the world around us. It is because of this dependency that our brains are always encouraging us to pursue areas that have more visual information, that is, lighted areas. The brain believes that the more we see, the better our experience in life will be. No doubt, there is also the residual belief that the more we can see, the more likely we are to find food, shelter, companionship, and the less likely we are to be eaten by predators.

When we investigate all of these emotional and behavioral effects that are unique to light, we see that there is much more to light than just sufficient quantity. In the realm of architecture and design, we can do much more than simply add light to a space so that people can function and perform visual tasks. Throughout this text, the knowledge that we will be exploring is based on making decisions about *what we want light to do* in a space.

Anything we introduce as design has to have justification for being, so we *justify* light by identifying the many benefits it serves in an environment. We then study the different types of light over which we have control. Lighting design then becomes the process of conceptualizing *what* light should be accomplishing in a space and *how and where* that light should be delivered.

Chapter 3

More Impact with Less Light

The most notable aspect of lighting design is *where light is directed*. As we deepen our understanding of how humans translate light to vision and ultimately experience, we become acutely aware of how to maximize the desired experience of our design through careful placement of light.

We live in a time when the resources required for electric light are becoming scarcer and more costly. In the design and construction industry, this trend has already led to significant study and legislation that controls how much electricity we dedicate to electric light. This concern for consumption usually takes the form of recommendations for light levels applied to tasks and environments. These studies and guidelines for how much light is appropriate for specific visual tasks are useful, but designers of complex spaces are likely to deal with far more than simply visual task performance. Some spaces can be effectively addressed by studying a visual task, like preparing food or filing paper work, and determining the exact amount of light appropriate for that task. A designer concerned with the overall experience, mood, interaction and visual impact of space, must take a much more holistic approach that involves putting the right intensity, color and texture of light onto the right surfaces to create maximum effect. When we place light with care, the result is a more profound statement likely created with less total light.

This *designerly* application of light has its foundation in four important relationships between light and human color vision:

1. Adaptation: adapting to bright or dark situations;

2. Brightness: contrast between surfaces and their surroundings;

3. Phototropism: attraction to lighted surfaces and objects;

4. Vertical Vision: tendency to look around us rather than up or down.

Relying on Adaptation

Adaptation refers to the ability of the human vision system to perform well under different light levels. All of us have experienced the phenomena of waiting for our visual system to adjust from one lighting scenario to another. When we walk from a sunlit parking lot to a darkened move theater, our eyes and brains work together to maximize the quantity of light entering our visual system. When we transition from the dark theater back to the bright parking lot, our eyes and brains work to limit the amount of light being translated. Although in both cases, this process takes time, eventually, our eyes and brains adjust so that we are able to function in both situations. The light levels that we are dealing with in the two extremes are drastically different. The variation between light levels under a high noon sky and a moonlit night are on the order of tens of thousands Hence, It is truly amazing that we are capable of reading a book in both of these situations.

The design implications of this adaptation work tremendously in our favor. Because our visual system is constantly at work adjust to the surrounding light levels, we can deduce that excess light introduced into a space loses effectiveness as our visual system works to adapt and even-out our experience. Thus, we can likely get away with far less light in many spaces as our visual system will change to make the most of what light is available.

These effects are most noticeable in evenly-lighted enclosed spaces. A room filled with flat, even light will appear very similar, no matter the light level, as the visual system adjusts.

Adaptation also tells us that a space full of surfaces receiving different amounts of light will always exhibit contrast, no matter what the actual light levels are.

Brightness through Contrast

Brightness is a common term used to describe the lighted effect of the surfaces in our day to day environments. Brightness is not, however, an absolute property of a surface. Because the human visual system adapts to each lighted situation, brightness is a subjective judgment made by an individual in a specific lighting situation. It is valuable to understand that *contrast* between objects is what defines vision and drives our brightness judgments. Our eyes tell us where one object begins and another ends because the objects reflect light differently. When we read a book, the dark ink reflects less light than the white paper, and we can distinguish the shapes of the letters on the page. As we apply more light to the pages of the book, the white paper reflects more light and appears brighter, while the dark text continues to reflect very little light. A simpler example is the corner of any room. Inevitably, we can tell where one wall meets the other because of the contrast between the two surfaces. If two intersecting walls exhibited the same brightness, our perception would be of one continuous surface. When we apply higher light levels to visual tasks or accented objects, it is an attempt to improve visibility by increasing the contrast between the objects or materials. Objects are not visible simply because they have light cast onto them; they are visible because they stand out from their surroundings.

Using Phototropism to draw attention

As discussed in Chapter 2, phototropism is the studied notion that human beings are attracted to light as a matter of instinct. This simple instinct can be relied upon to draw attention to the surfaces and spaces with which we want people to interact. Phototropism suggests that despite conditioning and expectation, in a room full of detailed furniture, intricate flooring, wall coverings and tile mosaics, the object that the casual observer will notice first is the shaded table lamp glowing in the corner. With this understanding, we realize that we have predictable control over where a viewer's attention is drawn in our designed spaces. Phototropism dictates that the eye of the observer will move from the brightest surface to the next brightest surface. It means that we can often convince an observer that a space is bright by simply drawing his/her attention to a few large, bright surfaces.

Lighting Vertical Surfaces

The third tool of human perception on which we rely is the premise that the human visual system is designed to translate the light reflecting off of the surfaces around it. The eyes aren't able to do much with the high levels of light that come directly from a light source. Thus, the perception of the brightness of a space has more to do with the light detected from the surrounding surfaces than the brightness of the light sources. This concept is exemplified by a stage performer under a spot light. This person has a large amount of light cast onto him/her, but he/she still feels like they are in the dark. Another example is a simple room with a glowing chandelier in the middle. The chandelier may attract attention, but it does not necessarily make a space feel bright.

Because we are upright, standing creatures, we rely on the light reflecting from the *vertical surfaces* that make up our surroundings and define our peripheral vision. In most of our day to day activities, our field of vision is focused directly in front of us. Even when we look around us, we are using the upright, vertical surfaces of our surroundings to define our environment. The feelings of confinement or freedom and overall light quality are defined by the conditions of the walls, ceilings, horizons and sky conditions around us. The only time we look down is to assess the safety of the path in front of us, so the only time we really need to apply light down and around us is to illuminate such paths.

Humans do not define brightness by the light level on the ground around them, and they do not define brightness by the light focused directly onto them. As upright, mobile creatures geared to learn from reflected light, we naturally focus on the upright, reflective surfaces around us to define our impression of place. If our goal is to create an impression of brightness, light applied around us will serve much better than light directed on us.

Figure 3.1 Light applied to vertical surfaces (left) increases the perception of brightness compared to the same amount of light applied downward (right).

A Summary of Our Lighting Tactics

Vision will adapt to make the most of low light levels and to mitigate excessively high light levels.

Brightness is a subjective judgment based on contrast between surfaces.

Human beings are instinctively attracted to bright surfaces, areas and objects.

Humans gain their definition of brightness from the vertical surfaces around them.

These four elements of human perception work together to form the foundation of how we design light into our environments.

With this basis, our design approach becomes a study of how to create maximum effect by directing light onto a few specific surfaces. This approach starts with identifying the surfaces that will best respond to light. Where can we create lighted goals to draw people through spaces? Where can we enhance the perception of brightness by lighting vertical surfaces and objects? Where can we rely on contrast of light levels to create visual interest? By answering these questions, we will create dynamic, visually-interesting spaces by painting specific *pieces* of light onto specific surfaces to accomplish the lighting design goals of a space. This lighting approach is the very opposite of creating even washes of high light levels to define a space. To accommodate the specific placement of light, many of the lighting tools available to the designer are discreet, architecturally-integrated luminaires that deliver a focused pool or plane of light onto a specific surface. By employing these hidden, directional light sources, we define our environment as a collection of lighted surfaces, rather than a collection of overly-bright light sources or a flat field of generic even brightness.

Because we spend so much time in offices and classrooms that typically have an even level of light throughout, we come to think that this design is the *correct* or *safe* way to light a space. However, as we learn to articulate our lighting goals, it becomes clear that the only reason spaces are treated with these even light levels is so that a person may conceivably sit down anywhere and perform a visual task for a long period of time. Because of this, we launch into our education with the understanding that light is our medium or more accurately that *lighted surfaces* are our medium. This simple building method of designing specific pieces of light will guide all of our designs.

THE FUNDAMENTAL TWO-STEP PROCEDURE OF LIGHTING DESIGN

This improvement in lighting understanding can be defined by a 2-step procedure of lighting design that we will adopt: Lighting specifics first and augmenting the ambience second.

Step 1: Light Specifics First

This step means taking time to recognize where we want to put light. We first identify the tasks, accents and local visual effects that are integral to our design. We visualize ourselves with the ability to "paint" light onto these surfaces as if with a paintbrush or spray can.

Figure 3.2 An unlighted space (left) with light mentally "painted" onto its surfaces (right).

Figure 3.3 How the lighted effect might look (left),
How it might look with an added ambient ingredient (right).

After lighting specifics, we assess the effect. After we have defined these surfaces and applied light to them, we step back and look at the overall lighted effect of our designed space. Every piece of light we direct into our space not only lights the intended surface, but goes on to bounce around and slowly fill our space with light. Understanding this "inter-reflectance" is crucial to visualizing how we are building light into our space

Step 2: Augment the Ambience or Perception of Brightness

It is only *after* we have assessed the overall effect of lighting our specific surfaces that we can determine whether our space needs supplemental lighting to introduce a different spatial ambience.

If we do determine a need for a greater overall perception of brightness, we now know that light onto the vertical surfaces will most efficiently achieve the goal.

YOU CANNOT LIGHT AIR

This procedure is in stark contrast to the idea of "filling up" a space with light only to go back trying to create visual interest after the fact. Our understanding of adaptation tells us that vision is based on contrast. We discern detail not by how much light is on an object, but how bright that object is compared to its surroundings. A statue that is twice as bright as the wall behind it will grab our attention, regardless of the actual measured light level. Therefore, if we flood our spaces with light first, we will end up wasting that much more light trying to draw out surfaces and objects within the already bright space. We find that if we identify and paint light onto specific surfaces and objects first, our lighting design falls into place more easily.

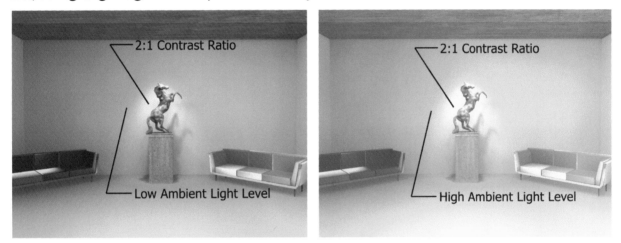

Figure 3.5 The 2-to-1 accent ratio (left) remains the same when light is added uniformly (right). Visual interest is created when the contrast is bumped up (below).

When our 2-step procedure is implemented, the result is a designed space filled with emotional impact, engaging visual interest, and logic. We create design that truly encourages interaction. This logic can prove useful even for our open office spaces and classrooms, but is exceptionally effective in our high-design interactive environments where visual impact and emotional effect are the primary programs.

The magic of this procedure and understanding is that it requires no knowledge of lighting products and technologies. It uses no calculations or light level measurement. Lighting in this manner is simply a change in perspective and understanding that will allow

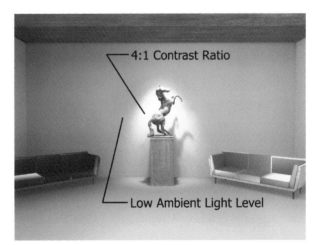

one to assess lighted effect better and to better define the lighting needs of a space.

We will build off of this procedure by introducing a system of determining where light belongs and articulating lighting goals. This simple, two-step process of lighting specifics first and then augmenting ambience will remain as the foundation.

Chapter 4

Adding Light in Layers

The design discipline is not nearly as spontaneous a craft as one would want to believe. Like all good art forms, design is much less an explosion of sudden creativity and much more a product of procedure and understanding. As designers concerned with light, we look to enrich our craft by expanding our possibilities to create room for great ideas. The maxim "form follows function" is as true in lighting as in any design discipline. To truly master lighting is to conjure up justifications for why we add light to a space. Design must have a reason for being, and to create opportunity for good design, we elaborate on the reasons for lighting to "be."

We touched before on the important mental practice of making lighting decisions *throughout* the architectural and interior design processes. To facilitate this goal, we will give ourselves as many opportunities as possible to stop and look at our design with fresh eyes. If we break up the process and focus on one aspect of light at a time, we have more opportunity to ponder the specific pieces of light that can be used to support our design goals.

One of the beauties of design is that there are no "wrong" answers, simply ideas that are not well thought through. If we study our ideas over a long enough period of time, the great ideas are sure to rise to the top. In lighting the best lighting is that which has been thought through, and the only wrong lighting is that which has not.

To truly get a feel for the importance of light integration, we need only visualize how powerful light is at changing the effect of a space. The moods of architecture are often subtle, and light can have a swift and potent effect on design. We must be keenly aware of what design goals are best fulfilled by light and what light is responsible for in our designed environment.

To these ends, the lighting procedure that we will implement is a method of identifying the reasons we add light to a space, and looking at them individually. This procedure has been refined and laid out here as a system of adding light in five distinct layers

THE FIVE LAYER APPROACH TO LAYERING LIGHT

Layer 1: Lighting to choreograph an experience

Use light to create goals, paths and destinations to encourage flow and movement

Layer 2: Lighting to define mood and ambience

Add intensity, color and texture to elicit emotion and encourage a specific use in a space

Layer 3: Lighting to accent objects

Create light that draws visual interest and encourages interaction by making interesting objects stand out even more.

Layer 4: Lighting to reveal architecture and space

Apply light to the features and details of a space to enhance spatial effects and reveal the mechanics of structure and form

Layer 5: Lighting for tasks.

Apply light to task areas to accommodate the basic functions of space

In a perfect world, the designer has the opportunity to look at these layers one at a time, with a mental break in-between each. For a lighting designer, the ideal situation is to surround oneself with the plans, elevations, diagrams and renderings that define the project. The designer then sets out to generate ideas for added light that might choreograph an experience through the space (layer 1). After exhausting those ideas, the designer takes a break. The designer then returns to the design and thinks of additions of light that contribute to mood and environment (layer 2). And so the process goes, designing with a specific purpose in mind, looking at the project each time with fresh eyes. This ideal is not always realistic, but to make the most of a layering system of design, each step should be addressed individually.

If we stare at a designed space and think merely of "lighting it up" in one fell swoop, we are bound to come up with generic lighting solutions based on utility and fear.

Just like a chef adds specific ingredients and flavors throughout the preparation of a meal, applying our designed light in layers gives us a depth of design that is not immediately obvious, and certainly not possible if we try to apply all of these ideas in one pass towards the end of the design process.

These layers will be outlined here to give an impression of just how much can be accomplished with each of them. The power of each layer will become evident as we go on to study the nuances of light and how humans interact with it. With the layer system to guide our thought process, lighting ideas come easily and with purpose. Our design process is more comfortable, and results are much more certain. This system is the single best tool I know of for empowering *any* designer to take command of how light is added to the designed environment.

LAYER 1: LIGHTING TO CHOREOGRAPH AN EXPERIENCE

To choreograph is to direct movement. In architecture we find ourselves responsible for encouraging people to flow though space in a specific manner. Thus the application of choreography is simply determining how we want a viewer to move through and interact with our design. Humans are phototropic. We are instinctively drawn to bright surfaces and objects. With this knowledge, we use the power of light to subconsciously convince a person to move toward a specific area just by placing light in that area. When we want to encourage flow, we can resort to blunt methods like signage and directional cues, or we can rely on the subtle, but powerful, human attraction to light.

The practice is as simple as lighting what we want people to move towards and leaving dark what we want them to move away from. In this manner, we use lighted end-points or goals to move people through a space. We place light at the ends of halls or light onto the entrance of a building. We light the far end of a room, and we light the coffee table in a gathering area. We find ways to use a single, lighted surface to attract attention where we might previously have illuminated an entire path. In this manner, choreographing attention and flow is one of the ways we reduce how much light we introduce into a space. For every directed movement that we want, we identify the one surface that will encourage that movement when lighted. When we want to draw attention and create visual hierarchy, we identify the few specific objects that we can light to accomplish this goal. When we combine this specific light placement strategy with our knowledge of the upright nature of human vision, we find that vertical surfaces, walls, partitions, furniture, and art features are the most effective surfaces for our choreography purposes. Suddenly, we find our space already taking form with visual interest created through identifying which specific vertical surfaces and central elements serve our choreography goals. Although choreography planning is but one layer of five, once applied, we already have a space that is intuitively self-guiding and has logical flow.

Images courtesy of Deltalight   www.deltalight.us

Figure 4.1 Lighting vertical surfaces and objects is an effective means of encouraging people to move towards a specific goal.

LAYER 2: LIGHTING TO DEFINE MOOD AND AMBIENCE

The second layer we study is the application of light into our space for the sole purpose of altering the emotional state of the viewer. It is easy to visualize how easily light can change the overall color, scale, or texture of a space. We get to work identifying the mood we want to create, and identifying lighting ingredients that will support that mood. Adding light to affect mood is a study in the controllable aspects of light and requires deliberate decision making. Remember the basic aspects of light that we use to guide our decisions:

Intensity: Dim vs. Bright.

Color: Warm vs. Cool (Or an obvious color).

Texture: Directional vs. Diffuse.

When we use this awareness to include an intensity decision, color decision and texture decision in each piece of light we add to a space, we can be sure that the light is sympathetic to the mood we want to create.

The idea is to approach our design on a room-by-room or area-by-area basis and determine the mood and emotional effect we desire for each of these spaces.

These subtle characteristics must be thought of for every piece of light that we introduce to avoid applying light that is accidentally in conflict with the desired mood. When we notice that cool fluorescent sources aren't conducive to intimate residential settings, we are simply addressing one aspect (in this case the color) that has not been considered carefully. We can look at numerous examples of light that are working against the desired emotion in a space, and very often it is only one of these three controllable aspects (intensity, color, texture) that has been neglected. Therefore, with only a minor change, the light could be remedied to contribute positively to the desired feeling.

This second layer will give you the opportunity to make meaningful decisions about the core qualities of light. It will also encourage you to articulate the specific intent of each designed area.

Image courtesy of Deltalight   www.deltalight.us

Image courtesy of Erco   www.erco.com

Figure 4.2 A few unusual applications of light can greatly affect the mood of a space.

LAYER 3: LIGHTING TO ACCENT OBJECTS

The third layer we tackle is, arguably, the most intuitive and readily-recognized. We are simply addressing light that we add to already-interesting objects and surfaces solely for the purpose of making those things *more noticeable*. The phototropic nature of humans can be used to draw human movement, but it is also effective on a small scale by drawing visual attention. By placing discreet shapes of light onto the objects in our space, we are creating a visual logic that will dictate how a viewer's eye travels over the visual landscape of our design. We can dictate a subconscious visual path from an accented wall mural, to a crystal chandelier, to a perfectly-appointed dining table. This organization of visual interest encourages a visitor to experience the environment in a specific order, taking time to interact with the design.

When we accent the objects in our space, we are also making decisions about what type of light is appropriate for that object. This encourages an understanding of the materials of our design and whether they respond better to particular intensities, colors and textures of accenting light. If we are interested in revealing texture, we want to use more directional light at steeper angles. If we want to conceal texture, we use more diffuse sources that scatter light in many directions. We should even be thinking of the shape of the light that we are casting onto an object.

When we speak of accenting objects to create visual interest and logic, we are also speaking about the decorative light sources that we use to add focus and sparkle to a space. Decorative pendants and wall sconces can serve as points of interest on their own.

When applied with care, the application of light to accent objects is yet another way we focus light onto specific objects to reduce the amount of light that we need to create visual clarity and function in our design.

Image courtesy of Erco   www.erco.com

Figure 4.3 Distinct pieces and shapes of light add to the interest of existing objects and materials.

LAYER 4: LIGHTING TO REVEAL ARCHITECTURE AND SPACE

The fourth layer of lighting in our system addresses light which defines, accentuates, and articulates the architectural effects and details that we have taken the time to design into our space. Vision is entirely dependant on light, so it is reasonable to say that the greatest of architectural concepts and spatial effects can be rendered meaningless without the proper application of light. With our understanding of the effects of light onto vertical surfaces, we are equipped to make meaningful decisions. Revealing architecture also requires us to think about the shape of the light we are creating. It is also an opportunity to think about where the light appears to be coming from.

Using light to affect and accentuate architectural decisions takes the form of two disciplines: lighting to define the architectural character and lighting to accent architectural details.

Image courtesy of Burke Lighting Design
www.burkelighting.com

Lighting to define spatial character

The first step to affecting architectural perception is to decide on a room-by-room basis just how we want a space to be considered. We must decide whether we want a space to feel tall and expansive, confining and intimate, wide and sweeping, etcetera. After we go to lengths to place our boundaries and objects in a manner that delivers a particular feeling of space, we can apply light to appropriate surfaces to enhance the desired effect.

We can wash light onto ceilings to define the height of a space. We can light the walls of a space to reveal the boundaries, or we can leave them dark to eliminate the perception of confinement. The application of light onto a specific set of architectural boundaries and surfaces carries a distinct spatial impact. We must take care and put purpose into our decision of how we treat each area. It is important to recognize that where light originates from has a significant impact on how people perceive a space and how they feel in a space. Humans are comfortably conditioned to the idea of light streaming down onto the world from the sky above. The advent of architectural lighting tools means that we can trump expectation and create light that emanates from the ground, wall, furniture, or wherever we choose.

Lighting to accent architectural details and features

The second element of revealing architecture is to identify the nuances and architectural features that help define what makes up a space. We are looking for the columns and soffits that define a space or the coves and coffers that we can highlight to define shape. Most of these architectural features will jump out at us from our plans and sketches. We treat them much the same as we treat other accentable objects. The only difference is that in addition to lighting them just to draw attention, we are helping to define what a space or structure is built from and how it is supported.

Image courtesy of Deltalight   www.deltalight.us

Figure 4.4 A few well-placed pieces of light add dimension and depth to architecture.

LAYER 5: LIGHTING FOR TASKS

The last layer that we discuss in our course of five layers is the light that we introduce to a space strictly for the sake of performing visual tasks. These tasks can be as articulate as reading paperwork or as subtle as navigating a lobby. We save this thought process for last because as we apply light to address all of the previous layers, it is likely that the light will interact with our space to deliver the light necessary for our visual tasks as well. If we design with consideration to all of our other layers of light, we will have a rich, dynamic emotional experience. If our design has failed to accommodate for our tasks, we can augment by adding additional fixtures or localized task lighting. However, if we neglect the more ethereal layers, like choreography and mood, it is unlikely that we will ever be able to regain those subtle aspects of functionality.

Image courtesy of Erco   www.erco.com

Lighting for tasks also happens to have an enormous wealth of precedent and information available to help a designer determine what light levels are appropriate for specific tasks. There are reference books full of charts and tables that can be used by anyone for solving task lighting problems.

What should be avoided is lighting for tasks being the *only* type of light considered for a space. In a good design approach, it is merely one of five layers, and the last one at that.

We will investigate the specifics of providing light for tasks as it is a critical component of the functionality of a space. But it must never overshadow the thought and design of the other layers that truly infuse unique experience into our environments.

Image courtesy of Deltalight   www.deltalight.us

Figure 4.5 Task illuminance should consider visual comfort and performance.

In order to get comfortable with the layer system, we must remind ourselves that none of the layers are complete solutions on their own. Knowing this, we can free ourselves to address light how and where we want it. If we isolate each of these layers as a unique thought process, we can stand back and watch our space nearly build itself as a collection of well thought-out applications of light onto specific surfaces.

Our success with this method relies on reminding ourselves, once again, that *lighted surfaces are our medium*. All of the light ingredients we add as a result of these layers of thinking are *pieces of light* painted onto specific objects and architectural elements. Additionally, our understanding of perception tells us that the most efficient use of our lighting resources is light applied to vertical surfaces and the upright accented objects that we place throughout our designed spaces.

Chapter 5

Physical Basics of Light

When we dedicate ourselves to incorporating light into our spaces, and claim it as a familiar medium, we also dedicate ourselves to understanding how light works. For our purposes, we will sail through a relatively succinct definition of what light is, how it interacts with the surfaces of our environment and how this affects our use of it. An understanding of light from a physical perspective will empower us to make good design decisions and avoid the perils and pitfalls of misapplied light.

Light is a member of a much larger family of physical phenomenon called Electromagnetic Radiation. In our discussion, we will simply call it "radiation." Radiation is responsible for many phenomena we encounter in our daily lives. It is all around us all of the time. X-Rays, Microwaves, Radio Transmission waves and even heat are all forms of radiation. "Light" is merely a name we have decided to give to the types of radiation that we are able to detect with our eyes.

LIGHT AS RADIATION

Radiation is essentially power and, as such, has no mass, no color, no taste, and no smell. All of the different types of radiation travel around our planet, and the universe, at the very same speed. We call this speed "the speed of light," but it is, in fact, the speed of every type of radiation. Light just happens to be our favorite type.

The only difference between one form of radiation and another is how fast that radiation vibrates as it travels. Thus the light we use to see differs from the microwaves used to for cooking only in how fast it is vibrating as it travels through space. Because this rate of vibration is the only discernible property of radiation, we symbolize radiation as little, squiggly lines flying around us. This allows us to describe radiation by the distance between peaks and troughs in our squiggly lines. The length from peak to peak or trough to trough is called the "wavelength" of the radiation, and it is the only sure way to distinguish one type of radiation from another. These lengths are very, very small, so they are often described in Nano-meters. A nanometer is so short that it takes one billion of them make a meter.

HOW WE VISUALIZE RADIATION

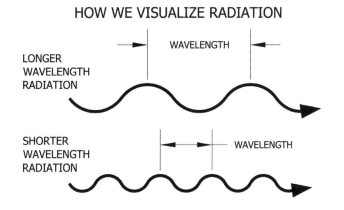

Figure 5.1 Radiation, including light, is best imagined as squiggly lines vibrating at different rates as they travel through space.

We don't need to visualize these units. We need only to know that in scientific circles, wavelength, expressed in Nano-meters, is a perfectly appropriate way to describe radiation. *Figure 5.2* shows the entire known spectrum of radiation and the corresponding range of wavelengths for the different types. You can see that "light" is a family of radiation at the "short" end of the spectrum, that is to say radiation which has shorter wavelengths and vibrates relatively fast.

COMPLETE ELECTRO-MAGNETIC RADIATION SPECTRUM

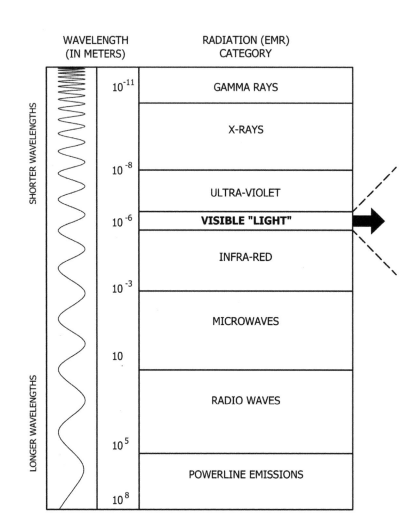

Figure 5.2 The complete spectrum of electro-magnetic radiation including the portion we call visible light.

Generally, we say that human color vision can detect radiation with wavelengths as short as 380 Nano-meters and wavelengths as long as 770 Nano-meters. So it is within this range that we have the "visible spectrum" or radiation we call "light." Anything vibrating faster, or vibrating slower, we no longer "see." The radiation is still there; we simply can no longer detect it with our eyes.

Humans do have mechanisms for detecting other types of radiation, but certainly not with the acuity of the "visible spectrum." Infra-red radiation, which lies just beyond the visible spectrum, is a good example. Humans don't detect it with their eyes, but they do detect it with their nerves as various levels of radiant heat. We are commonly told that heat rises, but, more accurately, *heated air* rises. Heat, itself, can be directed with reflectors just like other forms of radiation.

THE VISIBLE SPECTRUM

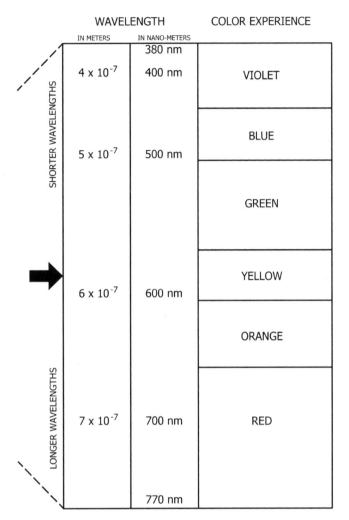

Figure 5.3 An articulation of the wavelengths of radiation that constitute the visible spectrum.

Most humans have an amazing ability to distinguish between different types and combinations of visible light. The articulation of our visual system is evident in the plethora of names that we have given to all of these light experiences. We name them as colors, and there is no shortage of subtle variation in our color experiences. It is important, however, to remind ourselves that "color" is simply a name for an experience. Light itself has no color. It is only when different wavelengths of radiation reflect off of surfaces in our environment and enter our eye that we have an experience that we can name as a "color." Hence every wavelength of radiation in the visible spectrum will cause a fairly predictable color experience. And so, rather than argue about whether an object is perceived as yellowish-orange or canary yellow, we could simply describe the radiation by its wavelength in Nano-meters to end the debate. It is also worth noting that the acuity of color vision varies from person to person depending on his / her physiological make-up. Various forms of color deficiency can drastically reduce the number of unique color experiences of which a person is capable. Studies show that about eight percent of males and less than one percent of females suffer some form of color deficiency.

EVOLUTION OF COLOR VISION

Describing radiation, light and color in this manner begs an explanation of why humans have come to "see" this radiation in the first place and why we are so good at discerning one type from the next. The explanation lies in the logic of life on earth. Historically, the sun has been the primary source of radiation here on earth. The sun exhibits a seemingly endless cycle of nuclear fusion, which emits a very elaborate spectrum of radiation: essentially, the complete spectrum as we know it, from x-rays to radio waves. The atmosphere that blankets our earth, however, blocks the vast majority of this radiation. Some of this radiation slips through, and as far as we can guess, has always slipped through. This band of sneaky radiation that actually makes it to earth's surface is a band that includes our visible spectrum and some of the ultra-violet and infra-red radiation just beyond the end of the visible spectrum. Color vision is an adaptation that humans have developed in response to radiation that has always been here. We have had a long time on earths surface to refine our ability to not only detect this radiation, but to articulate very minute differences, just as we can with smells and tastes.

This logic also explains why we do not readily detect or use all of the other forms of radiation; they were simply never on the earth's surface for us to care about. It is only the advent of modern science that has introduced many of these other forms of radiation to our lives.

EVOLVING TO THE SPECTRUM AVAILABLE

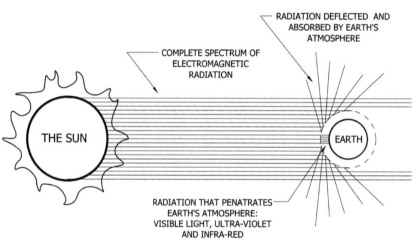

Figure 5.4 Humans have evolved to detect and use the small band of radiation that slips through the earth's atmosphere: visible light, ultra-violet, and infra-red.

Radiation that reaches the earth interacts with the surfaces around us in three ways:

Radiation can be "reflected" or bounce off of a surface.

Radiation can be absorbed by a surface.

Radiation can "transmit" or pass through a surface.

It is through these reactions that the complex spectrums from sunlight and electric light sources become different combinations of visible radiation that we translate into different color experiences.

Despite the complexity that can be attributed to the physics of radiation plays, the lessons are fairly basic:

"Light" is the name for a group of specific wavelengths of radiation that happen to be detected by our eyes.

Color is not a property of an object. Color is our brains' translation of the radiation being reflected from an object to our eyes.

BASIC LIGHTING INTERACTION TERMINOLOGY

To move forward and speak with clarity about the ways light interacts with our environment and our visual system, it is important to point out that in all cases of light, we are talking about the fundamental piece of light: The Lumen. Lighting science makes the task of talking about light a little bit tricky by lending different names to the phenomena of lumens of light interacting in different ways. The specifics of measuring lumens of light will be discussed later in chapter 18. For now, the critical knowledge is merely a bit of vocabulary.

*Illuminance is an expression of the quantity of **light falling onto** an object. The Illuminance onto a surface does not necessarily tell us what that surface will look like, as it does not define the amount of light that will reflect off of that surface. Knowing the illuminance level onto objects does, however, allow us to predict the contrast that will be created between the different materials of the objects.*

*Exitance is an expression of the total quantity of **light leaving** a surface. Exitance is easy to understand because it is simply a matter of counting up the number of lumens of light that leave a source or surface. This simplicity is also what limits the usefulness of exitance as a description. Exitance tells us how much light is leaving a source or surface, but it doesn't tell us in what direction or where that light ends up.*

*Luminance is the phenomena of **light leaving** a surface at a specific density in a specific direction. Although luminance is difficult to measure, it is extremely useful because it describes light coming off of a surface just as a viewer experiences it. Describing the luminance levels of a particular situation allows us to visualize the lighted effect of the space.*

The safest way to use these terms properly is to get used to the prepositions related to each. It is appropriate to talk about Illuminance "on to" a surface. We generally speak of the Exitance "off of" a surface. We generally talk about the luminance "of" a surface.

3 INTERACTIONS OF LIGHT

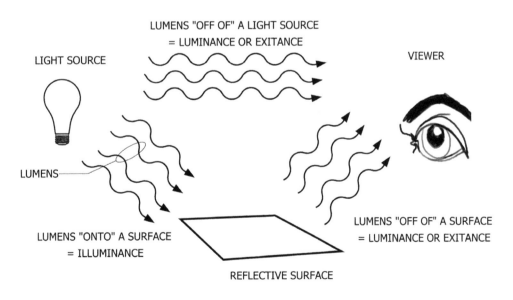

Figure 5.5 The interactions of light are always about the basic unit of light: The Lumen.

Chapter 6

Physiology of Vision

The human eye, with all of its mechanics, deserves a heavy book of its own. But, for our purposes we will focus on the components of the eye that detect and translate light. These components initiate the chemical process that transmits information to our brain, where it is processed into vision. To study these mechanics as designers, we must understand what our eyes and brains need to perform and feel comfortable in an environment.

To better understand the needs of our visual system, we start by studying some mechanical basics that we touched on earlier.

Adaptation

This term is the name we give to the mechanics of the eye and brain working to control the amount of light that enters the eye and is translated by the brain. We "dark adapt" when we walk into a dark room, as the mechanics of our eyes and brains work to make the most of what little light is available. "Bright adaptation" occurs when we transition into a brighter space and our eyes and brains work to limit the amount of light entering the visual system. Adaptation occurs unconsciously. It is worth knowing that dark adaptation can take a few minutes to occur completely. For this reason, we give extra thought to light levels when we transition people from bright spaces to dark spaces. Bright adaptation happens much quicker.

Accommodation

This is a fancy name for the ability of the eye to focus on objects at different distances. The eye has flexible components that change shape to bend light differently when we shift focus from an object in front of us to a tree off in the distance.

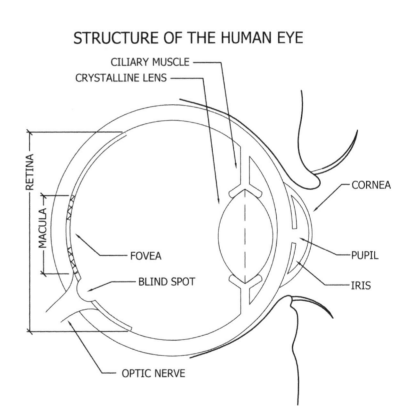

STRUCTURE OF THE HUMAN EYE

Figure 6.1 The major components of the human eye

STRUCTURE OF THE EYE

The human eye consists of a number of near miraculous components that perform all of these complex tasks. Nearly all of these functions can be understood by finding analogy with a camera.

The outermost component of the eyeball is the cornea, a fluid-filled bulge at the front of our eye that does a fair amount of gathering and focusing of light towards the back of the eyeball. The cornea also does a wonderful job of protecting the other components of the eye and filtering out harmful radiation.

Behind the cornea is the iris. The iris is the component of the eye that carries "eye color" and acts as a shutter device, opening and closing to control the quantity of light that enters the eyeball. It is the iris that is the first to act when the visual system "adapts" to different light levels. The pupil is the name for the aperture that the iris creates. So we see our pupil change in size to admit more or less light as conditions change.

SHAPES OF THE CRYSTALLINE LENS OF THE EYE

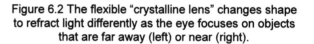

FAR FOCUSSED
MUSCLES TENSED
LESS REFRACTION

NEAR FOCUSSED
MUSCLES RELAXED
MORE REFRACTION

Figure 6.2 The flexible "crystalline lens" changes shape to refract light differently as the eye focuses on objects that are far away (left) or near (right).

Behind the pupil is the flexible, shape-changing lens that is responsible for a small, but critical, portion of our accommodation (focusing). This lens is attached to muscles that contract and relax to optimize the shape of the lens to refract light from far away or from nearby as we focus on objects at different distances.

All of these components are working in harmony at all times to deliver the ideal quantity of light to the elements at the back of our eyeball. These elements make up the retina. The retina is home to all of our light-detecting photoreceptors called rods and cones. The different types of photoreceptors are distributed in a very purposeful way that can be broken down into three areas of interest.

The periphery *of our retina is home to photoreceptors called "rods" that detect low levels of light.*

The central area of our retina is called the macula *and is home to a mix of rods and our more detail oriented photoreceptors called "cones."*

The very center of our retina is called the fovea, *and it is home exclusively to cones. Because cones are so critical for translating detail and color, the fovea is mildly regressed to maximize the surface area available. The density of cones at the fovea provides for greater detail and color perception at the center of the field of vision. It is this centermost area of the retina that all of the other mechanics of the eyeball are working to direct light towards.*

The cones and rods are the critical light detecting components of the eye. To understand how the two different systems work to contribute to vision in different light situations, we will expand on them here.

Rods

Rods are the photoreceptors that populate the outer perimeter of the retina and are responsible for our so-called "peripheral vision"

Rods are very large and very sensitive to subtle light changes and motion.

Rods are active in low light levels. We call these "scotopic" situations.

Rods populate the periphery of the retina and parts of the macula. The Fovea (center area) of the retina contains no Rods.

There is only one class of Rods, so they all contain the same photo-pigment. This photo-pigment is called Rhodopsin and is most sensitive to radiation with a wavelength of 504 Nanometers. This wavelength of radiation would translate to the color experience blue-green to normal color vision. Because all of our rods have the same sensitivity and respond to light the same, they only translate value information. Thus in low light level, "scotopic" situations, our rods translate only a judgment of bright or dark to the brain. Scotopic vision situations, therefore, appear mono-chromatic (one-colored).

Cones

Cones are the photoreceptors that populate the central areas of our eye and are responsible for all of our high detail and color vision functions. Cones are organized into three distinct classes, and each class contains a different chemical photopigment. The different peak sensitivities of the different classes of cones make color distinction possible. Understanding how light is detected by the different types of cones and translated to the brain is necessary to understanding color science and making appropriate light source decisions.

Cones are active in high light levels. We call these "photopic" situations.

Cones populate the central parts of the retina. The macula is primarily made up of cones, and the fovea at the center of our retina is exclusively made up of cones.

Cones are responsible for our color vision and are small in size in order to translate detail.

There are three different classes of cones, each named for the photo-pigment chemical that it contains. These three photo-pigments each have a peak sensitivity to a different wavelength of light and are named for the wavelength to which they are most sensitive. These unique sensitivities are what make discerning color possible.

Our "R" or Red Cones contain the photo-pigment "erythrolabe," which is most sensitive to radiation of wavelength 580 Nano-meters. Not surprisingly, this wavelength on its own would elicit the color experience we call "red."

Our "G" or Green Cones contain "chlorolabe," which is most sensitive to radiation of wavelength 540 Nano-meters.

Our "B" or Blue Cones contain the photo-pigment "cyanolabe," which is most sensitive to radiation of wavelength 450 nanometers.

Photopic Color Vision from our Cones

The key to understanding cones and rods is in visualizing how these photoreceptors work together to transmit information to our brain, where it is then translated into vision.

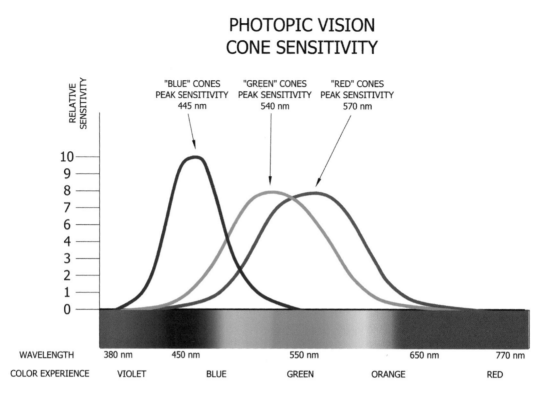

Figure 6.3 Approximate sensitivities of the three classes of cones.

Figure 6.3 shows the entire spectrum of visible radiation (on its side). You may remember that on the short end of the spectrum (380 Nano-meters in wavelength), we have radiation that elicits the color experience "violet." On the right side of the diagram is the long end of the visible spectrum (radiation of wavelength 780 Nano-meters) which is radiation that translates to the color experience "red." On the left-hand axis of the chart is a simple measurement of quantity or intensity. The three sensitivity spectrums of the three types of cones are overlaid onto the diagram. As expected, the peak sensitivities of each occur at radiation types that deliver the color experience we would expect. The most effective way to visualize the workings of the cones is to picture each class of cones as an individual person or group that casts a vote of intensity based on how much of their favorite radiation they detect.

As an example, if we could isolate a specific wavelength of radiation, in this case 520 nanometers, we could predict how each class of cones would vote based on where the line of the wavelength intersects each of the three sensitivity curves. We see that the Red cones vote 4, the Green cones vote 7, and the Blue cones vote 1. These three votes form the three digit number that is transmitted to the brain for processing; in this case "471".The brain translates each unique 3 digit code as a unique experience. To keep them straight, we name the experiences as colors. In the event that our classes of cones all detect the same quantity of their favorite light, they all vote the same, and the number sent to the brain looks like 333 or 555. In this case, the brain's translation is a neutral value, some shade of gray or black or white.

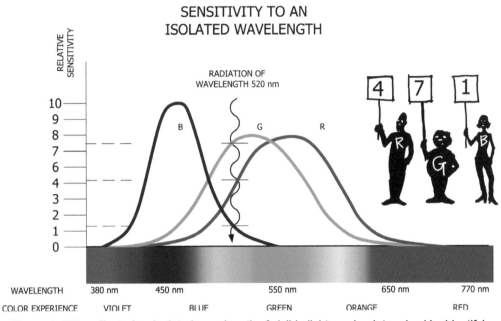

Figure 6.4 The effect of an isolated wavelength of visible light can be determined by identifying where it intersects the sensitivity curves.

Far more likely than a few isolated wavelengths of light is a group of many different wavelengths that may be reflecting off of an object or coming from a light source. In the case of a broad spectrum like this, we find the intersections of all of the different wavelengths and consider an average value that represents them. In this fashion, every imaginable combination of light can be boiled down to a vote from each of the classes of photoreceptors and transmitted as a three-digit number to the brain. The fact that there are three digits is what makes color space such a large place with so many combinations.

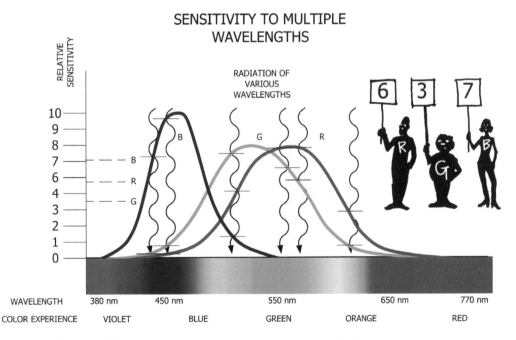

Figure 6.5 Even a very complex spectrum is translated by the photoreceptors

as a single 3-digit number.

Although the wavelength characteristics of light are absolute, the detection of light and translation of color are far more subjective. Every person's visual system has slightly different peak sensitivities and different ranges of detection. There are individuals who detect certain wavelengths of light that other people do not. They, therefore, have color experiences that some people may never have.

This model of color vision leads to the understanding that the sensation of "color" is merely the brains translation of the retina's detection of different quantities of different wavelengths of light. This has important ramifications in that we can artificially create any color experience we want through an engineered combination of many different wavelengths of light.

Scotopic Vision from our Rods

If we can visualize the interaction of our cones, understanding how rods work is very simple. In the case of our rods, there is only one class, one photo-pigment, and, therefore, only one vote. The information that is transmitted to the brain is a single number. Because of this, low-level "Scotopic" vision is monochromatic. The brain is being furnished with only enough information to make a value judgment: simply dark or light.

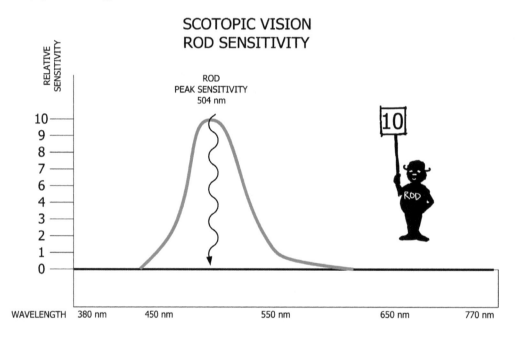

Figure 6.6 All rods are sensitive to light in the same manner.
Thus, they translate only a value judgment.

THE TROUBLE WITH WHITE LIGHT

This science needs to be most thoroughly understood as it relates to so-called "white light." With the advent of modern, highly-engineered electric light sources, we have harnessed technology that allows us to create light sources that can appear as a pleasing version of neutral when viewed directly, yet render colors very poorly.

Figure 6.7 shows that if we create a light source that emits just the right color of blue light and just the right color of orange light, our cones will send a three-digit number to our brain that will be translated as neutral.

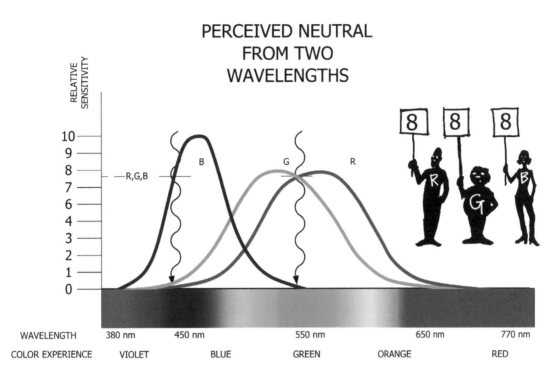

Figure 6.7 The perception of neutral from a light source can be created through a combination of as few as two wavelengths of light.

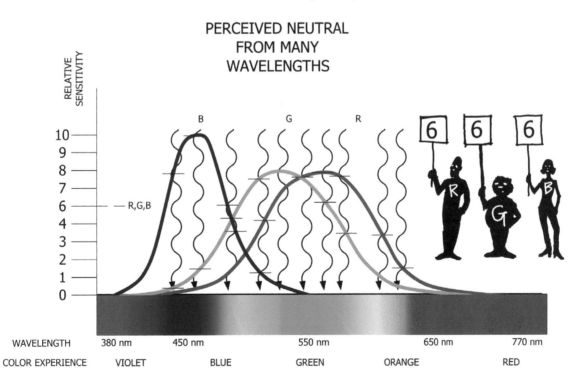

Figure 6.8 The perception of neutral light is more commonly the product of a wide variety of visible wavelengths.

What is inherently dangerous is that when our brain detects a "neutral" light source, we are tempted to believe that this light source will render all of the potential colors in the environment around us. But if we created the light source illustrated in *figure 6.7*, it would accurately render only two colors; the rest would be muddled and gray. We would successfully have created a source that appears perfectly neutral to the eye, but renders only oranges and blues. For this reason, a designer should avoid describing light as simply "white." To speak accurately of light sources, we must discuss two distinct properties:

> *The completeness of the spectrum of a light source or "Color Rendering Index," and*
>
> *the balance of spectrum of light source or "Color Temperature."*

Chapter 7

The Color Science of Light Sources

Like all color experiences, "white" or neutral, is relatively subjective, and people may experience it slightly differently. In addition to the variation in individual color sense, there are two other factors that contribute to "white" being a dangerous term to label a light source.

The first of these factors is a simple physical shortcoming of photoreceptors. Our cones rely on chemical photo-pigments to cause the chemical reaction that translates vision. When we exhaust the supply of photo-pigments the cones can no longer "vote." This temporary exhaustion is called "bleaching" of the photoreceptors and is the reason that after staring at a saturated color for a long period of time, we see the "inverse" of a color when we look away.

The second shortcoming is based on our brains' habit of ignoring repetitive information that it deems of little use. Your brain is a device of efficiency, and if it feels that a repetitive signal is being ignored, it will stop sending it. In this manner, as you stare at an object, your brain grows bored of telling you that the object is colored. The brain starts to ignore the signals sent by your eye, and your perception of the object's color begins to shift towards neutral. More appropriately, your brain is deciding that the color of that object is the "new white," and, thus, every other color is judged from it.

These factors together mean that an object appears to be most saturated with color the instant we look at it, and fades as our cones run out of photo-pigment. This subjectivity also means that we can do much arguing about the color of an object or light source. We have already pointed out that we can eliminate argument about color by labeling individual colors by their corresponding wavelength. Here we are interested in applying this simplicity to light sources. We specifically care about the light sources that we rely on to reveal the colors of the world around us. In an attempt to limit confusion and argument, we insist on describing two unique properties of every light source: Color Rendering Index and Color Temperature.

Color Rendering Index:

This term describes the complexity or completeness of the spectral output of a light source.

Color Temperature:

This phrase describes the color that a light source appears to the eye due to an imbalanced spectral output.

COLOR RENDERING INDEX

Color rendering index is rather simple in principle and expression. The color rendering index, or CRI, of a light source is expressed as a number ranging from 0 to 100, where 100 is a spectral output that contains the entire visible spectrum and, therefore, renders all colors accurately. If a light source emits every wavelength in the visible spectrum, then the materials in an environment have the opportunity to reflect all of those wavelengths to the eye, and, thus, express all of the potential color in the environment.

The lower the CRI value, the fewer distinct wavelengths the source emits. Therefore, fewer potential color expressions can be reflected from materials in the environment. When we go on to investigate various electrical light sources, we will see that color rendering capabilities (and corresponding CRI values) vary greatly from source to source. This variety is of huge significance to the designer. Since designers are responsible for making many critical material and color decisions, it is imperative that they are aware of the possible shortcomings of the light source under which they are making their decisions. Many a person has been shocked to find that two materials that look to be the same color under a specific electric light source look utterly different under daylight. Daylight represents a complete spectrum and, therefore, has a Color Rendering Index (CRI) of 100.

Incandescing sources like the common "light bulb" and halogen sources are engineered to also emit the entire visible spectrum, so they also have a CRI of 100. A bad fluorescent source may have a CRI of 60. We will discuss the specific CRI values of various electric light sources in chapter eight when we investigate each source individually. Suffice it to say for general understanding that the following guidelines can get us through the system:

Color Rendering Indices (CRI) in the 60's and 70's are relatively incomplete and are unacceptable for making critical color decisions.

CRI values in the 80's do a reasonable job of revealing colors

CRI values in the 90's render colors very accurately and are appropriate for color critical environments.

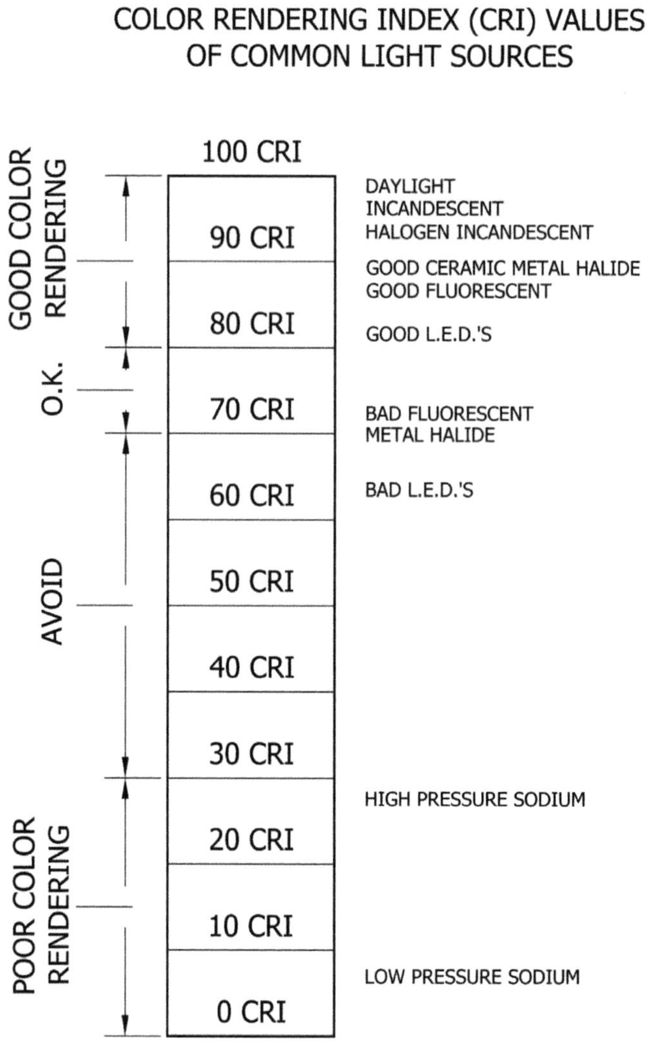

CORRELATED COLOR TEMPERATURE

COLOR RENDERING INDEX (CRI) VALUES OF COMMON LIGHT SOURCES

Figure 7.1 Color Rendering Index (CRI) of different light sources expressed from 0 to 100.

This is a method of describing the apparent color of a light source that is very nearly neutral. When a light source appears colored to our eye, it is due to an unbalanced spectral output. If a source emits little or no green light, it may appear reddish or "warm." A source may also appear "warm" or reddish if it emits every color, but emits a higher proportion of red.

Color Temperatures are expressed in Degrees Kelvin or simply Kelvins (because The Kelvin scale is absolute, it needs no units).

The reason that we express this color appearance as a temperature is a result of the experimenting that led to the scale. The color temperature scale is expressed as the colors that a black body radiator exhibits as it is heated to extreme temperatures. A black body radiator is simply a fancy block of iron that won't melt. As this fancy block of iron is heated to high temperatures, it begins to glow. The first color that the iron block will glow is a dull, deep red. If heated further, the same block of iron will begin to glow orange and then yellow. Experiments show that if heated even higher, the color exhibited by this block of iron will travel all the way through the color spectrum. Thus, the next stop is green, onward to blue. The path that this color transition makes is not linear, so the green happens to be very, very pale and is, for our purposes, considered a colorless neutral.

The glowing red color of the iron occurs at a temperature of about 2500 Kelvins. With this logic, when a light source exhibits this reddish color, rather than call it reddish, we describe the light source as having a Color Temperature of 2500 Kelvins. In this system, orange occurs at about 2500 Kelvins, followed by yellow at about 2800 Kelvins. Following the progression of temperature and the color spectrum, keeping in mind that we use the pale green as our neutral, the Color Temperature translations follow the table in *Figure 7.2*.

We most often use this system of color description for our engineered light sources like fluorescent lamps, Light Emitting Diodes, and High Intensity Discharge lamps. These color associations are only approximations and differ in meaning from source to source and even brand to brand. This leaves plenty of room for discrepancy, but the basics of Color Temperature to describe the slight color of engineered sources like fluorescent remains useful.

2500 Kelvins: warm

3000 Kelvins: neutral

4100 Kelvins: cool

It is worth noting that with these engineered sources, the color temperature description has no relationship to the operating temperature of the source itself. However, when we discuss incandescent or halogen incandescent sources, color temperature has more meaning. Because these light sources are the product of heating a metal filament, the color temperature exhibited is related to the temperature of the filament. When we heat an incandescent filament to 2800 degrees Kelvin, we get light that we would describe as the "color" 2800 Kelvins (warm).

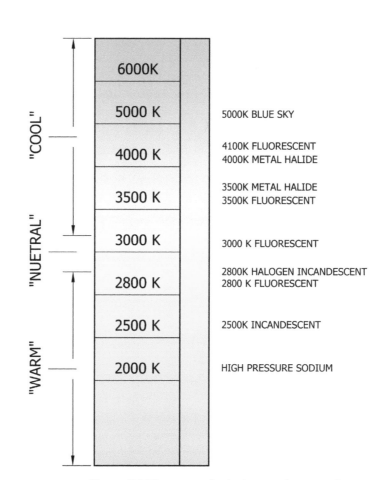

CORRELATED COLOR TEMPERATURES (CCT) OF COMMON LIGHT SOURCES

Figure 7.2 The range of color temperatures used to describe common electric light sources

Where our engineered sources cause difficulty is when they are not labeled nor described by their Color Rendering Index, or numeric Color Temperature. Unfortunately, many consumer grade fluorescent light sources are labeled with marketable names like "daylight white" or "designer white." These names give no real hint as to the color temperature to expect and certainly tell nothing of the color rendering index. Thus, these products should be avoided when color rendering and source color are critical.

Knowing the Color Rendering Index and Color Temperature properties of a light source is necessary for gaining a full understanding of a light sources capability. It is reasonable to say Color Rendering Index is the more impacting of the two. If a source emits a complete spectrum of visible light and reveals every color accurately, it is really a matter of preference as to whether that source needs to appear warm or cool. This is just like daylight which changes color drastically from pale sunrise to deep sunset, but is always useful for revealing color. Conversely, if a light source reveals colors poorly, it is of little significance whether the source, itself, appears warm or cool to the eye. Many unsatisfactory lighting situations can be remedied by implementing light sources with a better color rendering index. Very few lighting problems can be solved just by addressing color temperature. To make complete lighting decisions, it is necessary to understand and specify both the Color Temperature and Color Rendering Index of a light source.

Chapter 8

Electric Light Sources

At the core of every electric luminaire is the lamp that actually converts electricity into radiant light energy. Since the commercial success of the standard Incandescent lamp in 1879, modern science has developed a number of ways to electrically create light. Each technology has pros and cons that should be understood by the designer interested in making lighting decisions. Just as it is important to understand the priorities and program of the design job, it is necessary to know which light sources are going to serve those priorities. The topic of light source technology has become more complex as technologies have progressed. If we consider how long humans have relied on the sun as the primary source of illumination, it is easy to see why our visual system might struggle to deal with the different types of light delivered by all of our newer, technologically advanced sources.

We will discus each of these technologies with the intent of understanding how each performs, and where each should be used or not used. "Lamp" is the proper name for what most people call a "light bulb." In our discussion we care about vocabulary as much as anything else, so we will refer to our sources as lamps.

Let's summarize our working knowledge of the different light source technologies by describing their properties in the following manner.

Initial Cost: how expensive is the source to purchase?

Operating Cost: the expense of providing electricity and replacing the source

Color Rendering Index: (CRI on our scale of 1 to 100.)

Color Temperature: expressed in degrees Kelvin or Kelvins, indicating warm, neutral or cool

Ballast and Transformer Requirements: some sources rely on these special components to operate. They are usually mounted in or near the luminaire.

Dimming: how easily can the source be dimmed?

Instant on / off: does the source require time to warm-up?

Directionality: how easily can we direct light from this source?

Efficacy: a fancy word for efficiency: How much light do we get out for the electricity we put in? Expressed as lumens of light out for watts of electricity in or "lumens per watt"

Lamp Life: how long before we have to replace the source: We express this in thousands of hours and assume that 1000 hours translates to roughly 1 year of typical use. This estimate assumes about 3 hours of use per day, so adjustments can to be made accordingly.

Temperature requirement: some sources perform better in different temperatures

Heat Generated

Noise Generated

INCANDESCENT / STANDARD INCANDESCENT SOURCES

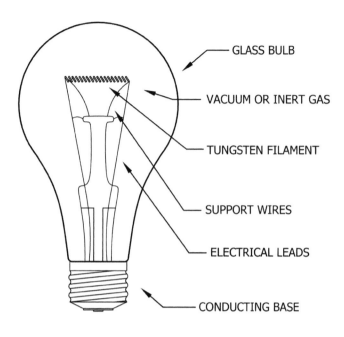

GLASS BULB

VACUUM OR INERT GAS

TUNGSTEN FILAMENT

SUPPORT WIRES

ELECTRICAL LEADS

CONDUCTING BASE

Figure 8.1 The working components of standard incandescent light sources

Cheap, hot and inefficient; standard incandescent lamps are used for soft, diffuse blobs of warm light that render colors well.

Standard Incandescent sources represent a very basic technology that has changed little in the 100-plus years since its refinement. *Figure 8.1* illustrates the basic working components that enable these sources to function. Very simply, electricity is passed through an engineered metal filament. As with many materials, the metal filament "resists" the flow of electricity. This resistance causes friction, which, in turn, becomes heat. Once this resistance and subsequent heat become great enough, the metal filament "incandesces"; it gives off radiant energy in a broad spectrum that includes the visible spectrum. Understanding that the radiant energy given off also includes a huge quantity of heat (infra-red radiation) explains many of the undesirable properties and inefficiencies of incandescent sources.

The Properties of Incandescent Sources:

Initial Cost: *cheap!*

...Dirt cheap. This is the primary reason incandescent sources are so common. The small price tag compels us to reach for incandescent lamps despite our knowledge or their inefficiencies.

Operating Cost: Expensive;

The first flaw of incandescent sources is the amount of electricity that is transformed into heat rather than light. Only one-third of the electricity pushed into an incandescent source is converted to visible light. The remaining two thirds leaves as heat. When we consider also the short lamp life, the result is a source that is expensive to electrify and needs constant replacement.

Color Rendering Index: 100 (great);

The filament of the incandescent source is engineered to incandesce in a manner that delivers every wavelength of visible radiation. This means that the light contains every color component, so it can reveal all of the colors that our environment has to offer. The color - rendering ability is another reason we are so reluctant to move away from these sources.

Color Temperature: warm;

Incandescent sources actually operate at the temperature that corresponds to their color temperature. Standard incandescent filaments are heated to about 2800 degrees Kelvin, so the warm, orange light given off by the source can be described as 2800 Kelvins. This warmth is another reason we seem to be attracted to these sources. The warm color temperature translates well in intimate, relaxed environments.

Ballast and Transformer requirements: None;

Incandescent sources require no special components to operate. Electricity is simply driven through the filament, which heats to a point of incandescing.

Dimming: Cheap and Easy;

Incandescent sources can be dimmed simply by lowering the amperage (quantity) of electricity that is pushed through them. This can be accomplished with a simple wall box dimmer that can be installed in place of any common light switch

Instant on / off: Yes;

Incandescent filaments heat up to incandescence very rapidly as electricity is applied to them. For our purposes, we will consider it as instant.

Directionality: Poor;

Incandescent sources are, by nature, very large to accommodate the relatively large filament within. Generally, the larger the source, the more difficult it is to build a reflector around the source to gather up the light and drive it out in a specific direction. Think of using a common "light bulb" to accent a sculpture, and you begin to get the picture.

Efficacy: Very Poor (10 Lumens per Watt);

Incandescent sources do much more to deliver heat than they do light. This factor results in a large quantity of wasted energy. We say that incandescent sources create about 10 lumens of light for every watt of electricity we put into them.

Lamp Life: Poor;

Another significant drawback of standard incandescent sources is the frequency with which we replace them. Incandescent sources are expected to have a lamp life of about 1000 hours. Using our estimates, this translates to about 1 year of regular use before the source "burns out." As incandescent lamps operate, the metal filament is heated so that is literally boils away. As the filament boils away, it becomes thin and brittle and, ultimately, breaks, causing failure.

Temperature requirements: None;

Incandescent sources operate equally well in any temperature condition.

Heat Generated: Lots;

Incandescent sources emit more infra-red radiation than visible light. They are truly heat lamps by nature. Hence, we often see them being used to keep our onion rings warm.

Noise Generated: Some;

Incandescent sources have a tendency to "buzz" when they are dimmed down. This generally comes from the filament buzzing due to vibration as electricity flows through. Incandescent sources are fairly silent under full-power operation.

Incandescent lamps are inexpensive to purchase, render colors well, have a pleasing warm color cast, and are easy to dim. They are, however, wildly inefficient, produce a tremendous amount of heat, and are short-lived.

We use incandescent sources when we are trying to create soft, diffuse, warm floods of light. Incandescent sources are good for distributing an even quantity of warm light in all directions. Occasionally, we build reflectors around incandescent lamps to create downlights and accent luminaires, but the large nature of the source makes them ill-suited for this task. Incandescent lamps are often the heart of diffusing fixtures like floor lamps, table lamps, and decorative sconces. The limit in size and wattage of incandescent sources also limits the size of application. These lamps are usually suited to smaller environments and low (10'-0" and under) ceilings.

COMMON INCANDESCENT LAMP SHAPES

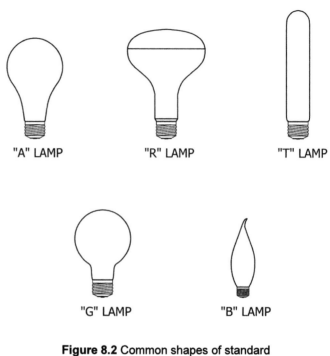

"A" LAMP   "R" LAMP   "T" LAMP

"G" LAMP   "B" LAMP

Figure 8.2 Common shapes of standard incandescent light sources.

HALOGEN INCANDESCENT SOURCES

Small and hot, Halogen sources deliver clean, crisp, easily-directed light that is commonly used for creating pieces of accent light onto surfaces and objects or for twinkling on their own.

Called by many names, Halogen, Quartz Halogen, Tungsten Halogen, we are talking about a light source that is essentially a refined version of the basic incandescent lamp. Halogen incandescent sources are named for the halogen gas that they contain and the quartz outer bulb that surrounds their filament. Both of these advancements allow the filament in these sources to operate at a higher temperature. This has the surprising benefit of allowing the source to run more efficiently and also extends the life of the lamp. The other benefit these advancements provide to the designer is a smaller source package which can more easily be harnessed into directional light. *Figure 8.3* shows the working components with the expected similarities to standard incandescent sources.

Halogen Incandescent sources are basically a refined version of standard incandescent; they offer higher color temperatures described as nearly neutral pale yellow and less orange. These lamps offer longer lamp life, greater efficacy, and a smaller package that can be better directed to accent and light specific objects.

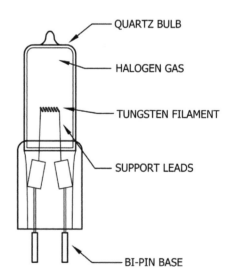

QUARTZ BULB

HALOGEN GAS

TUNGSTEN FILAMENT

SUPPORT LEADS

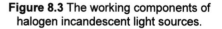

BI-PIN BASE

Figure 8.3 The working components of halogen incandescent light sources.

The Properties of Halogen Incandescent Sources:

Initial Cost: Moderate;

Halogen sources are moderately expensive to purchase. This expense comes from the cost of the technology and because they are less common than the standard "light bulb."

Operating Cost: Expensive;

Although more efficient than standard incandescent, Halogen sources are still wasteful and still short-lived when compared to sources like fluorescent and HID.

Color Rendering Index: 100 (great);

Halogen sources also rely on heating filaments to a point of incandescing. These filaments are designed to emit a spectrum that includes all of the visible wavelengths that objects in our environment may reflect to our eye.

Color Temperature: warm to neutral;

The higher operating temperature of halogen incandescent sources creates light that is described as a higher color temperature. The filament is heated to about 3000 degrees Kelvin and, therefore, creates a pale yellowish light that we can describe as 3000 degrees Kelvin.

Ballast and Transformer requirements: Some;

Many halogen incandescent sources are engineered to operate at a lower voltage than is commonly delivered to electrical circuits. These "low voltage" sources require a transformer to "transform" the electricity from standard line voltage (120 volts in the U.S.) to a lower voltage like 12 volts or 24 volts. These transformers can be as small as a candy bar, but must always be considered as they have to go somewhere and must be accessible.

Dimming: Cheap and Easy;

Just like standard incandescent sources, halogen incandescent sources can be dimmed with simple wall box dimmers, which regulate the quantity of electricity delivered through the filament.

Instant on / off: Yes;

Halogen Incandescent filaments also heat up to incandescence nearly instantaneously.

Directionality: good to excellent;

One of the most notable by-products of Halogen technology is the ability to build a smaller lamp around a smaller filament. These small lamps are ideal for building into precision reflectors that drive out light in a single direction. The small size is the reason halogen incandescent lamps are so commonly used for accenting, stage lighting, and precision flood lighting.

Efficacy: Poor (15 Lumens per Watt);

When first developed, Halogen incandescent sources were heralded for being fifty percent more efficient than standard incandescent. In the face of sources like Fluorescent, this number is less than impressive.

Lamp Life: medium to good;

The higher temperature of Halogen Incandescent lamps creates a situation in which the metal of the filament recycles within the lamp, thus, extending lamp life significantly. Halogen sources generally last about 3000 hours, but can be engineered to last as long as 10,000 hours (10 years by our basic assumption of 1000 hours per year)

Temperature requirements: None;

Halogen incandescent sources will operate well in any temperature condition.

Heat Generated: Lots;

Halogen incandescent sources create a tremendous amount of heat.

Noise Generated: Some;

Halogen incandescent sources "buzz" when they are dimmed down. In addition to the buzz of the filament, some magnetic transformers required for low voltage sources can also create noise.

Halogen incandescent lamps are moderately expensive lamps that, like incandescent, are rather inefficient and create excess heat. We use halogen sources where we want the excellent color-rendering capabilities and the nearly neutral color. Halogen sources are very small, so they can be incorporated into smaller luminaires and into precision accenting luminaires that drive out a directional beam of light for accenting specific surfaces and objects.

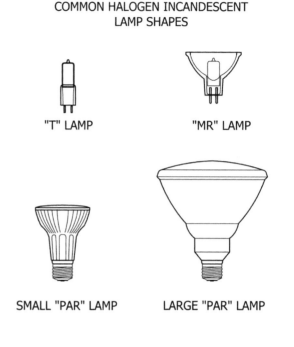

COMMON HALOGEN INCANDESCENT
LAMP SHAPES

"T" LAMP   "MR" LAMP

SMALL "PAR" LAMP   LARGE "PAR" LAMP

Figure 8.4 Common shapes of halogen incandescent lamps.

FLUORESCENT LAMPS

Cool and efficient, fluorescent lamps create diffuse light that can have many different color temperatures and different color-rendering capabilities.

Fluorescent technology has come a long way since the days of flickering, humming blue light. The most significant aspect of fluorescent lamp technology is the vast range of color and color rendering properties in which they are available. Consequently, care must be taken in specifying them. Generally, if a designer does not request a fluorescent source with a specific color temperature and a good color-rendering index, the product delivered will be less than desirable.

Fluorescent lamps work through a very novel management of technology based on phosphorescence. *Figure 8.5* shows the components that are at work in all fluorescent lamps. Long, linear fluorescent lamps and twisty, compact fluorescent lamps are all basically hollow glass tubes filled with vaporized metal. When this "cloud" of metal vapor is excited by a bombardment of free electrons, it gives off a limited spectrum of mostly ultra-violet radiation. The magic of the technology is the white powdery coating of mineral phosphors that line the inside of the glass tube. These phosphors glow by translating the ultra-violet radiation into a much broader spectrum of visible light. The quality and make up of the phosphor coating is what determines the color-rendering properties and color temperature of the lamp. This phosphor coating can be engineered to deliver light that exhibits any version of cool or warm: bluish, violet, pinkish, orange-ish, yellowish, etc. Using electricity to excite the metal vapor and the translation made by the phosphor coating are efficient processes that create very little heat.

Fluorescent lamps also require a device called a ballast that starts the lamp and stabilizes the electricity delivered to the lamp. These electronic or magnetic devices range in size and must be located in or near the fluorescent luminaire.

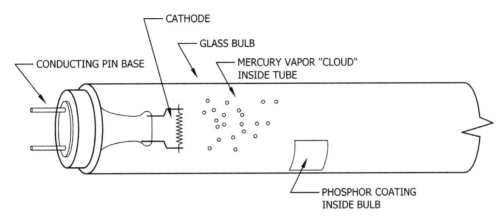

Figure 8.5 The working components of fluorescent light sources.

The Properties of Fluorescent Light Sources:

Initial Cost: Moderate;

Fluorescent lamps get less expensive to purchase as they become more commonplace. There are also many government funded programs that subsidize fluorescent lamps to encourage their use.

Operating Cost: Cheap;

Between the high efficiency and long time between re-lamping, these sources are among the most economical to operate.

Color Rendering Index: 70 - 90 (moderate to good);

Fluorescent lamps can be engineered to render colors well, but are, unfortunately, far more common in versions that don't.

Color Temperature: warm to cool (all sorts);

Fluorescent lamps can be engineered to exhibit any color we want. What is critical to understand is that the color a lamp appears to our eye does not tell us how well that lamp will render colors. Fluorescents generally have some slight color cast that may look odd when compared to incandescent and halogen sources.

Ballast and Transformer requirements: Yes;

All fluorescent lamps require a device called a ballast to operate. The ballast can be built into the luminaire or mounted remotely. Some fluorescent lamps, like those intended to replace screw-in incandescent lamps, have the ballast built in to them. Ballasts operate either magnetically or electronically, and it is worthwhile to specify electronic ballasts for most uses. Magnetic ballasts are responsible for the flickering, humming, and buzzing that are associated with fluorescent lamps. Electronic ballasts are small, light, quiet, start nearly instantly, and are more efficient.

Dimming: yes ...but expensive;

Many fluorescent sources can be dimmed, but this requires an expensive dimming ballast and, often times, a specific type of dimming switch.

Instant on / off: Yes (with an electronic ballast);

An electronic ballast will allow a fluorescent lamp to start nearly instantly. Magnetically ballasted lamps tend to flicker and stutter when turned on.

Directionality: Poor;

Because of their large size, fluorescent lamps are best used for a diffuse glow of light and are hard to direct as accents.

Efficacy: Excellent (70 Lumens per watt average);

Fluorescent lamps have been refined to be exceptionally efficient. Ranging from 50 to 100 lumens per watt, these lamps consume as little as 1/10th the electricity of incandescent lamps while providing the same amount of light.

Lamp Life: Excellent;

Fluorescent lamps are designed to last anywhere from 10,000 to hours to 30,000 hours, anywhere from 10 to 30 years between re-lamping.

Temperature requirements: prefer warmth;

Fluorescent lamps operate better in warm environments and actually get brighter as they warm themselves up. Fluorescent lamps often don't work in cold environments, so care should be taken when specifying them for such.

Heat Generated: Very little;

Efficient technology means that very little electricity is converted to heat, but these lamps still become warm to the touch.

Noise Generated: Some;

Lamps with magnetic ballasts can click and buzz. Electronic ballasts can also hum slightly. Lamps labeled as "high-output" can also give off a significant amount of noise.

COMMON FLUORESCENT LAMP SHAPES

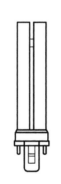  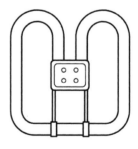

"TWIN TUBE"
LAMP

"TRIPLE TUBE"
LAMP

"2D" LAMP

Figure 8.6 Common shapes of compact fluorescent lamps.

COMMON LINEAR FLUORESCENT LAMP SHAPES

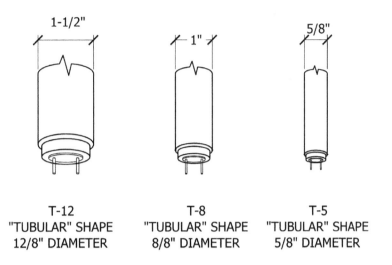

T-12	T-8	T-5
"TUBULAR" SHAPE	"TUBULAR" SHAPE	"TUBULAR" SHAPE
12/8" DIAMETER	8/8" DIAMETER	5/8" DIAMETER

Figure 8.6.5 Common shapes of linear fluorescent lamps. T-12's are older technology, T-8's are the most common, and T-5's are the newest technology.

Fluorescent sources represent an efficient way to produce soft, glowing light akin to the diffuse texture we would get from an incandescent source. They are good for the same diffuse blobs of light. These lamps last an exceptionally long time. Fluorescent lamps require care in specifying because of the variety of color temperatures and color-rendering index values available. It is necessary to be specific about these two properties when using fluorescent lamps.

We most commonly use fluorescent lamps for large, open areas like classrooms and open office workspaces that need a consistent level of diffuse light throughout. We use fluorescent light on shelves to wash up onto ceilings or in slots and coves to wash down walls. Like incandescent lamps, it is difficult to harness the light of these large lamps and focus it as accent light.

HIGH INTENSITY DISCHARGE (HID) LAMPS

This high wattage, high output, efficient source ranges in use from streetlights to retail accent. Most notably, they all require some war- up time and are not easily dimmable.

High intensity discharge lamps represent a large family that includes sources like High Pressure Sodium, Metal Halide, and Ceramic Metal Halide. We will focus our discussion on the Metal Halide and Ceramic Metal Halide family, as these produce relatively complete color spectrums that are used for color critical environments. The technology behind HID relies on creating an arc of electricity in an environment of metal vapor. It is fair to consider HID sources as a compressed version of fluorescent technology just as halogen sources are a compressed version of standard incandescent. Light from HID sources does not rely on phosphors to translate light, so the light

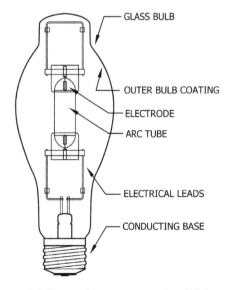

Figure 8.7 The working components of high-intensity discharge (HID) light sources.

color and rendering capability are products of the blend of metals that make up the vapor in the lamp. All of this occurs in the arc tube of the lamp, as electricity is passed between electrodes. *Figure 8.7* shows the components.

The Properties of High Intensity Discharge (HID) lamps:

Initial Cost: High;

These lamps represent a lot of technology packed into a little package and therefore are relatively expensive.

Operating Cost: Cheap;

Like fluorescent, these lamps are efficient and have long lamp lives.

Color Rendering Index: 70 - 90 (moderate to good);

Standard metal halide lamps have CRI values in the 70's or 80's. Ceramic metal halide can have CRI values in the 90's. Other HID sources, like high pressure sodium and mercury vapor, have notoriously poor color rendering properties represented by CRI values of 30 to 50.

Color Temperature: warm to cool (pink to green);

Metal halide lamps tend to have a greenish or bluish cast regardless of the color temperature rating. Ceramic metal Halide lamps tend to have a pinkish or violet cast.

Ballast and Transformer requirements: Yes;

HID sources all require an electronic or magnetic ballast to operate. Electronic ballasts have desirable features like improved efficiency and less noise.

Dimming: seldom;

The dimming of HID sources is just now becoming viable, and is very expensive

Instant on / off: No!

The most notable downside of HID sources is that they all require time to warm up. This time is generally 2 to 5 minutes. For this reason, these lamps are primarily used where they will be left on for long time periods. When specifying HID sources, they should generally not be relied upon for instant-on operation.

Directionality: Good to great;

HID sources are compact by nature (relative to their light output). Many of these sources are put into lamp shapes similar to halogen sources. All of them have very small cores, so they are easily controlled and directed.

Efficacy: Excellent (70 Lumens per watt average);

HID covers a broad array of source types, but all of them have very good efficacies. Sources with good color rendering capabilities like ceramic metal halide have efficacies on the

COMMON HIGH INTENSITY DISCHARGE
(HID) LAMP SHAPES

HID "T" LAMP   HID "PAR" LAMP

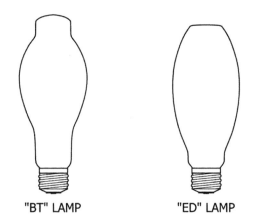

"BT" LAMP   "ED" LAMP

Figure 8.8 Common shapes of
high-intensity discharge (HID) lamps

lower end (70 lumens per watt), but less color-considerate sources like high-pressure sodium have efficacies as high as 120 lumens per watt.

Lamp Life: Good;

HID sources are rated to last anywhere from 10,000 hours to 30,000 hours, which can mean anywhere from 10 to 30 years between re-lamping.

Temperature requirements: none;

HID sources will work equally well in most any temperature condition.

Heat Generated: Relatively little;

HID sources are efficient and don't create much infra-red radiation, but the large wattages available mean that the little bit can add up to be quite hot. HID lamps also produce a fair amount of UV radiation. HID lamps implement an outer shield to contain this, but lamps should be discarded if this outer glass is ever compromised.

Noise Generated: Some;

Larger HID lamps have ballasts that can click and buzz. Even newer, smaller HID sources that use electronic ballasts can have a slight hum. It is safest not to consider HID sources in spaces where extreme quiet is required.

HID sources are undergoing constant refinement. The current generation of HID sources is focused on ceramic metal halide technology, which offers great color-rendering capabilities. These sources are engineered to come in small packages like the PAR lamps, MR lamps, and "T" lamps, usually associated with halogen sources. HID sources are finding their way into hotels, casinos, and retail operations. They still, however, require warm-up time and are rarely ever silent.

LED SOURCES

LED's, or Light Emitting Diodes, are undergoing the most vigorous advancement of the electric lighting technologies. What was once used as the indicator light on your VCR has now been born into a nearly full spectrum source used for its Red-Green-Blue Color mixing capabilities and as a neutral source for tasks and accents. LED technology is based on electrifying a diode that emits a single wavelength (color) of radiation depending on the compound of the diode. To gain a broader spectral output, these diodes are mated with phosphor technology in the same manner as fluorescent lamps. These diodes are tiny so that in a cluster of many diodes, each diode can have unique beam spread and output properties.

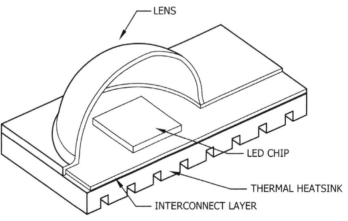

Figure 8.9 The working components of light emitting diode (LED) light sources

The General Properties of Light Emitting Diode Sources:

Initial Cost: Very High;

> LED sources are the cutting edge of technology, and, as such, they are expensive to buy. Like all things economic, prices will likely dro0070 as volume and popularity grow.

Operating Cost: Cheap;

> LED sources are gaining ground as very efficacious means of creating electric light. Pair this with amazing lamp life, and you have a very low operating cost.

Color Rendering Index: 70 - 80 (moderate to good);

> As of press time, LED's are primarily heralded for their saturated colors and color mixing properties. There are neutral sources out there, but they require careful scrutiny if you plan on using them in color critical situations. See for yourself how a particular product looks and renders colors before specifying it for a project.

Color Temperature: cool to cold (greenish to bluish);

> LED products claim to provide color temperature from 2800K up to 5000K. To have faith in the color temperature, it is important to actually see samples of LED products before specifying them.

Ballast and Transformer requirements: Yes;

> LED sources run at odd voltages, and most manufacturers provide a proprietary transformer or driver that must be accommodated.

Dimming: Yes;

> LED's can be dimmed, but similar to fluorescent sources, the dimming is in the driver or transformer technology and must be specified as such from the manufacturer.

Instant on / off: Yes;

> LED sources are truly on or off, with no warming up or fading out.

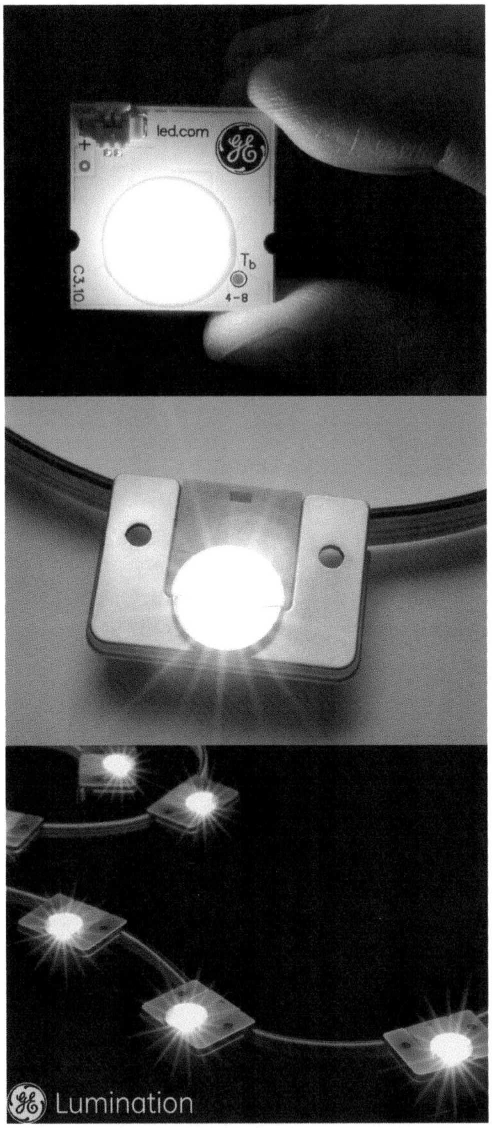

Directionality: Great;

> LED sources are directional by nature, so they can be controlled with lenses. A trickier task is getting LED sources to diffuse evenly, but this too has been accomplished.

Efficacy: Good (30-50 Lumens per watt as of this printing);

> We can generalize the efficacy of LED sources as being somewhere between halogen and fluorescent. LED's undergo so much development that their true efficacy is a moving target and should be confirmed for use on each job.

Images courtesy of GE Lumination
www.led.com

Figure 8.10 Common shapes and packages of light emitting diodes (LED's).

Lamp Life: Great

Many LED source are marketed as having lamp lives in the 50,000 to 100,000 hour range. This translates to 50 to 100 years, which is more time than the technology has been around, so time will tell.

Temperature requirements: none

LED sources will work well in any normal temperature condition. Care must be taken to dissipate heat however. A quick way to shorten the life to an LED is to expose it to too much heat.

Heat Generated: Relatively little

LED sources tend to be small and low wattage for now, so their heat contribution is also low. But LED luminaires are really just big heat sinks to dissipate the heat that they generate. As the size of LED's grows, the small amounts of heat will add up to a fair contribution.

Noise Generated: None

Both LED sources and the electronic components that drive them operate very quietly.

It takes research and sampling to determine if LED's are appropriate for a design application. As a light technology, they are all over the charts in terms of their color-rendering capabilities and color temperature. It is certainly advisable to see LED products first hand to assess these properties when considering using them as a source. LED technology is efficient and long lived. The major drawbacks are the sheer cost and small wattages and outputs available. LED sources tend to cook themselves if they get too big. Common uses for LED light sources are as continuous linear sources for coves and slots. LED's are also being incorporated into directional luminaires like downlights and accent fixtures. Because LED's are monochromatic by nature, they make a natural replacement for neon and colored lighting effects. Functional neutral sources are a work in progress as of this printing.

LAMP NAMING LOGIC

One of the more helpful elements of lamp technology comes in understanding the naming convention that is used to describe the shape and sizes of common electric lamps.

Most lamps are given a description code of 2 or 3 letters followed by 2 or 3 numbers. In most cases, the letters are some manner of describing the lamp shape, and the numbers are a manner of describing the size.

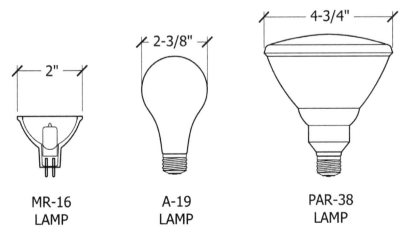

MR-16 LAMP   A-19 LAMP   PAR-38 LAMP

Figure 8.11 Most lamp names describe the lamp diameter in 1/8" increments.

Lamp Size

The sizing of lamps is very simple, if not utterly logical. Common electric lamps sizes are indicated by a two-number code that describes their size in ⅛" increments. By this logic, our common light bulb, which in lighting circles is referred to as an A-19 lamp, is ¹⁹⁄₈" in diameter or 2-⅜" in diameter. This measurement turns out to be accurate as we go down the line from small lamps like MR-16 lamps (¹⁶⁄₈" or 2" in diameter), to larger PAR-38 lamps (³⁸⁄₈" or 4-¾" in diameter). Figures 8.11 and 8.12 illustrate a few examples of these size codes.

Lamp Shape

The system for describing the shape as a code is a little more varied. Inevitably, the two or three letters leading a lamp code are meant to give some literal indication of the shape of the lamp. A stroll through the family illustrates some examples.

A-lamps, which include the A-19 (common light bulb), A-21, and A-23, are named such that "A" stands for "arbitrary." This is presumably due to its irregular shape.

Next in the lineage of directionality are so-called "R" lamps, like R-20, R-30, and R-40. In all of these cases, R stands for "reflector," presumably to describe the generic silver backing common of these lamps.

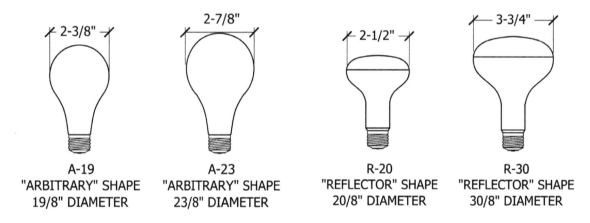

Figure 8.12 Common sizes of the arbitrary shaped "A" lamp (left) and reflector "R" lamps (right).

Then we encounter our PAR lamps, like our PAR-20, PAR-30, and PAR-38. PAR stands for Parabolic Aluminized Reflector and refers to the engineered parabolic surface built into each of these lamps.

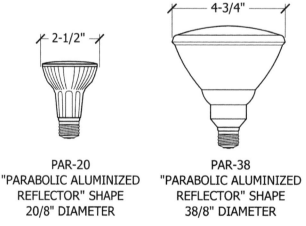

Figure 8.14 Common sizes of parabolic aluminized reflector "PAR" lamps.

When we discuss MR lamps, like the ubiquitous MR-16 and the smaller MR-11 and MR-8, the MR stands for Multifaceted Reflector and is, indeed, a very highly-engineered reflecting device.

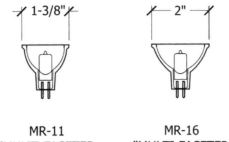

MR-11
"MULTI-FACETED
REFLECTOR" SHAPE
11/8" DIAMETER

MR-16
"MULTI-FACETED
REFLECTOR" SHAPE
16/8" DIAMETER

Figure 8.15 Common sizes of multifaceted reflector "MR" lamps.

T-lamps tend to be "tubular" in shape, as is the case with our linear fluorescent T-8 and T-5 lamps. T-lamps can refer to smaller, tubular halogen or HID lamps as well.

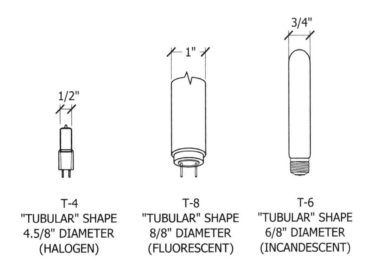

T-4
"TUBULAR" SHAPE
4.5/8" DIAMETER
(HALOGEN)

T-8
"TUBULAR" SHAPE
8/8" DIAMETER
(FLUORESCENT)

T-6
"TUBULAR" SHAPE
6/8" DIAMETER
(INCANDESCENT)

Figure 8.16 Common sizes of tubular (T) lamps.

The parade of names and codes goes on, but the lamps mentioned above represent most of what we run into in the world of architectural lighting.

LAMP CODES FOR COLOR RENDERING INDEX (CRI) AND COLOR TEMPERATURE

It is important to point out that lamps truly are the core of all of our light creating devices. The design industry puts much focus on luminaires and their behaviors and aesthetic appeal, but at the heart of every electric light creating device is a lamp of some sort. It is perhaps more valuable to dedicate brain space to knowing about lamp technologies and properties than to clutter one's head with the glut of luminaire literature that circulates. Lamp technology tends to change slower than luminaire technology, and there is an inherent logic to the way lamps are designed, marketed, and manufactured.

The key to successfully specifying the right lamp is caring tremendously about Color Temperature and Color Rendering Index properties of the lamp. Remember that once we step outside of standard incandescent and halogen incandescent sources, science can cook up any color and color rendering properties desired. As per our earlier discussion, it is imperative to boil down lamps to their two primary properties of concern:

Color Rendering Index or CRI (from 1-100)

Color Temperature (in Degrees Kelvin or Kelvins)

Luckily for us, most engineered electric light sources like HID and fluorescent are described by a three digit code that is stamped right on the lamp or lamp packaging. This three digit code contains information indicative of both the Color Rendering Index and Color Temperature.

The first number in the series indicates the Color Rendering Index or CRI. If the 3-digit product code starts with a 7, the CRI of that product is in the 70's. If the code starts with an 8, the CRI is in the 80's. A 9 indicates a CRI in the 90's. We tend to give more merit to the color-rendering capabilities of our fluorescent and HID sources, and so we can assess the CRI code like this:

7 = CRI in the 70's: This is acceptable, but should be used only in non-color critical environments.

8 = CRI in the 80's: This is typical and reasonable to use in most day-to-day applications.

9= CRI in the 90's: This is very desirable for color critical environments, but also relatively expensive.

The second component of the code lies in the last two digits. These two numbers are indicative of the Color Temperature in degrees Kelvin. The system breaks down like this:

28 = Color Temperature of 2800K = warm (imitating the color of incandescent sources);

30 = Color temperature of 3000K = neutral (imitating the color of halogen sources);

35 = Color Temperature of 3500K = cool;

41 = Color Temperature of 4100K = cool;

50 = Color Temperature of 5000K = cool;

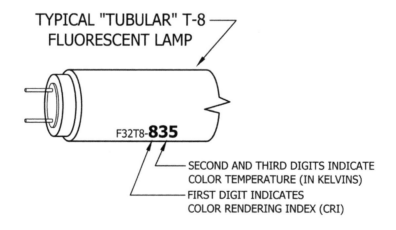

TYPICAL "TUBULAR" T-8
FLUORESCENT LAMP

F32T8-**835**

SECOND AND THIRD DIGITS INDICATE
COLOR TEMPERATURE (IN KELVINS)
FIRST DIGIT INDICATES
COLOR RENDERING INDEX (CRI)

Figure 8.17 Most fluorescent and HID products are labeled with a three digit code expressing color rendering index and color temperature.

Keep in mind that color temperatures are really meaningful only as guidelines within a family of products. One brand of 2800K fluorescent lamp may not look like another brand of 2800K fluorescent lamp and will certainly not look like a 2800K Metal halide lamp nor the incandescent lamp it is trying to imitate.

Source Efficacy Estimates

Identifying source technologies with their general efficacies or efficiencies is a useful and often neglected piece of information. In some lighting design guides, it is a recommended practice to design appropriate light levels for spaces based on a watts-per-square-foot density of installed luminaires. This practice tends to be tactically deficient. Designing light on a power density basis is ignorant of the different efficacies of the different source technologies. It can lead to uninspired designs of flat, even illuminance levels where they may not be welcome. The closest thing to designing to a density is the Lumen Method Calculation which recommends light density based on lumens per square foot (we will discuss calculation methods in Chapter 20). For the time being, we will introduce a basic set of numbers that will paint an approximate but useful picture of how various sources compare to one another in terms of efficacy (light-out compared to electricity-in). In common lighting design practice, we make use of four source technologies. Below are *rough approximations* of efficacy for each that we can use for comparisons.

Standard incandescent efficacy = 10 lumens per watt (lpw);

Halogen incandescent efficacy = 15 lumens per watt (lpw);

Fluorescent and HID efficacy = 70 lumens per watt (lpw);

LED efficacy = 30-50 lumens per watt (lpw);

This simple table shows why we tend to group all of our high-efficacy sources together. It also illustrates why fluorescent sources consume only 1/5th to 1/7th the amount of electricity as the incandescent products they are replacing. If you can mentally hang-on to these four numbers, you will have an invaluable foundation for visualizing, estimating, and calculating lighting effects.

All of these properties together give the user fairly good insight into making lamp decisions. Lamp literature is also, thankfully, more straight-forward than that of luminaires. By grasping the basic concepts of color rendering, color temperature and efficiency, one is much better prepared to make decisions about suitable sources for accomplishing lighting goals.

Part II
Designing Light

Chapter 9

Textures of Light

Texture is one of the most neglected concepts of understanding light. It also happens to be one of the most useful for designers desiring a quick intuitive knowledge base for making lighting decisions. This understanding is based on the ability to visualize and describe the various textures of light that we paint onto our surfaces. Many bad lighting decisions come from the lack of understanding texture of light. You will recall that the basic spectrum of light texture has soft, diffuse light on the one hand, and directional, focused light on the other hand. It is useful to understand how our specific lamp and luminaire technologies deliver light so that we can make good decisions from the beginning.

DIFFUSE LIGHT

When we talk about diffuse light, we are talking about light that leaves its source equally at all angles and, as such, reflects off of surfaces at all angles.

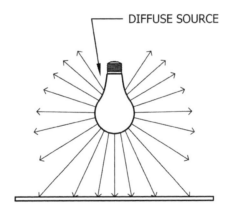

DIFFUSE SOURCE

Figure 9.1 Diffuse sources deliver light evenly in every direction.

This light is usually the product of large glowing sources like incandescent globes and fluorescent tubes. We can diffuse light even further by placing diffusing lenses like frosted glass and acrylic on our light source, as in the case of decorative pendants and sconces.

Diffuse light fills in shadows and, therefore, reduces the appearance of texture changes. We use this light to render people as it is flattering and forgiving of textural imperfections. We use soft, diffuse light to create comfortable, intimate environments where we want long-term visual comfort. Diffuse light tends to be even light, which reduces eye strain that comes from high-contrast environments. Diffuse light also works well for task environments by eliminating shadows and, again, reducing contrast that causes eye strain.

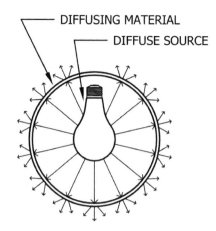

Figure 9.2 Diffuse sources can be further diffused to deliver even softer light.

Diffuse light applied as the only ingredient can become monotonous, boring, and visually un-interesting. When a space is filled with even, diffuse light, there is little visual interest to direct the order that you experience a space. Diffuse light can also cause a unique type of eye strain that comes from having too little contrast. Over long periods of time in purely diffuse environments, the eye tends to strain to pull out detail and find visual acuity. It can feel as if one's eyes are straining to find more detail in the scene around him / her.

DIRECTIONAL LIGHT

Directional light is the product of lamps and luminaires that have purpose-built reflectors that harness light from a source and push it out in a single direction.

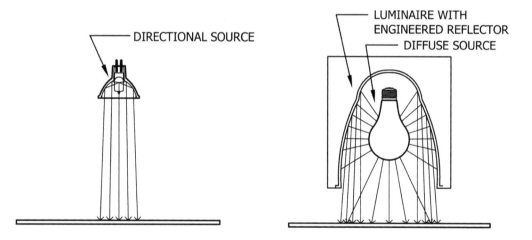

Figure 9.3 Directional lamps (left) and directional luminaires (right) utilize reflectors and optics to deliver light in a controlled manner.

This effect is often accomplished with an engineered luminaire, or simply within the lamp itself. Directional light is most notably delivered in a shape that has distinct boundaries. Our directional light sources create pools and beams and scallops of light that tend to be brightest in the center, and fade to a clear-cut border. As designers of light, these sources are the primary ingredient of our thought process, as they are able to deliver specific pieces of light to specific surfaces and objects in our space. The light arrives from one direction and has a tendency to reflect off of objects in one direction. Hence, directional light creates distinct shadows between light and dark and, therefore, introduces contrast that shows off material texture.

Figure 9.4 Diffuse light sources (top) hide texture and limit contrast. Directional sources (bottom) create shadows, contrast, and visual interest.

We use directional light sources to cast accent onto art, objects and unique architectural features. Directional light makes objects glow and makes metals and glass shimmer and sparkle. It is these sources that add visual interest and hierarchy to environments by creating objects and surfaces that are distinctly brighter than their surroundings. The contrast created by directional light can, however, become uncomfortable over long time periods. Excessive contrast causes the eye to constantly re-adapt when looking from bright elements to dark elements. Directional light is also undesirable for many tasks since excessive shadows (often from a person or his / her own hand) can obscure the task on which you are trying to focus.

THE SPECTRUM OF LIGHT TEXTURES

The fundamentals of making good luminaire and lamp decisions are as simple as identifying light sources by the type of light they deliver. The diagram below exhibits what we will consider as the four levels of light texture, ranging from directional to diffuse.

Very Directional Light

At the directional end of the spectrum, we have reflector driven lamps like halogen MR lamps that have precision engineered reflectors that drive light out. This light is perfect for accenting art and decorative objects, but creates glare and contrast that may be unsuitable for lighting a social gathering space. We can also create this directional light with accent fixtures that have precise reflectors around a small halogen or HID source. We can compare this light to the harshness of direct sunlight.

"MR" LAMP

LUMINAIRE
WITH "T" LAMP

Figure 9.5 Effects of very directional light (left) are often the product of very directional lamps and luminaires with engineered reflectors and small sources (right).

Directional Light

Slightly softer and directional light can be created with PAR type lamps. These lamps also have a reflector, but incorporate diffusing lenses and less-precise optics that create a slightly more diffuse quality of light. PAR lamps are built around small Halogen or HID sources. We can also create this quality of light by placing diffusing filters in front of MR type lamps. This light is perfectly functional for painting light onto art, gathering areas and architectural features; it is acceptable to some for creating even levels of task light. It is similar to the quality of unfiltered skylight.

"PAR" LAMP

Figure 9.6 Effects of directional light (left) are often the product of directional lamps.

Diffuse Light

Towards the softer end of the spectrum are luminaires that use reflectors to harness the light of diffuse lamps. When we take an otherwise diffuse incandescent lamp or fluorescent lamp and build a large reflector around it, the product is a subtle wash or pool of slightly diffuse light. We also get this light from our family of incandescent "R" lamps that are little more than a common light bulb with a generic reflecting surface built into the back. Diffuse light is unsuited for making an accent statement, but delivers a nice quality of light for gathering areas and task situations. We might liken this effect to the soft light of daylight diffused through sheer curtains.

BARE "R"-LAMP

LUMINAIRE
WITH "A" LAMP

Figure 9.7 The effects of diffuse light (left) are often the product of diffuse lamps (right) and luminaires with engineered reflectors and larger sources (right).

Very Diffuse

On the very diffuse end of the spectrum, we consider glowing sources that put out light in every direction and often include diffusing materials to encourage the spread of light. We get this light from bare incandescent and fluorescent lamps. We also create this light with diffusing sources like shaded table lamps, floor lamps, diffusing pendants and sconces. This is like the light we get on a cloudy, overcast gray day. Diffuse light is suitable for filling an entire room with a homogenous glow, but is certainly not useful for accenting objects.

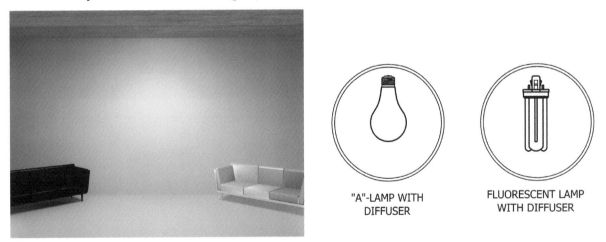

"A"-LAMP WITH
DIFFUSER

FLUORESCENT LAMP
WITH DIFFUSER

Figure 9.8 Effects of very diffuse light (left) are often the product of luminaires with diffusers and diffuse sources (right).

With these four textures committed to our intuitive knowledge base, a designer is well-prepared to articulate the quality of light envisioned for a space. Once you get used to the idea of making a texture decision about light, you will wonder how you ever got by without doing so. The designer who can visualize and describe different textures of diffuse and directional light can also identify light sources, lamps and luminaires that are not going to meet the needs of the design.

Chapter 10

Shapes of Light

The next ingredient in our intuitive understanding of light is the articulation of shapes of light that we add to our designed spaces. It is impossible to deliver visual interest in a space without making distinct statements through the shape of light and lighted surfaces. The easiest way to understand the different shapes of light we use as tools is to identify the following three categories: pools of light, planes of light and glowing objects.

POOLS AND PIECES OF LIGHT

Most of our directional sources emit beams of light that deliver some type of pool of light onto the objects we illuminate. These round shapes of light can have relatively soft borders or well defined boundaries between light and dark. We use these shapes to cast pieces of light onto specific objects like art, sculpture, furniture pieces, and convening areas. Creating distinct pieces of light is certainly a way to add detail and interest, but care must be taken to not overuse the treatment. Light shapes tend to come across as artificial and contrived, as they are rare in the natural world. When not used with restraint, pools of light can give galleries, restaurants and other high contrast environments an "over-done" appearance.

Image courtesy of Deltalight   www.deltalight.us

Figure 10.1 Distinct pools of light add visual interest and contrast, but can become overwhelming or visually "noisy."

PLANES AND LINES OF LIGHT

We have a vast array of continuous linear sources that are useful for creating long lines of light that follow the long lines of our architecture and materials. Linear sources, used properly, allow an entire geometric surface to glow evenly and can enhance the way materials are perceived. Slots and washes of light bleed across surfaces and create shapes of light very similar to what we might encounter from daylight devices like skylights, light wells and windows. We tend to have an affinity for these shapes because they deliver a sense of connection to the natural skylight and sunlight to which we are accustomed.

Image courtesy of Deltalight   www.deltalight.us

Figure 10.2 Planes and lines of light can harmonize with architecture and are reminiscent of natural daylight.

GLOWING OBJECTS

Glowing objects like pendants, sconces and shaded lamps make up the last shape we consider. We call these self-contained pieces of light art "self-luminous" sources, and we distinguish them from the architecturally-integrated light sources that we use to create pools and planes of light. The most certain thing that we can say of self luminous sources is that we must use them with care. When we combine decorative intrigue with brightness, the result is an object that draws immediate attention to itself. These shapes of light can be useful for instructing visual flow and encouraging way finding, but if we try to use these glowing objects as our primary sources of light, we end up with overly bright decoration that works against our lighting goals. Once these glowing sources have attracting one's gaze, the eyes adapt to the brightness, so the space, as a whole, is consequently perceived as darker. It is good practice to use these sources in conjunction with luminaires that direct light onto surfaces. This combination of effects allows us to use our decorative fixtures at lower levels for the visual effect we truly desire without having to rely on them to create brightness in a space.

Adding a concern for shape to our lighting decisions gives us one more specific ingredient for matching light application to the function of our space, and the shape of our space. We can now identify how we want to add light so that it harmonizes and emphasizes the geometry, scale and materials of our design. Designing with shapes of light also has a profound effect on the mood and feeling that a space translates.

Image courtesy of Deltalight   www.deltalight.us

Figure 10.3 Glowing sources serve as visual interest, but can overpower a space and be a source of glare.

Chapter 11
Location of the Light Source

The last frontier of decision making about adding light is designing where the light appears to be coming from. It is important to ponder this decision because recent trends and technologies have led to the misconception that all lighting devices belong in the ceiling, washing light down onto the ground below. To make the most of our lighting resources, we must take time to investigate all of the other ways of delivering light that we can conceive. Many successful lighting designs are, indeed, based on ceiling-mounted downlights as they are certainly a versatile way to deliver pieces of architectural light. We will strive for innovation, however, by opening our mind to the variety of methods for delivering light. It is a good practice to investigate uncommon techniques, first, to avoid the tendency to migrate back towards the generic means of recessed downlights.

LIGHT FROM THE CEILING ONTO WALLS

The quickest change we can make to the generic downlighting tactic is to use light sources that can be aimed to direct light onto the vertical surfaces of a space, rather than simply straight down. These pieces of light go a long way to increase the overall perception of brightness in a space. Vertical lighting also expands a space and shows off the architectural boundaries.

Image courtesy of Erco   www.erco.com

Figure 11.1 Lighting vertical surfaces creates a distinct impression of brightness.

LIGHTING FROM THE GROUND UPWARD

We can implement light sources that recess into the ground or floor plane and create beams of light that wash the walls and cast pools of light up onto ceilings and canopies overhead. This flavor of light delivers a unique light quality that is rare in the natural world, where daylight from above is the norm. Upward directed light can contribute to the perception of height and verticality. It can also create a more intimate feeling if the light further reveals the ceiling above.

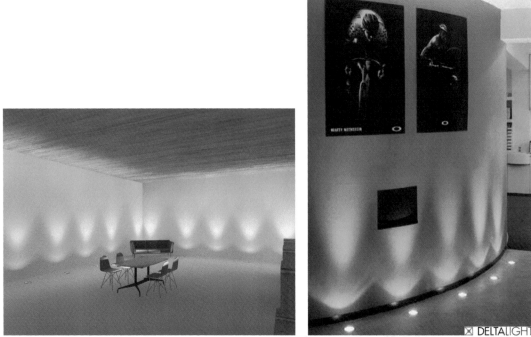

Figure 11.2 Lighting upward from the ground is at once unusual and creates a unique environment.

LIGHTING FROM THE WALL UPWARD

These sources are mounted to the surface of a wall or regressed into a wall and cast light up onto the ceiling plane above them. Light onto the ceiling plane opens up a space and increases the perception of volume. A bright ceiling lends a feeling of openness by mimicking a bright sky above. The even light from a glowing ceiling is sometimes all the light needed for a simple environment where little task or accent lighting is necessary.

Figure 11.3 Lighting from the wall to the ceiling adds volume and height to a space.

LIGHTING FROM THE WALL BACK ONTO THE WALL

We have a vast array of decorative and functional fixtures with shielded sources that paint light back onto the wall to which they are mounted. These differ from our purely-decorative sconces in that they wash light onto the wall, rather than simply glow. This treatment of light is useful where ceiling or floor mounted luminaires are not an option. These fixtures can be mounted in rows and patterns to help the flow of a long space or corridor.

Figure 11.4 Lighting back onto the wall creates brightness without glare.

LIGHT FROM SLOTS AND COVES ONTO WALLS AND CEILINGS

These are the architecturally integrated lines of light that create even washes and unique glows onto entire surfaces of a space. These shapes of light go a long way to enhance the geometry of space. The long, clean lines can show off the joints and connections of structure. Lines of light also do a good job of mimicking the clean light we receive from daylight openings like skylights and light shelves.

Image courtesy of Erco   www.erco.com

Figure 11.5 Slots of light from above create brightness onto vertical surfaces and are reminiscent of daylight.

SUSPENDED GLOWING SOURCES

Glowing sources add a haze of light to our spaces and a distinct focal point. They must be applied with care to avoid glare and generic floods of light. These sources are often the crowning elements of visual interest that we apply after our other lighting needs have been met. There are environments where a single, well-placed glowing source can solve most of our lighting needs, but they are more often misused to draw attention and leave a space feeling dark.

Image courtesy of Erco   www.erco.com

Figure 11.6 Glowing pendants act as focal points, but can also deliver controlled
light up and down.

LOW LIGHTING ONTO THE FLOOR

Localizing light onto the floor plane can be accomplished with luminaires that mount low on the wall. These so-called "step lights" are usually considered for lighting stairs, but they are just as effective in delivering light onto the floor plane. These luminaires typically recess into the wall and work to get the light source closer to the surface being lighted.

Image courtesy of Erco   www.erco.com

Figure 11.7 Low, wall-mounted area lights keep light down where it is needed.

The goal of considering a simple list of lighting applications like this is to avoid the repetitive and static environment that is the product of over-using recessed lighting. Certainly, a complex space can be lighted entirely with the right adjustable, ceiling-mounted fixture, but if we start by experimenting with ideas of unusual light application, we are much more likely to innovate. The result can be a space with a truly special and unique design character. There are certainly numerous ways to deliver light other than the manners we have listed, but if we can add these distinct methods to our intuition, we will be much more likely to consider them as we design.

Chapter 12

Building Light from Darkness

With our new-found intuition for the texture, shape and source of light, we can further expand on our decision-making process to make sure that we are considering all of our options when adding light to a space. If we consider each of these aspects every time we look to add light to our design, we can be sure that the light will support what we are attempting to convey through the design. The convenient aspect of this intuitive knowledge is that it doesn't yet require knowledge of light levels, calculations, or luminaire technologies. We are still simply addressing the light itself and how that light will interact with the surfaces of our designed environment. *As long as we can visualize light and communicate design ideas for it, we can find a way to implement it.*

Our expanded list of the controllable aspects of light now looks like this:

Light intensity: Bright vs. Dark;

Light Color: Warm vs. Cool;

Light Texture: Directional vs. Diffuse;

> We now have a visual understanding of what texture means and what types of sources create these textures.

Light shape: Pools of light, Planes of light, Points of light;

> We can now make decisions about how we match the shape of light to the shape of our architecture, surfaces and objects within a space.

Light origin: Where is the light coming from?

> Thinking beyond basic downlighting, we are more likely to come up with lighting systems that are truly complementary of the designed space.

BUILDING LIGHT FROM DARKNESS

An effective mental exercise for enhancing the design process is to step back and approach a space as a collection of surfaces that can receive light. This process can be broken down into two steps: seeing an environment as a collection of surfaces and seeing those surfaces for the materials of which they are made.

Seeing our environment for the surfaces that make it up

Once we have adopted all of the subtleties of lighting design decisions into our intuition, we are ready to start placing light with meaning, conviction, and true relation to the design goals of our project. The helpful process for making lighting additions to our environment is to take what we know about our architecture and surroundings and visualize this environment as a collection of surfaces in darkness. From this starting point, we picture ourselves with the ability to *paint* light onto the specific surfaces that make up the space.

The more we know about the use and layout of a space, the better, but this visualization can be done with only the walls, floor and ceiling in our mind. We picture ourselves placing light onto each surface because this is exactly what all of our architectural luminaires are designed to do. All of the engineered reflectors and precision lamps have been tweaked and refined to give us total control of delivering light exactly where we want it. We can place light onto a wall, onto a table, onto a piece of art, up onto the ceiling, anywhere we feel the light belongs. A space visualized in total darkness is a blank canvas waiting for lighting design. The designer can imagine painting light onto surfaces as if with a brush or spray can. One-by-one, surfaces are lighted in this manner until the desired lighting effect begins to emerge. *Figure 12.1* illustrates the mental process of visualizing darkness and adding light one surface at a time.

Image courtesy of Deltalight   www.deltalight.us

Figure 12.1 The mental progression of visualizing a space as a collection of surfaces and painting light onto surfaces one by one.

Seeing surfaces for the materials that make them up

Once we have established the mental picture of our environment as the surfaces that make it up, we take the next step and visualize the materials that make up these surfaces. This is where we implement our intuitive knowledge of matching light texture, color and intensity to the specific materials with which we are building.

Texture: Think of the material texture and whether it should be revealed our concealed. Organic stone, concrete and wood may benefit from directional sources that show off the subtle textures by creating shadow through grazing and steep aiming angles. Imperfect walls or materials intended to appear smooth and flawless may benefit from diffuse sources located far from the material.

Color: Think of material color and what color light source will complement it. Cool-colored materials can be emphasized by cool sources like cool fluorescent, metal halide and LED's. Warmer, richer materials, like wood and warm stone, benefit from warm sources like Incandescent. Keep in mind that warm fluorescent sources often appear warm to the eye, but actually do a poor job of rendering warm materials. Mock up any critical situations where the source needs to complement the color of the material.

Intensity: Think of material finish and what light intensity is suitable. Often times, light colored surfaces need very little additional light to make them stand out as bright surfaces and focal elements. Darker materials may require considerably more light to serve as focal points. Some dark surfaces reflect so little light that they may not be worth lighting at all.

Shininess or specularity of a material should always be considered. Shiny materials respond to light by reflecting an exact image of the source that is lighting them. This can be desirable as in the case of accenting jewelry, glassware and other shiny products. Large architectural surfaces of glass or metal may, however, reflect undesirable glare or reflect the light source. Such surfaces may be better off applied with little or no light.

This mental process of visualizing a space in-depth effectively draws out lighting concepts and ideas that will enhance an environment. Taking just a few moments to break a space down into its constituent materials and surfaces makes it easier to address the specific nuances of each lighting addition. This thoughtfulness leads to a designed environment with lighting applications that respond to each surface and perfectly support the design intent.

Chapter 13

Developing Lighting Ideas

When we consider the process and decision-making that we can now apply to our lighting design, we begin to see the steps in a more articulate manner. If abused, this can lead to lighting design that is overly complicated. If we make decisions carefully, however, the result will be a unique synergy of light and material in space that meets the goals of our program and becomes the framework of truly great design.

Take, for instance, a common residential bedroom. If we use our knowledge to determine where light actually belongs in the space, we can very quickly establish a number of appropriate applications. We can consider any or all of the "Five Layer" approach that guides our design. We may think of choreography, mood, and accent, or we may think only of visual tasks.

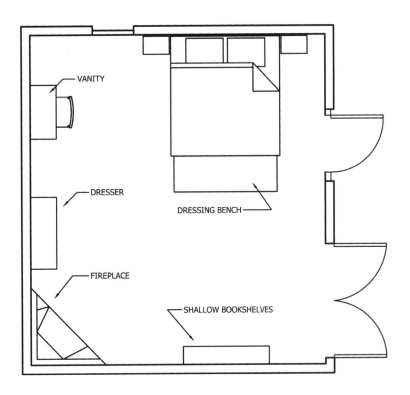

Figure 13 1 A typical residential bedroom.

Consider the following applications of light in this space:

Accenting art on the bed wall to provide a visual focus;

Light onto the vanity for tasks and rendering faces;

Light onto book shelves to read text and highlight the objects;

Light at the bench at the foot of the bed to accommodate dressing.

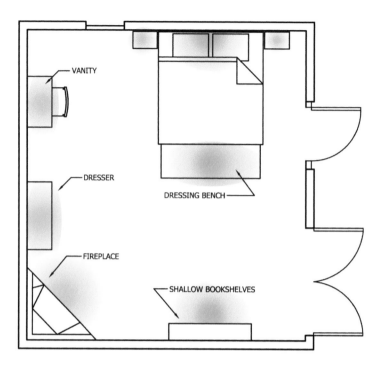

Figure 13.2 One way the space might be rendered to show numerous lighting options.

Now consider all of the applications of light that we have articulated and consider the most commonly seen method to solve all of these problems: a single fixture in the center of the room.

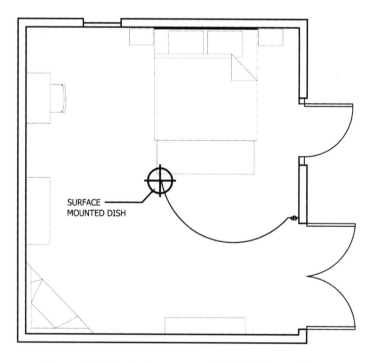

Figure 13.3 A typical economy-minded lighting solution.

Suppose this fixture is a simple recessed downlight. Which of these goals are being addressed? Nearly none, as the light is simply pushed down to the dark surface of the floor in the middle of the room.

Suppose this fixture is a surface mounted decorative dish. Now which of our identified applications are we addressing? Perhaps none directly, but it could be argued that we are creating *some* amount of light on nearly every surface. Hence in a very generic manner, it may be a suitable solution.

Now, what if we articulate and place luminaires to specifically address all that we have identified?

We begin to see what lighting design can look like. But it is certainly reasonable to say that such a solution is overly complex and self indulgent. The effort and expense required to install, electrify and maintain such a solution is excessive. Additionally, the lighting

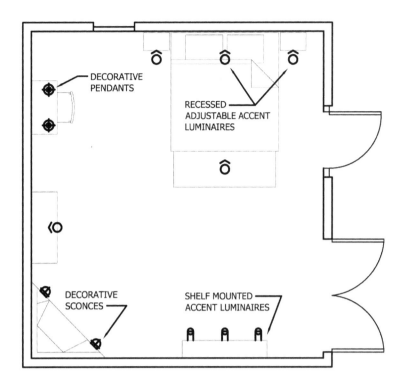

Figure 13.4 An example of an over-developed solution for the space.

solution may be too specific and customized to the current layout and use of the space. In spaces of this type our lighting solutions may need to be more universal and flexible.

It is easy enough to select from among the solutions that we have identified to come up with a reasonable blend of function and versatility.

If we start experimenting with combinations of the effects and applications we have identified, we are bound to refine our options into the exceptional solutions that will support the rest of our design.

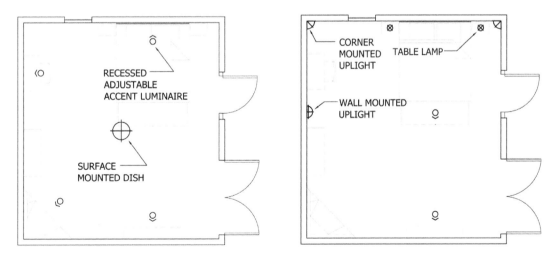

Figure 13.5 Examples of a few prudent lighting solutions.

The process we have just walked through is one for a very common and misunderstood space. This same methodology can be applied to all of the environments, large and small, that we will design. We have allowed ourselves to rely on our intuition and brainstorm in a fashion to identify lighting goals and then the methods for implementing them. No matter how complex our spaces and environments become, lighting design is simply a matter of using design knowledge to determine where light goes, what kind of light it is, and how to get it there.

If we look carefully at the steps above, we will see that we are giving ourselves the opportunity to apply all of our procedure:

We think spatially and see our room as a collection of surfaces.

We identify specific objects first and visualize light on those specifics.

We consider the five layers of light (choreography, mood, accenting, architecture and tasks.)

We consider the controllable aspects of light (intensity, texture, shape)

We consider all of the ways we can deliver the light we are after.

All the while, we are considering the real world aspects of efficiency, economy, maintenance, flexibility, and any other factors that may be a reality for this type of space. We may go on to solve lighting challenges with cost effective luminaries or high-efficiency sources, but since we have already identified where light will go, the integrity of the design solution will stay intact. By designing with light, rather than attaching ourselves to specific luminaries or a specific layout or tactic, we can respond to the changing program of the project. Deciding where light belongs affords us the confidence to deal with changes in budget or schedule that might otherwise derail a developed lighting design.

With a thorough knowledge of our design requirements, and an intimacy with the environment we are designing, all we need is the willingness to be thoughtful with light, and our intuition will do the rest.

This gives us great confidence to explore all of our ideas and lighting design goals without an extensive knowledge of specific luminaires, specific light levels or complex lighting calculations.

Chapter 14

Identifying Concepts in Light

Before delving into specific applications of light in typical spaces, it is well worth exploring lighting application concepts in a broader sense. The strength of lighting design lies in how the individual designer applies his or her knowledge of lighting cause and effect. Rather than present a collection of generic lighting solutions for generic spaces, the following chapter represents a portfolio of lighting concepts that can be applied to many spaces. Confidence in making design decisions comes from experience and familiarity or from the genuine belief that we have thought of every option. There are no shortcuts to familiarity and experience, but the following visual concepts can help lay a foundation that will strengthen a designer's ability to conceptualize and investigate numerous lighting options.

For the majority of designers, the goal is not to grasp every shred of lighting knowledge possible. The goals are more practical and focused: visualization and communication.

A designer must be able to visualize lighting effects.

(This is the reason we present light as visual concepts).

A designer must be able to communicate and describe the light that he/she desires.

(This is why we emphasize lighting vocabulary)

If a designer can visualize light and successfully communicate lighting goals to others, there are consultants and experts who can assist the designer in bringing those lighting ideas to reality.

The images and descriptions presented here are targeted towards this hypothesis. By providing visual concepts of what light can do, the designer is left to decide where these ingredients are best put to use in the design.

"LIGHT A WALL AND LIGHT AN OBJECT"

This basic concept can be implemented in even the simplest spaces. It is applicable at any scale for any architecture. The large *vertical surface* to which you apply light will define the bright character of your space. It will contribute to your mood and the architectural effect of the space. The *object* that you focus light on will create visual interest, likely accommodate tasks, and will organize and choreograph your space. *Figures 14.1 and 14.2* show spaces lighted generically beside the same space with this tactic applied.

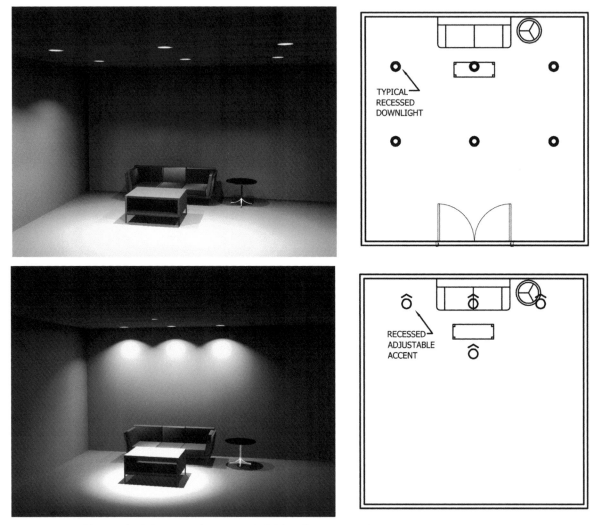

Figure 14.1 A generic layout (top) yields a flat quality of light in a seating area. Lighting a vertical surface and a focal object (bottom) creates perceived brightness and visual interest.

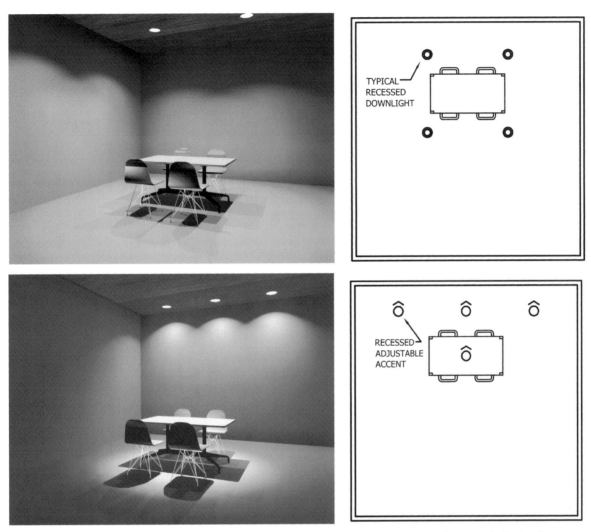

Figure 14.2 A generic layout applied to a dining area (top). A more focused approach (bottom) creates contrast and mood.

MOVE LIGHT TO THE PERIMETER

One of the simplest ways to transform a space is to apply light to the walls and other vertical surfaces. When we consider the bare-bones lighting tactic of placing a group of recessed downlights in the center of a room, we need only change our tactic slightly to get greater effect. Thoughtlessly placing luminaires in the center of a space is a poor use of light resources. By simply shifting the location of these luminaires, light is painted onto the high vertical surfaces that deliver the perception of brightness. This simple shift is an effective example of using the same luminaires in a different way to make an impacting difference on how a space feels. Observe how different these basic spaces feel as a result of this shift.

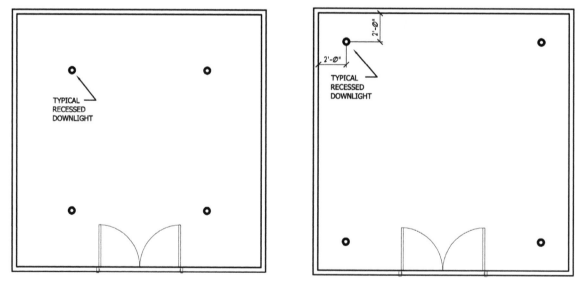

Figure 14.3 Light directed downward (left) can create a cave-like effect. The same amount of light applied to vertical surfaces (right) adds to the perceived brightness.

CHOREOGRAPHING HALLS AND CORRIDORS

Passageways are often treated with the same thoughtless application of regularly-spaced luminaires marching down the center of the space. These luminaires lose most of their light into the dark floor surface and do little to organize the space or create brightness. If we use our light to address the vertical surfaces, we can create both visual interest and definite way-finding by creating lighted goals. We can experiment to identify the lighted surfaces that create the mood and effect we are after, but, invariably, the best use of our light will not be on the floor. A single piece of light at the end of a hallway is often more compelling than an entire row of recessed downlights. Consider also what happens when we implement asymmetric lighting or even a linear slot of light down one side. Lighting the wall of a hallway creates a continuous light shape that encourages flow.

Images courtesy of Erco and Deltalight

Figure 14.4 A lighted goal and a lighted surface are all that are needed to make a corridor attractive and functional.

UPLIGHTING WALLS AND CANOPIES

Walls and vertical surfaces aren't the only surfaces that have a profound effect on our spaces. We can create a dominating presence and alter mood by washing light up onto the ceilings and canopies in our space. Lighting the ceiling overhead can make people feel safer, can expand space, and can lend a sense of lightness to an environment. Using our lighting resources in this manner can often deliver dramatic effect with very little light used.

Images courtesy of Deltalight   www.deltalight.us

Figure 14.5 Light directed upward onto an overhang or ceiling creates an encompassing environment of light.

SLOTS, COVES AND LIGHT SHELVES

The last two decades have truly seemed to be the era of the recessed downlight, and because of this trend we have gotten very used to the idea that scallops of light and pools of light are the proper shapes to add to our space. More and more, the geometry of contemporary architecture seems to pair better with linear planes of light. Spaces that tend to become visually cluttered can be organized by applying light as large geometric statements.

Large clean geometric shapes of light lend our designs the same clean, efficient feeling as our contemporary architecture. Slots, coves, and light shelves are all examples of architectural features that can conceal light sources that create the large, glowing shapes that define our perception of brightness in a space.

Image courtesy of Deltalight   www.deltalight.us

Figure 14.6 Spaces usually treated with pools of light take on new feeling when lighted with lines and planes.

LIGHTING THROUGH GLASS

Lighting glass can be understood by recognizing that as a transparent material, we cannot light glass itself. Light directed toward glass either passes through or reflects directly back. Because of this property, if there is nothing to see beyond a piece of glass, the glass will simply act as a mirror. This has two important design consequences.

First, it is worth noting that luminaires placed close to windows tend to reflect a direct image of the bright source right back at us. For this reason it is good practice to avoid placing interior luminaires right next to glass and windows. Secondly, it means that our best chance of drawing attention through glass is to create bright surfaces and objects *beyond* the glass. This leads us to light exterior features to draw attention through glass openings. It also leads us to wash light onto exterior eves and overhangs just beyond our windows.

SUPPLEMENTING DECORATIVE FIXTURES

Hopefully, it is clear through all of our discussions that glowing decorative sources of light are not ideal stand-alone tools for our version of integrated architectural lighting design. Decorative fixtures do have an important place in our lighting tool vocabulary, but, on their own, they tend to be sources of glare and leave a room gloomy. To make better use of these decorative fixtures, we need to support them with more directional luminaires nearby. When we have concealed sources that we can use to place specific pieces of light where we want, we are free to use our decorative sources at lower light levels for the subtle visual effects and mood effects we desire.

Figure 14.8 Providing directed accent light frees up glowing sources to serve as decoration.

Image courtesy of Erco   www.erco.com

DIRECTIONAL DECORATIVE FIXTURES

In order to avoid tiptoeing around decorative lighting elements, it helps to be deliberate in the types of decorative luminaires specified. It is useful to draw a clear distinction between self-luminous glowing sources and shielded decorative luminaires that direct light back onto nearby surfaces. Luminaires that appear as glowing bright spots tend to be overly self-serving and don't always support the space as a whole. Decorative luminaires that direct light can be used like our other architectural light sources for lighting surfaces. For every glowing decorative pendant, wall sconce and floor lamp, there is a version of this fixture that shields the source and directs the light onto the surfaces of the space.

Figure 14.9 Decorative luminaires like the linear pendant shown here can be
designed to provide functional light for tasks and ambience.

The ideas presented here are just a head-start toward familiarity of the ways light can be effectively delivered to add emotion and experience to our designed environments. With a dedication to dissecting designed environments, the designer is sure to steadily build a repertoire of lighting ideas and concepts that will work for him/her. As this knowledge base grows, it is a helpful practice for a designer to pinpoint what works and what could be changed to improve the interaction of light in the spaces he/she visits.

There are no absolutes in design, and even fewer in lighting design, but the images and concepts discussed in this chapter should encourage you to think a bit deeper about what options are available and should get you to question that status quo that gets applied to so many spaces.

Chapter 15

Lighting That Works

The deeper our familiarity with the basics of lighting science and design, the more we can learn from lighted, designed environments all around us. Take time to investigate design and articulate what elements of design are responsible for the way things are functioning. Each of the following images has identifiable lighting elements that play a strong role in the design as a whole. There is a saying in lighting design that "Good lighting gets a space noticed, and bad lighting gets itself noticed." This speaks to the power of architecturally-integrated light and warns us to be cautious with our decorative lighting elements and strongly-themed lighting statements.

The surest way to create a predictable effect is to integrate something that has been successfully implemented before. But a designer must be sure that he/she is implementing something because it works and is desired, not simply because it seems to be a commonly-used solution.

The following images are accompanied by numbered items that point out the key lighting elements in each scenario. The scenarios focus on integrated lighting that is well thought-out and supports the needs and goals of each space.

Museum / Gallery Space

Image courtesy of Erco   www.erco.com

1. *Pools of increased light levels move the eye from one important object to the next.*
2. *Slender, indirect sources fill the ceiling volume with diffuse ambient light*
3. *Aimable, directional luminaires provide accent light on art and vertical surfaces*
4. *Indirect uplight reveals the volumes and shapes of the vaulted ceiling system.*
5. *The combination of directional, accent light and diffuse light provide for long-term visual comfort.*

High-End Retail Display

Image courtesy of Deltalight   www.deltalight.us

1. The combination fixtures in the room center provide both comfortable diffuse light and aimable accent light for visual interest.
2. Adjustable accent luminaires in running slots provide punch onto the displayed objects.
3. Planes of light in each display niche define the space and create the perception of brightness.
4. Glowing lines of light in the display niches define the depth and form of the space

High-End Dining / Lounge

Image courtesy of Erco   www.erco.com

1. *Uplight and reflective surfaces define the entry of the space, while darker materials and light directed downward provide more intimacy and a lower scale in the dining area.*
2. *Recessed decorative downlights provide a twinkle on the ceiling and a pool of light for mood and accent down at the task.*
3. *The bright vertical surfaces keep the space bright, so the lighting is free to be applied only where necessary.*

Chapter 16

Designing with Daylight

When we talk about the importance of making decisions about where light will go and how light will interact with architecture, we are talking about the controllable aspects of daylighting, as well as electric light. The most critical component of daylight to remember is that as a source, it is hugely intense. As such, the misuse of daylight can be amazingly detrimental to a project. For this reason, daylight design is primarily a study in control.

There are numerous texts discussing the fine, technical aspects as well as the more philosophical side of the sun as a light source.

We will focus here on basics that are useful as intuitive knowledge. Also presented here is a fundamental procedure that will encourage you to think through all of the factors and decisions that will lead to successful use of daylight.

Daylight can be assessed and controlled, and, as such, it deserves the same type of design scrutiny that we apply to electric light. We should approach our spaces with the intent to visualize our effects and determine what surfaces and objects will benefit from the addition of daylight, just as we do with electric light.

OBVIOUS BENEFITS OF DAYLIGHT

A primary aspect of daylight systems is to consider the benefits that may serve your design. In order to actually make use of these benefits, the daylight systems we integrate must be as well-conceived as our electric light systems.

First and foremost, daylight is a means of producing light without the consumption of electricity or other fossil fuels. This is a huge benefit to all manner of projects where sustainability, minimal maintenance and environmental concern are part of the program. Daylight consumes no electricity and also eliminates the need for changing lamps. Daylight can also be harvested with relatively little heat gain, which means that we can reduce our need for the electricity associated with air conditioning and cooling that offsets heat contributed by electric light.

Daylight is also a special source of light because of our long standing relationship with it. When we consider how long humankind has had only daylight (and occasional firelight) as a light source, it is easy to imagine why we have a special fondness for it. Daylight connects us to the natural world and brings us into contact with a way of life for which we are readily equipped. Small quantities of daylight stave off depression, allow us to synthesize Vitamin D, and can invigorate our spirit and energy level. Certain forms of daylight also have the uncanny ability to deeply relax us.

Daylight is inherently dynamic and changes throughout the course of the day and the year. This factor benefits our natural rhythms and stimulates our active mind. One of the most depressing aspects of poorly-executed electric light is the static, unchanging nature. Daylight is dynamic by nature, so even a small amount can have a huge impact on the interest and stimulation of an environment. The changes in daylight quality are so effective in encouraging different mental states that many electric light systems strive to mimic similar changes in texture and color over the course of a day.

FLAVORS OF DAYLIGHT

In order to visualize and implement the integration of daylight into design, it is helpful to categorize two types of daylight systems: Functional Daylight and Daylight Accenting.

Functional Daylight is the careful introduction of daylight into a space to serve task and spatial-defining functions. This is generally diffuse, even light that can accommodate long term visual comfort.

Figure 16.1 Controlling daylight through diffusion or shading (left) turns it into a tool for solving lighting challenges. Direct sunlight components (right) are useful for impact and interest.

Daylight Accenting is a more dramatic and obvious use of daylight to inspire certain moods and create distinct visual interest. These features may be integrated into high-design spaces where emotional impact is the priority.

These two types of daylight are accomplished through distinctly different types of systems and have very different effects on our environments. There are systems that introduce both simultaneously, but when we visualize a design effect, it is important to identify our target and distinguish between the two.

COMPONENTS OF DAYLIGHT (TEXTURES)

The other basic intuition that a designer should carry is the distinct difference in light quality that is obtained from the different components of daylight. Daylight enters our spaces in a number of different ways and takes on different texture accordingly. Just as we distinguish between the directional beam of an accent luminaire and the soft diffuse light of a glowing globe, we break down the components of daylight into three textures: Direct Sunlight, Skylight and Diffused Sunlight

Direct sunlight Is, arguably, the least useful as a functional light source and most hazardous to design. Light received directly from the sun is excessively bright and leads to situations of glare and unacceptable contrast. Direct sunlight can also introduce heat and UV radiation that can

damage materials and fabrics. As creatures of reflected light, sunlight into our eyes or off of a bright surface into our eyes is simply too bright for our visual system.

Skylight is the product of sunlight diffusing and scattering though various states of our atmosphere. Skylight takes on many different qualities depending on time of day, time of year, weather and atmospheric conditions. From clear blue skylight to soft, diffuse cloudy daylight, most forms of skylight suit our visual system well as a sustained light quality for long durations. (This is no surprise, given our long history with skylight).

Diffused sunlight is the product of introducing sunlight into our spaces after it has interacted with some sort of diffusing material. Once we have passed sunlight though tinted or frosted materials, we gain a much more manageable source of light.

SITE LAYOUT AND MASSING

The dynamic nature of the sun and sky demand that we consider the daylight-harvesting goals for a project very early. The first step in recognizing how to make use of daylight is to identify the opportunities based on the project's orientation and proportions.

There are a few quick rules of solar geometry that will have significant impact on the potential uses of daylight on a design job. Daylight is simple at its heart, and the relationship created by project orientation is equally simple.

Architectural layout and massing must be considered with daylight implications in mind. Height and width of forms and facades greatly affect the surface area available for daylighting opportunities. Glazing must be considered for its daylight implications and not simply for its view considerations. Sight lines and shadow lines should also be investigated in deciding how and where to locate a project.

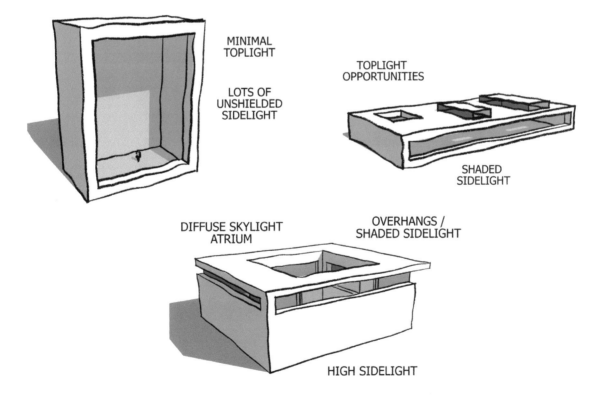

MINIMAL TOPLIGHT

LOTS OF UNSHIELDED SIDELIGHT

TOPLIGHT OPPORTUNITIES

SHADED SIDELIGHT

DIFFUSE SKYLIGHT ATRIUM

OVERHANGS / SHADED SIDELIGHT

HIGH SIDELIGHT

Figure16.2 The massing of a structure will determine the opportunities for various forms of daylight harvesting

Latitude

The closer you are to the North and South Pole of the earth, the lower the sun will be in your sky throughout the year. Without burdening ourselves with solar geometry, we can safely say that a project on the equator has the potential for the sun to be directly overhead much of the year, while a project in the Arctic will never see the sun high in the sky.

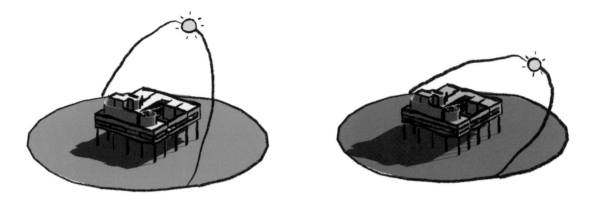

Figure 16.3 High Latitudes and summer months (left) mean a high sun angle and short shadows. Low latitudes and winter months (right) mean a low sun and long shadows.

Cardinal Orientation

The sun rises in the east and sets in the west. Spaces facing these directions have the potential for direct sunlight exposure in the mornings and evenings of every day.

Figure16.4 In the northern hemisphere, the sun will reliably arc across the south sky, casting shadows to the north.

Seasonal Sun Angles

Daylight also has a predictable dynamic behavior over the course of the seasons in a year. The sun will ride higher in the sky in the summer months and will ride lower in sky over the winter months. This means that with a little studying, we can design physical overhangs and shading devices that affect daylight differently throughout the year.

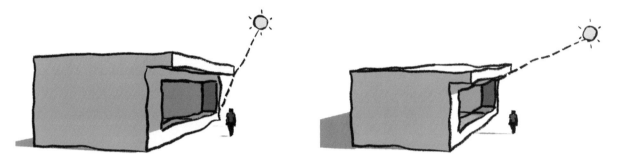

Figure 16.5 A well designed overhang can shade high summer sun (left) and allow in low winter sun (right)

North Light / South Light

Living in the northern hemisphere means that the sun will always arc across the sky to the south. This means that south facing spaces have the potential for direct sunlight all day, while north facing spaces will receive exclusively skylight.

It is good practice to create a simple diagram of the project site in reference to the cardinal directions. This will give the designer guidance as to where he/she can use certain techniques and where to watch out for potential problems.

It is also helpful to draw the elevations of the project site in reference to solar angles and the structures that may shade daylighting opportunities. Do some research on the solar angles that occur at the project latitude through the year to gain a specific understanding of the sunlight variance.

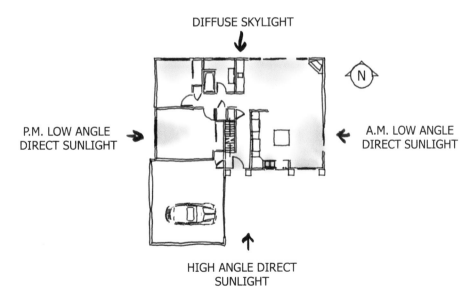

Figure16.6 A simple map of what types of daylight can be expected on a project in the northern hemisphere.

When it comes to actually implementing and designing daylight systems into a space, it pays to think the solutions and concepts through all sun positions. Visualize not just the ideal situations, but every potential sun angle condition to which the design will be subjected. *Think the project through morning and night, sunny and cloudy, and winter to summer.* Far too many daylight ideas are conceived in one dimension and are successful only on the one day a year when the sun and the project are perfectly aligned.

DAYLIGHT SYSTEMS

The next step in making daylight decisions is to determine what types of light character will serve the design intent. The controllable aspects of intensity, color, texture, shape and origin are just as valid with daylight as they are with electric light. Daylight systems can be lumped into two basic categories: side-light and top-light. We then identify the technologies and geometries that we use to control, modify and enhance each.

Side-light Systems

Common wall windows are the clearest example of side-light entering a space. Side-light systems are unique in the many ways that they can transform daylight into a useful form. If we receive direct sun sidelight, we must consider diffusing techniques like tinting, frosting, and fritting. Side-lighting systems are effective high up on vertical surfaces to impart a glow that lights up ceilings and walls to translate volume. Side-light systems can also be designed with geometry in mind so that different components of sunlight and skylight are delivered differently through the year. These systems can incorporate overhangs and shelves to shade direct sunlight. *Figures 16.7 through 16.11* illustrate various systems for harvesting and controlling side-light.

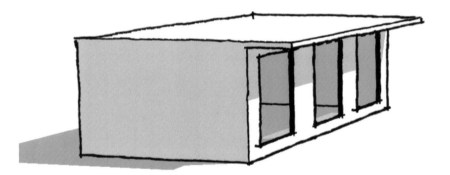

Figure 16.7 Side-lighting daylight systems: **Overhanging soffit**.

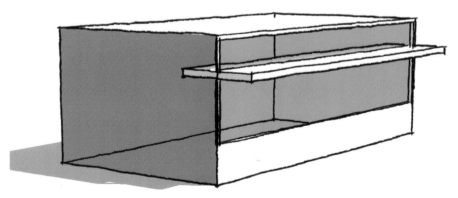

Figure 16.8 Side-lighting daylight systems: **Light shelf**.

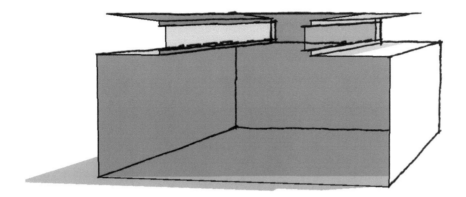

Figure 16.9 Side-lighting daylight systems: **Light monitor.**

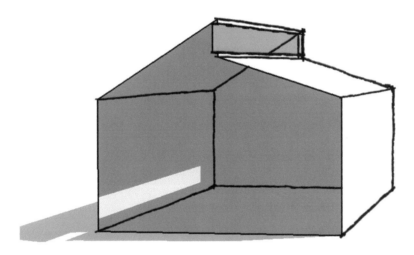

Figure 16.10 Side-lighting daylight systems: **Clerestory window.**

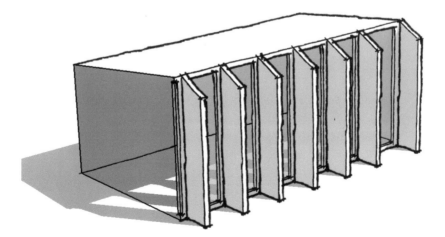

Figure 16.11 Side-lighting daylight systems: **Vertical shading.**

Top-light Systems

Most designed spaces have access to high angled downward daylight, regardless of orientation and neighboring structures. Daylight from above can be shaped much like the recessed luminaires we use so much. High daylight is easy to incorporate into long, linear slots and clean planes. The guidelines for such systems are the same as any daylight:

Direct sunlight should be diffused and controlled;

Skylight is welcomed and easier to put to use;

Study of solar geometry and diffusing materials are the key to good daylight textures.

Figures 16.12 through 16.14 illustrate various systems for harvesting and controlling Top-light.

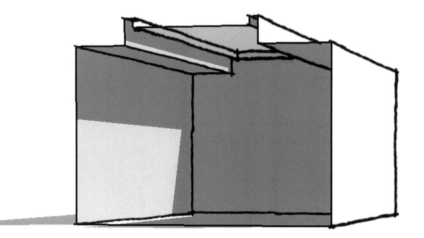

Figure 16.12 Top lighting daylight systems: **Skylight.**

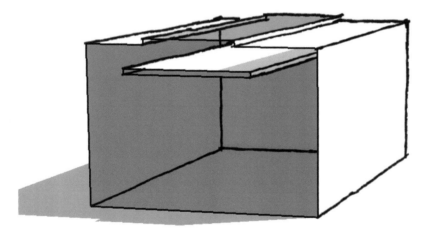

Figure 16.13 Top lighting daylight systems: **Bounced skylight.**

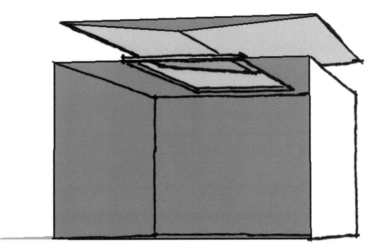

Figure 16.14 Top lighting daylight systems: **Shielded skylight.**

LIGHT CONTROL TECHNIQUES

The last ingredient to making use of daylight is an understanding of the technologies that we use to alter the light textures we receive.

Diffusing

Diffusing daylight can be accomplished though the use of translucent acrylic, frosted glass and a host of other slightly opaque materials. This treatment tends to create a soft, even texture similar to skylight on a cloudy day.

Tinting

Tinting is the simple act of reducing the transmittance of a transparent substrate. Tinting films and laminates come in a variety of colors and are often mirrored. In many cases they receive mixed reviews as they impart a strange sort of gloomy or dark perception of the outside world.

Fritting

Fritted materials are otherwise transparent materials with lines etched or embedded in them. Good fritting can act like a series of miniature light shelves or louvers, using geometry to reduce the transmission of light at certain angles. Bad fritting behaves similar to diffusing materials or prismatic lenses.

Daylight at Work

There are, of course, situations where the raw, unbridled effects of natural daylight are exactly what a space needs. When daylight is used as an accent feature, the challenge is often in studying exactly what type of system is most effective. Daylight for the sake of energy conservation is a noble cause, but there are just as many valid emotional and experiential reasons to work daylight into your design. Many of the most amazing natural and designed spaces hang much of their greatness on the inclusion of daylight. The ethereal connection we hold with daylight makes it a powerful ingredient that can turn an otherwise sterile environment into a truly moving experience.

INTEGRATING WITH ELECTRIC LIGHT

Whether our daylighting ingredients are functional or aesthetic, it is necessary to consider how they can substitute or work in harmony with electric light. In design applications it is worth investigating how a particular daylight effect can be recreated with electric light, or vise versa. It allows a space to have similar light textures in varying sky conditions throughout the day and the year. Consider how shelves, slots, coves and coffers can be fitted with components of both electric light and daylight. Consider also the decisions that help the two systems work in harmony: intensity, color and shape.

Intensity:

Technology allows us to respond to the daylight we are receiving by automatically reducing the intensity of the complementary electric light system. Photocells can send signals to dim or step down the output level of the electric light system. Photocells can also activate shading systems in the case of excess daylight. If your goal is to use daylight to reduce or replace electric light, a thorough study of technologies like photocells, dimmers, and time clocks is in order.

Color:

Coordinating daylight use with electric light also demands careful consideration of the color temperatures of light that are being introduced to the space. The color of both skylight and sunlight are entirely variable. Skylight can range from the pale blue of a clear morning to the murky cool of a cloudy day to the violets and pinks of a sunset. Direct sunlight can vary from a warm glow to a brilliant orange. Both, however, seem to have an uncanny knack for showing off the unnatural look of the colors of our electric sources. Because daylight components by nature have perfect color-rendering capabilities, they tend to show off the deficiencies of our electric systems. Electric light can look very un-natural when it is shown up by daylight. Because of the great variance of daylight, it is not suggested that your electric light sources necessarily try to match the color temperature of your daylighting ingredients; it is simply one more facet of light to consider.

Shape:

Integrating daylight and electric elements together also requires consideration of the shape of light. Daylight tends to be delivered in long, clean pieces and planes. Our long, linear electric sources can do a good job of harmonizing with these elements. Daylight can also be delivered in clean directional beams and pools when produced by small apertures and devices like solar light tubes.

The point is to take control of daylight and expand concepts of what can be accomplished with it. Almost any source of electric light has a proper daylight counterpart. The responsibility is simply to investigate the possibilities and think through every design decision.

Some common daylight integration details can be found in chapter 30

HAZARDS OF DAYLIGHT

For all of its power and charm, it is important to remember that there are distinct hazards of daylight applied improperly. Keep at the forefront of your mind the perils that can befall a space with poorly-controlled daylight contributions.

Heat Gains

Unmitigated direct sunlight generally contributes a fair amount of heat, in addition to excessive light. There are low-emissivity glasses and coatings that can transmit visible light without the heat contribution, but these are not commonplace. If you want direct sunlight, you get heat, or you make use of these expensive glazing technologies.

Glare and Contrast

Sunlight is an obvious culprit, creating light hundreds of times brighter than our brightest electric sources. As a task light, direct daylight is simply too bright. As an accent light, sunlight can still cause glare and contrast to which the human visual system simply cannot adapt. Skylight and diffused sunlight can also present problems when not carefully considered with the material reflectances, colors, and visual criteria of a space.

Damage to Art, Fabrics and Other Materials

Sunlight and daylight contain a quantity of ultra violet radiation that will deteriorate dyes, inks, pigments and the integrity of organic materials. Glazing blocks all but a small quantity of UV radiation, but even this small quantity has damaging effects over time.

Excessive Window Light

Daylight windows are not necessarily view windows. Windows placed for clear views of the exterior environment should always be considered for the daylight that they will receive. Far too often, glazing is designed for views with no consideration for the intrusion of daylight that will result. Daylight systems should be designed independent of view windows and vice versa. Simple wall glazing can certainly serve both purposes, but careful study and consideration are necessary.

DAYLIGHT AS A CONTROLLABLE ELEMENT

The bottom line is that sunlight and skylight are controllable, predictable sources of light that can be used to satisfy the needs of all of our five layers when implemented properly. There are daylight ingredients to serve the needs of way finding, mood, accenting, spatial revelation and tasks.

The key is to take control of daylight and design systems that use it. Even simple wall windows deserve the consideration of diffusing curtains, blinds and shading devices. Daylight should never be an accident, nor should it be neglected. Like many other aspects of light, fear keeps designers from confidently implementing daylight. Daylight is such an elemental material that there are numerous simple ways to successfully put it to use.

Unlike electric light devices, there are few product catalogs that illustrate daylight systems. Good daylight use is often the product of unique situations and a fair amount of experimenting. If you come across an application that you like, take note, sketch it, and start a collection of daylight systems that you can draw from the next time you need to lean on the sublime character of sunlight and skylight.

I am a strong believer in the unique mood and visual attraction of daylight. I go to great lengths to study the opportunities for introducing skylight and diffuse sunlight into my environments. I think this affinity is so strong that I tend to design my electrical lighting systems to mimic the intensity, shape and texture of controlled daylight systems. This also offers the advantage of seamless integration between electric light and daylight. Despite all of the caution encouraged regarding daylight integration, remember that a little bit of daylight can go along way towards a positive effect in the designed environment.

Chapter 17

Graphic Tools: Rendering and Light Maps

We mentioned earlier that the designer's ability to *visualize* lighting ideas is only one of the necessary skills. In order to implement lighting design, the designer must also be able to translate those ideas to other designers and ultimately back to themselves. Communicating ideas is necessary for working through challenges, getting feedback and assistance, thinking innovatively, and, ultimately, being free to think creatively. For a designer, it is understood that representing ideas *visually* is the fastest, clearest way to get them out of our heads and into the design process. The credo that a designer should adopt to ensure lighting success is:

> *"Draw your light."*

Far too often, people see light as a product of luminaires, and they, therefore, design by staring at a space plan and placing symbols that represent luminaires. This process inevitably yields repetitious, static solutions. The little circles and squares do little to explain to us or anyone else how light is behaving in the space. In our design process we should vow never to design by drawing lighting *symbols* straight away.

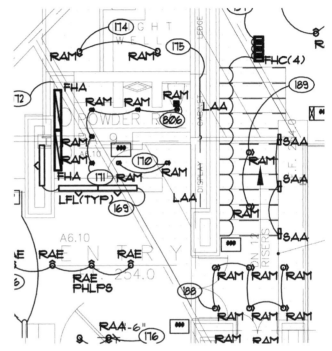

Figure 17.1 Lighting symbols on a construction document do very little to describe how the space will look, feel, or function.

The first step in expressing light ideas is to graphically represent light as *light*. We draw this light how we envision it, where we envision it. We identify the surfaces and objects that we want bright, and we draw brightness onto them. If we can make a habit of expressing our ideas through drawing light, we will always head down a more complete path of designing that will yield more inspired and innovative designs.

Drawing light onto surfaces, object and spaces requires only the simplest of tools. A yellow colored pencil can represent "light" in its most generic form. With this single colored pencil, we can sketch light onto architectural elevations, sections, plans and perspectives. We can print out images and sketch onto them. We can sketch light onto our own hand-drawn scribbles. I make a habit of carrying around a small army of yellow, colored pencils so that as soon as a lighting idea comes to mind, I can communicate it immediately without a lot of big words and hand waving. When one draws light onto plans and sketches the eyes of fellow designers, clients and peers light up with comprehension and understanding. I know of no easier tool for communicating light ideas, and so this will be our first. *I call this process of expressing light through graphics "Light Mapping"*

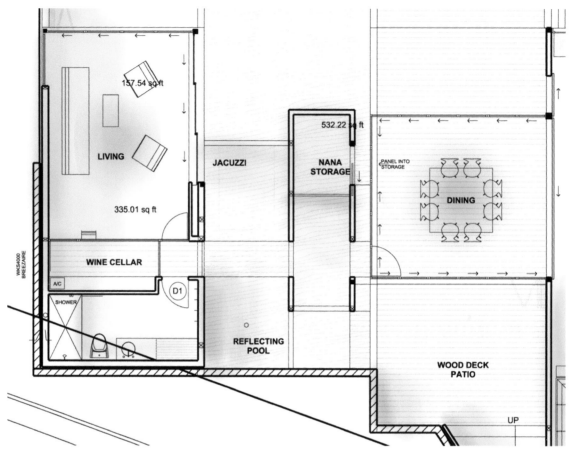

Figure 17.2 A light map detail example of a contemporary residence.

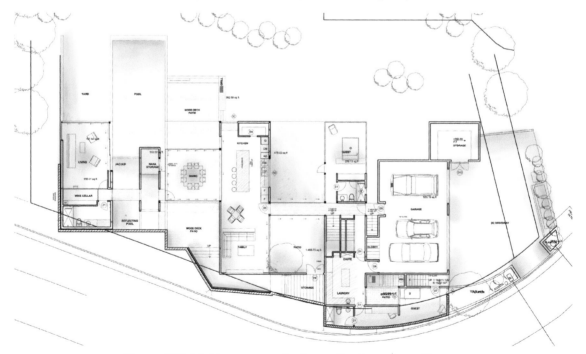

Figure 17.3 A light map example of an entire floor of a residence.

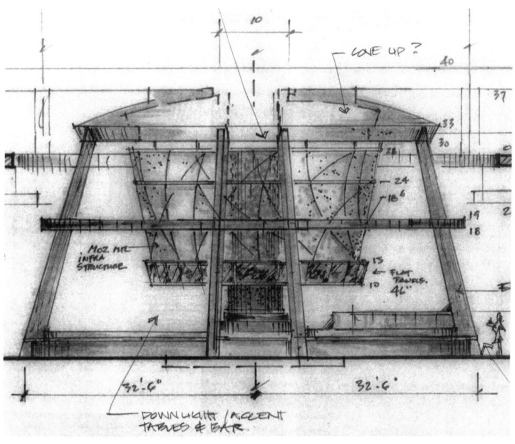

Figure 17.4 A light map example of an elevation of a central bar area in a casino.

Our design process should always revolve around a dimensional understanding of our environments as a whole. One of the best practices to commit to is pinning up, displaying, and surrounding oneself with all that he/she knows about a specific project and space before starting to design within it. This allows the designer to render lighting ideas in all dimensions and to understand the ramifications of lighting decisions and concepts.

THE LIGHT MAPPED PLAN

The most basic form of a light map is simply whatever architectural or environmental information the designer has available with lighting graphics applied on top. After we have exhausted all of the information we have available and have made light maps of all of the elevations, sections and perspectives, we set our sights on creating a light mapped plan. The light mapped plan can be based on a floor plan, furniture plan or ceiling plan. This simple, graphic tool will help to communicate light ideas and will serve as a roadmap when we move forward and lay out our lighting equipment. When we go to solve lighting challenges and identify locations and types of luminaires, a good, light-mapped plan will solve itself.

The Keys to Success in Creating a Light Map:

Think only in terms of light. Don't worry about practicality, constructability, luminaire location, or even the luminaire itself.

Think about the quality of light and where it goes

Focus on surfaces and objects and how they receive light.

Adding to the Impact of a Light Map

When we set out to translate lighting information on plan in two dimensions, it is imperative that we keep our mind open and our ideas fresh. We can add rendering techniques like additional colors and patterns to represent different lighting techniques. It is often helpful to graphically distinguish between directional accent lighting, diffuse lighting, light up onto ceilings and lids, as well as color casts. *Figure 17.5* illustrates a few ideas for ways to represent lighting. One may want to create a legend on the light map that helps translate the different lighting applications.

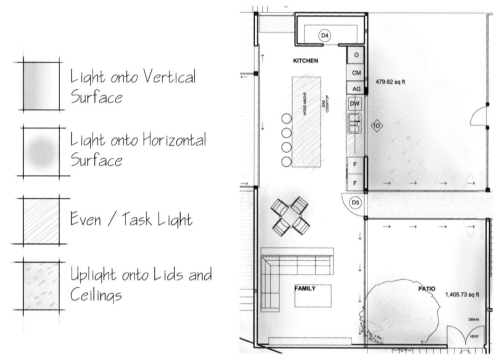

Figure 17.5 an example of a legend (left) used to clarify colors and patterns used on a light map (right).

With only a yellow pencil, an orange pencil, and some imaginative patterns, a designer can translate a wealth of lighting concepts in plan.

As one can see from the preceding figures, the goal is to truly represent light where it ends up. More to the point, we could say that we represent the surfaces that receive the light. Our Light Map plan becomes a map of specific "Lighting Events," one specific lighting concept after another clearly identified.

Describing Light

In order to create Light Maps that can truly stand on their own to translate information to others, we add articulate descriptions to the graphics of our lighting "events". Describing light doesn't need to be a study in poetics and superlatives. We are simply clarifying what it is that light is doing. The better our descriptions, the less we have to rely on specialized graphics to get our ideas across. Lighting descriptions are like architectural notes; they need be detailed only enough to get information across clearly. On the other hand, even a brief description is better than the ambiguity of no description at all. Take pride in descriptions and dole them out generously. There is a rule in design that says, "when in doubt, create a note." We will translate this guideline to be one of our mottos in graphics and creating light maps: *"When in doubt, add a description"*.

To help forge the right level of information into a lighting description, I recommend considering the following elements that are included in a good description:

Color, texture, and intensity of the light;

How the light affects mood;

How the light interacts with the surface.

If a lighting description includes these elements, it will be that much easier for other designers to understand the intent of the design. It will also be easier to solve lighting ideas and select the luminaires that will bring the idea to life. If one finds him/herself short on adjectives to add life to a lighting description, consult the list of descriptors in appendix C.

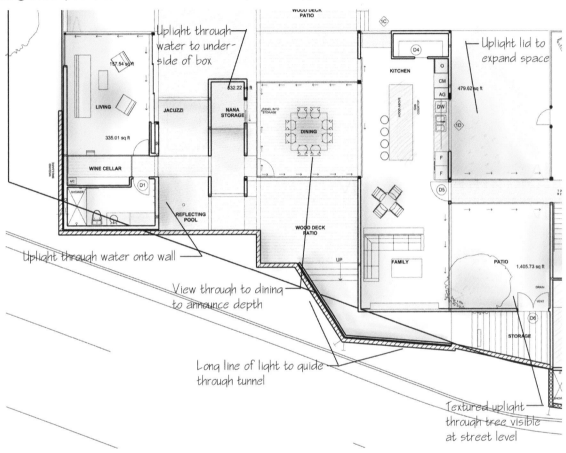

Figure 17.6 Descriptions of lighting intent are a crucial step towards defining lighting challenges.

It is good visual practice to study environments that feature good lighting design and imagine how one would represent them graphically as a Light Map. This analysis really shows off the idea that it is the surfaces receiving light that define a space. *Figure 17.7 and 17.8* show images of lighted spaces and how we might translate them to a light map. We rarely work this way in design, but it is good practice.

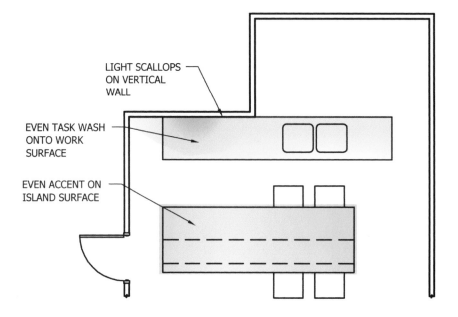

LIGHT SCALLOPS
ON VERTICAL
WALL

EVEN TASK WASH
ONTO WORK
SURFACE

EVEN ACCENT ON
ISLAND SURFACE

Figure 17.7 A contemporary kitchen (below) can be quickly represented in a light map (above).

Image courtesy of Deltalight   www.deltalight.us

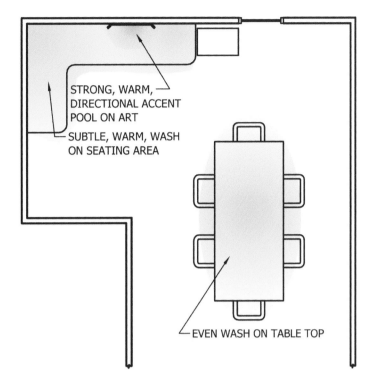

STRONG, WARM,
DIRECTIONAL ACCENT
POOL ON ART

SUBTLE, WARM, WASH
ON SEATING AREA

EVEN WASH ON TABLE TOP

Figure 17.8 A living room (below) can be quickly represented in a light map (above).

Image courtesy of Deltalight   www.deltalight.us

Remember that when we create our lighting map, we should be thinking in terms of the 5 layer system we have developed.

Light to choreograph an experience;

Light to affect mood;

Light to accent objects;

Light to reveal architecture;

Light for tasks.

As one designs, he/she will recognize that particular lighting events serve many purposes across our five layers. If we keep in mind the purpose of the light we are adding, our space will evolve with maximum effect and function with the right amount of light out in the right places.

Light Mapping Choreography.

The good first step to implement when creating a light mapped plan is to show light for the sake of choreographing a path of experience for a visitor (the first of our five layers from chapter three). Choreography benefits greatly from the light mapping process because it requires a large scale overview of the project. The choreography step is a quick and simple application of light on just a few large surfaces or objects in space to create distinct destinations that serve as lighted goals for people to move towards. The choreography intent can be further clarified by adding symbols to represent the location of a person as he/she interacts with the space. *Figure 17.9* shows these symbols as blue cones indicating where a visitor's attention should be directed. This process of creating a path helps to identify what it is that should be lighted in order to draw a person through the space. Light can be rendered onto one surface after another in sequence to map how the lighted surfaces encourage a person to flow through the space.

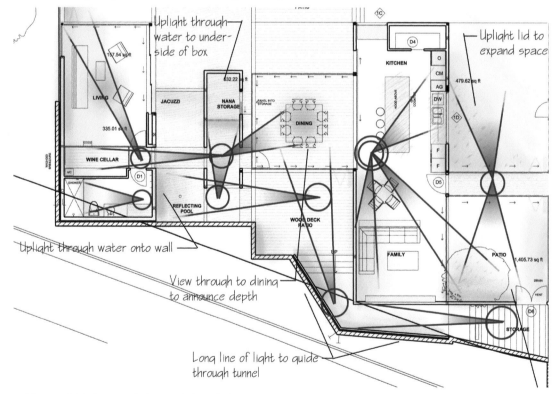

Figure 17.9 Cones of view and descriptions explain how we intend to use light to lead a visitor from one space to the next.

Once a designer is satisfied with the lighting additions and descriptions that have been added to choreograph the space, he/she can move on to rendering graphics to represent the remaining five layers. Think of the specific objects, architectural features and surfaces that one will use to create the lighted effect. Think in terms of the overall mood of the design on a space-by-space basis. Identify whether each space should feel calm, relaxed, sterile, cold, etc. Take time to review all of the aspects of light and lighting tactics that we have discussed thus far. The more a designer focuses on the decisions that need to be made, the more meaningful the lighting graphics and descriptions will be.

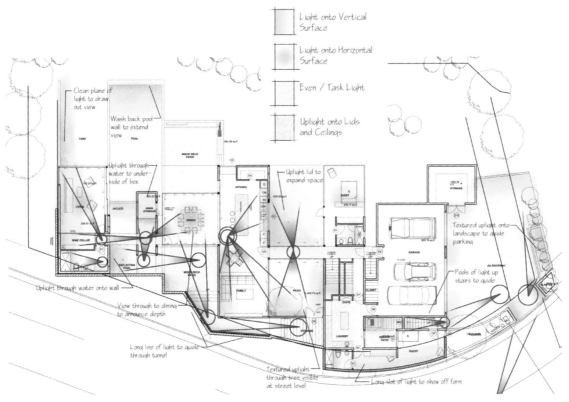

Figure 17.10 A completed light map of a residential floor.

The goal of the light map is to communicate ideas to others and to create a visual map of light that will help to make luminaire decisions easier. If the light map is thorough, with bold, clear graphics to represent light, it sets the designer up nicely to move forward and make quick work of laying out the luminaires that will create the lighting events.

Chapter 18

Lighting Units and Measurements

Up to this point, we have managed to explore the depths of lighting design concept and application without having to burden ourselves with the specifics of lighting science and the systems of units and measurements that go with it. In order to speak knowledgeably about lighting effects and lighting solutions, it is necessary to have a basic understanding of light levels and how they translate visually. In order to engage in this discussion, we must first take a look at lighting science and some of the fundamental building blocks of lighting metrics. This will help us not only communicate our lighting ideas more precisely, but will also allow us to recognize appropriate tools and tactics as they are presented by others.

When we go on to discuss light levels in design, we almost always refer to the lighting unit of the foot-candle. A foot-candle is a measurement of Illuminance cast onto a surface in a space. The unit of the foot-candle is, indeed, based on the light produced onto an object a "foot" away from a very special candle. We however are not really concerned with what a foot-candle is, but rather what different illuminance levels, expressed in foot-candles, look like. Let's start with the basics.

IT'S ALL ABOUT THE LUMEN

Light comes in pieces, or at least we consider that it does for most of our science and study. Scientists call these tiny pieces of light photons, and they exhaustively study all of the ways that photons interact with the physical world.

In lighting science, we are not just concerned with light generically; we are concerned with how these pieces of light affect human vision. Our visual system is more sensitive to some types of light than others, so we measure a unit of light energy as it affects the sensitivity of the cones and rods in the human eye. We call these modified pieces of light "Lumens." The lumen is the basis of all lighting study, and we can always be safe talking about light in terms of lumens. We study three common ways that lumens interact with the environment:

We study the number of lumens onto or striking a surface;

We study the number of lumens off of or leaving a surface;

We study lumens of light leaving a surface in a specific direction with a specific density.

When we talk about lighting effects, we generally talk about light density, and, therefore we talk about how many lumens are acting per area. An unfortunate part of lighting science is that we have come up with different names for the measurements of light interacting in different ways. *Figure 18.1* shows the three interactions as lumens of light striking and reflecting off of a surface.

Figure 18.1 shows that illuminance and exitance are both measurements of light density; specifically, a measure of lumens per square-foot. The difference between the two phenomena is simply whether the light is striking a surface (illuminance), or leaving a surface (exitance).

Luminance, however, is a more thorough measurement of how densely light is leaving in a specific direction.

To completely understand the nuances of these three methods of measuring light, we will elaborate on them here.

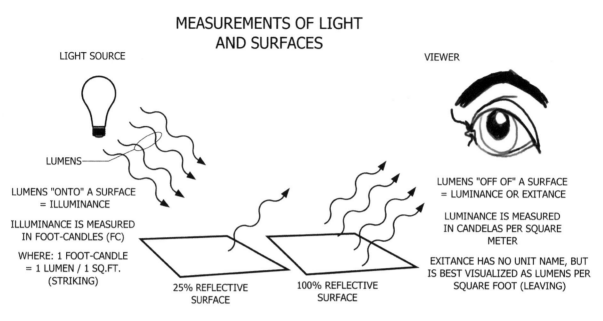

Figure 18.1 The two common ways we consider light interacting with simple surfaces.

Illuminance:

Illuminance is the measurement of lumens of light striking onto a surface.

Illuminance is measured and expressed in foot-candles (FC).

1 foot-candle is the equivalent of 1 lumen of light distributed evenly onto a 1 square foot surface.

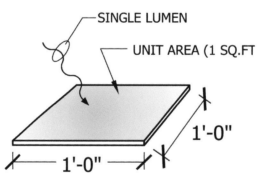

Figure 18.2 Diagram of one foot-candle (density of light onto a simple surface).

Exitance:

Exitance is the measurement of lumens of light leaving a surface or source.

Exitance has no unit of measurement; it simply accounts for the total number of lumens leaving and gives no information about the density or direction in which the light is leaving. The exitance of a reflective surface is the illuminance onto that surface multiplied by the reflectance of the surface. If a surface is 50% reflective, the exitance off of the surface will equal half of the illu-

minance on to the surface. In the case of a light source, the exitance is the sheer number of lumens that the light source is creating and emitting.

Exitance is seldom used to describe light levels, but understanding it is useful for visualizing how lumens interact with surfaces and objects.

Luminance:

Luminance is the measurement of a specific density of lumens of light leaving a surface or source in a specific direction.

Luminance is measured and expressed in candelas per square meter (CD/sq.M).

In order to understand what luminance represents, it is necessary to understand what a candela represents.

The candela is the unit of light density. It is a useful way to express how densely light leaves a source or surface. One candela is the equivalent of light leaving a source with a density of one lumen per "steradian," of spherical area. A steradian is a contoured area made of a portion of a sphere. The area of a steradian is such that there are always 2π (two pi, or about 6.3) steradians in any sphere. As a sphere grows larger, the size of a steradian carved from the sphere grows larger. *Figure 18.3* shows two different

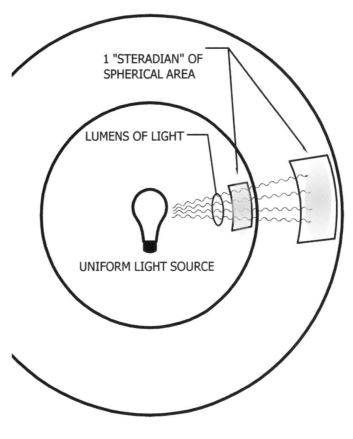

Figure 18.3 Diagram of Candle-power (density of light leaving a light source)

spheres and one steradian of area carved out of each of them. Because light spreads out spherically as it leaves its origin, the same number of lumens passes through each steradian despite the area difference. Though not easy to visualize, candela output is very useful for describing light sources like accent luminaires that direct far more light in front of them than off to the side. Knowing the candela value that comes from the center of an accent luminaire is useful for calculating the illuminance level that will occur at a point on a surface or object due to that specific luminaire.

The nature of the candela means that the luminance value exhibited by a light source or surface differs based on the angle from which the source or surface is being viewed. It is luminance that the eye detects and uses as the basis for decisions about source or surface brightness.

Although we have crafty names for all of these interactions and their units, the most important and commonly-encountered in lighting design is *illuminance* expressed in foot-candles. This expression of light onto objects is easy to measure and helps us to understand the levels of contrast we can create in an environment. Illuminance values onto a surface are independent of the color or reflectance of the surface, so an illuminance value alone does not indicate how an object will look. A black book and a white book, side by side on a table, may be experiencing the same Illuminance level from the luminaires above them. The drastic difference in appearance between the books is a product of their reflectance. To successfully visualize a situation, we must be told the reflectance of the objects (values and colors), as well as the Illuminance level onto the objects. This gives us enough information to interpolate the exitance from the objects. If we also know the texture of the books and how they will direct reflected light, we can estimate their luminance, which is much more closely related to our description of object "brightness." It is worth noting that all of these measurements of light do not dictate objectively how bright a surface will appear. Brightness is a judgment made by a viewer and is dependant on the adaptation of the viewer and the contrast of the environment.

In all three of these cases of lighting measurement, we are talking about lumens interacting with objects, so if all else fails, it is always safe to describe light as lumens.

Chapter 19

Understanding Illuminance Levels

The vast majority of our quantitative lighting study and discussion will revolve around measurements and expressions of illuminance (the study of light *onto* objects). Therefore, we will commonly express light levels in terms of foot-candles (the unit of measuring Illuminance).

ILLUMINANCE LEVEL INTUITION

There is a wealth of published information about what specific illuminance levels are appropriate to provide onto surfaces to accommodate different types of visual tasks, and many people use these guidelines as the basis of their design. Adhering to prescribed illuminance levels for tasks and neglecting the lighting effect of a whole space can, however, lead to a very one-dimensional experience.

Because we are after a much more holistic approach to our design, we are interested in an intuitive ability to visualize different Illuminance levels and what they represent. Though prescribed illuminance levels are intended to be considered for a specific surface or surfaces, a designer can put Illuminance levels to good use by utilizing them to describe the ambient glow of a space where many surfaces are experiencing a similar illuminance level. This is technically an abuse of the intention of illuminance level prescription, but is such a useful way for designers to communicate lighting intention that we take the liberty. When one describes an entire space as exhibiting an "average" illuminance level, one must account for contrast, accent, and areas of higher and lower light levels within it.

Assembled here is a short list of illuminance levels (expressed in foot-candles) that can help a designer to visualize what these different light levels can mean to a design. As you consider each space type, close your eyes and visualize the space described if it were lighted fairly evenly. What you are visualizing on the surfaces of the space is likely the illuminance level listed. Remember this is not a list of recommendations, but rather a reference for visualizing.

Designed Space	illuminance Level
Full Moon Light	0.1 Foot-candle
Exterior Parking Lot	1.0 Foot-candle
Dim, romantic restaurant	5.0 Foot-candles
Comfortable Living Room	10-15 Foot-candles
Residential den / study	20-35 Foot-candles
Classroom / Open Office	50-70 Foot-candles
Laboratory / Exam Room	100 Foot-candles

It is uncommon to light an entire interior space to Illuminance levels beyond 100 foot-candles. Once we start dealing with these higher illuminance levels, we are usually talking about light that would be applied to small areas of localized task. We may provide 200 foot-candles of light onto an operating table or an accented object, but it is unlikely that we would light an entire space to this level.

ADDING ILLUMINANCE VALUES TO A LIGHT MAP

If one can keep these light levels in mind while designing and discussing light, he/she will have all of the intuitive knowledge needed.

With just this small amount of familiarity, one can start adding these values as targets for specific surfaces and whole room effects in designed spaces. A logical progression of design is to label these Illuminance level targets on the light map. Illuminance levels are best used to describe the quantity of light cast onto a surface, but they can also be used to give an impression of the overall ambient glow that one may perceive in a room. This can be put to use by mentally walking through the design, room by room, determining the overall ambient glow that is desired for each room.

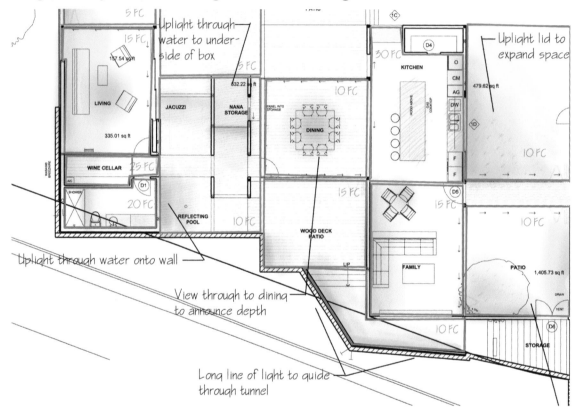

Figure 19.1 Adding ambient illuminance level targets (shown here in green) helps to refine design goals.

In residential settings this process can be handled very easily. For spaces like residences that don't have to support critical tasks, it is safe to use a limited range of illuminance values between 5 and 35 Foot-candles as targets for whole room ambience. You can reference the table above to see that these values cover most of the moods and environments we try to create in a residential setting. These illuminance levels can also serve as the overall ambient glow for spaces like restaurants, galleries, hospitality and museums. For more task oriented spaces, like open office areas, classrooms, civic and conference spaces, average illuminance levels in the 35 to 55 Foot-candle range tend to be common. When visual tasks are a critical component of the lighting design program, a designer is advised to consult more technical reference material for Illuminance level recommendations onto specific task surfaces.

The illuminance guidelines above are a gross simplification of a topic that encompasses much study and engineering. For our basic understanding and ability to visualize, these numbers will suffice.

It is important to realize that whole room illuminance levels are just reference targets off which to build. The hope is that all of the specific task and accent lighting that gets added to the space will inter-reflect to create this glow. Our design procedure in not to create an ambient light level first, and add accent or task affects later.

We define lighting goals for specific surfaces and objects for task and accent first and then assess the effect. Only after we have done this, do we design lighting intended to increase ambient light levels or perceived brightness.

As illuminance level targets find their way onto the Light Map, designers will find their lighting design fall into place much easier.

LIGHTING FOR VISUAL INTEREST

As designers primarily interested in adding impact and emotion to our environments, much of what we light are accented surfaces and objects that must stand out from the surfaces around them. When we paint light onto objects with the intent of drawing attention to them, it is helpful to identify specific light level targets to make sure the impact of design stays intact.

Now that we have a basic understanding of what illuminance levels mean, we will introduce a useful rule-of-thumb for designing accent and feature lighting. We call this rule the *"2 times"* contrast rule, and we use it frequently for creating accents and visual interest. The rule is based on fundamental vision science that tells us that an object must be twice as bright as a surface adjacent to it to appear noticeably brighter. When we light an object or surface with the intent to make it "pop" or serve as a focal element, we implement a simple version of this theory by illuminating the accented object with at least twice as much light as the surrounding environment. This simplified solution of addressing only the amount of light cast onto an object ignores the reflectance and color of the object, but it is a good starting point. There are more complex ramifications of this rule that have to do with object value, color, and reflectance, but for our design purposes, we can safely rely on the broad version of this rule. Generally, the more light we cast onto a surface, the greater the accented effect.

The other end of the contrast rule comes from the desire to not create too high a level of contrast that might be translated as glare. To avoid uncomfortable glare and excess contrast, we avoid lighting an object to be more than 5 times as bright as the surrounding environment.

So the *"2 times"* contrast rule really becomes the *"2 to 5 times"* contrast rule. We say that for creating visual interest in designed spaces, we want to light our objects to be twice as bright as their surroundings, but not more than 5 times as bright. We accommodate this in a very simplified manner of illuminating objects to two to five times the illuminance of the surrounding environment.

The effects of this rule can be written onto the light map to further clarify the lighting design intent. The process is as simple as identifying the objects and surfaces one wants to use as focal elements in each space. Because the designer has already assigned a desired ambient glow to these spaces, he/she has an illuminance value to use as the basis for the "2 to 5 times" contrast rule. Mentally walk through the design, space by space, and identify objects and label them with a target accent illuminance level.

An example might be a dining room where the design calls for a minimum ambient glow of the space to be around 10 foot-candles. Using the 2 to 5 times rule, we see that our accented objects should be illuminated to levels between 20 and 50 foot-candles. The "2 to 5 times" rule requires that we have first established an ambient illuminance level with which to work. This is why we went through the process of targeting overall ambient illuminance levels for the whole space. These two simple steps of defining an ambient glow for a space first and then using that as the basis for accents are quick and effective.

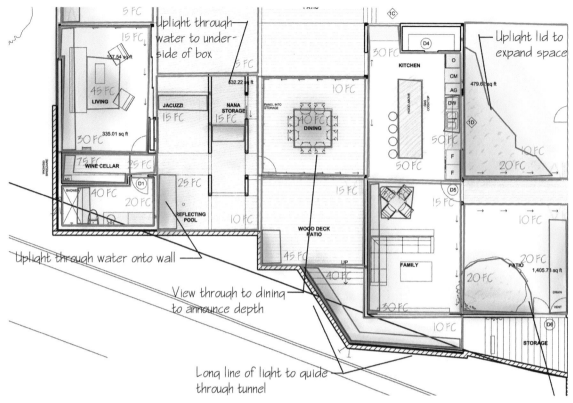

Figure 19.2 Establishing ambient illuminance level targets (in green) allows a designer to go back and define areas of heightened light levels (in pink).

How we will actually get the light there can be worked out later. For now, we are simply adding more information to our Light Map to make it increasingly easier for us to locate and select luminaires.

IES ILLUMINANCE LEVEL CRITERIA

A more specific way to arrive at illuminance level targets for specific tasks and critical effects is to use the well established system put forth by the Illuminating Engineering Society of North America (IESNA). The IESNA is a scientific body dedicated to the study of lighting and its effects on human visual performance. The IESNA has committed significant resources to the study of illuminance levels onto tasks.

Remember that Illuminance levels are descriptions of how much light we are putting onto an object. Illuminance levels don't account for reflectance or how light will leave a surface. This limits their value in trying to describe how a surface, object or space will look.

Illuminance levels are exceptionally useful when determining appropriate light levels for tasks. This works primarily because visual tasks involve objects with known reflectances. If we know the reflectance of the materials involved in a task, it is safe to prescribe a quantity of light that should be cast onto the task to create the necessary contrast. Reading, for example, involves dark text on light-colored paper. As we cast more light onto a reading task, the light-colored paper reflects more light back at us, while the dark ink continues to reflect very little. In this manner, the contrast between the two increases. This is the fundamental basis for the long list of Illuminance values that the IESNA provides. The IESNA publishes a book that categorizes a variety of tasks articulated with a variety of materials. For each of these task and material combinations, the IESNA provides a recommended Illuminance level. IESNA literature can be ordered from its website: www.iesna.org.

The IESNA recognizes that there are many factors that dictate what is appropriate lighting. Another significant aspect of the IES illuminance selection procedure is the assessment of the designed space and consideration for all of the other visual performance issues that must be addressed. This includes concerns like color rendition, evenness, and glare. It is helpful for a designer to develop his/her own list of lighting issues and concerns like the one presented in *Figure 19.3*.

LIGHTING DESIGN CONCERNS CHECKLIST

☐ DESIRED CONTRAST / DISTINCT ACCENTS   ☐ DAYLIGHTING INTEGRATION / CONTROL

☐ DESIRED SPARKLE / VISIBLE SOURCES   ☐ GLARE REFLECTIONS / SPECULAR MATERIALS

☐ ACCURATE COLOR RENDERING   ☐ SENSITIVITY TO FLICKER / STROBING

☐ COLOR APPEARANCE OF ENVIRONMENT   ☐ SENSITIVITY TO GLARE

☐ MOOD AND EMOTIONAL ATMOSPHERE   ☐ ENERGY CONSERVATION / EFFICIENCY

☐ MODELING OF OBJECTS AND FACES   ☐ MAINTENANCE CONCERNS

☐ VISUAL TASK PERFORMANCE   ☐ HEAT CONCERNS

☐ SYSTEM CONTROL AND DIMMING   ☐ NOISE CONCERNS

☐ LIGHT LEVEL EVENNESS (REDUCING SHADOWS)

Figure 19.3 A list of lighting concerns that should be considered for every project

The IES selection procedure can certainly help a designer avoid under-lighting critical situations, but it is really intended as a procedural guide for visual tasks (the fifth layer of our 5-layer system).

For visual effect, aesthetics, mood, and spatial organization (The remaining four layers from our 5 layer system), intuition and experience will serve us better than exact numbers. This is the reason we have gone to great lengths to voyage through a thought process that leads to understanding and intuition. Illuminance values are a welcome level of information to add to our design intent, but they are only one part of a much bigger picture that has its foundation in visualization and graphic rendering of lighting concepts.

Remember to visualize lighting effect first and then draw and describe the lighting effect. Only if the designer feels the need to further articulate does he/she need to move on to specifying target Illuminance levels. We add these values to our light map to clarify our intent and make the selection and placement of lighting equipment easier. If targeting a specific task or accent light level does not serve to progress our design, it is not worth taking the time to identify.

Chapter 20

Lighting Calculations

It is imperative before delving into the world of lighting calculations to step back and remember the reason for using calculations in design. We use calculations to help us arrive at specific solutions to critical lighting challenges. If a calculation will help us select a luminaire, and apply that luminaire to create the lighting effect we are after, we welcome it. It is important not to rely on calculations too heavily as they are merely a supplement to good lighting instinct and experiential knowledge. It is also important not to assume that every lighting element we are designing can benefit from performing a calculation.

Light calculations can assist us in selecting lamps and luminaires when we are tying to obtain a specific light level. Lighting calculations also help us predict the lighting effect we may get from a specific lighting scenario.

We will investigate two lighting calculation methods that help us in two types of lighting situations: Lumen Method Calculations and Point Calculations.

Lumen Method calculations are used for determining average light levels in large, open areas.

Point Calculations are used for determining light levels at a specific point on an object or surface.

These two calculations cover the two ends of the design spectrum: broad, spatial light levels and minute, point-specific light levels.

To understand how we make use of lighting calculations, we must first investigate more specifically the way we count and measure light.

In the case of both types of calculations, we will be using Illuminance as our measurement of light level. Illuminance is, of course, the measure of light falling onto surfaces. Specifically, illuminance is the measure of the number of lumens that are falling onto a square foot of area, which is the definition of a foot-candle, the unit of measurement of illuminance. A foot-candle is one lumen of light received evenly over an area of 1 square foot.

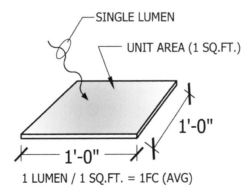

SINGLE LUMEN

UNIT AREA (1 SQ.FT.)

1'-0"

1'-0"

1 LUMEN / 1 SQ.FT. = 1FC (AVG)

Figure 20.1 One lumen onto a one square-foot area is one foot-candle of illuminance

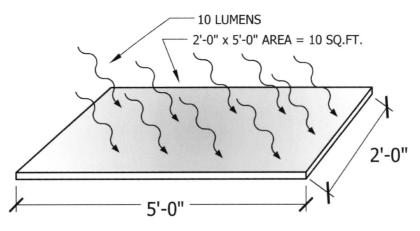

10 LUMENS / 10 SQ.FT. = 1FC (AVG)

Figure 20.2 Ten lumens onto a 10 square-foot area is also one foot-candle of illuminance

LUMEN METHOD CALCULATIONS FOR LARGE, OPEN AREAS

The lumen method of calculating light levels is really not a calculation all, but rather an extrapolation of the unit definition of the foot-candle. When we dissect the foot candle, we see it is simply a measurement of light density in lumens per square foot.

1 Foot-candle = 1 Lumen ÷ 1 square foot

or

1 FC=1 Lm ÷ 1 sq.ft.

Therefore, we can generalize

Illuminance = Lumens ÷ area (in square feet)

or we can express it as mathematical abbreviations

E = Lms ÷ A (sq.ft.)

Putting this together tells us that to calculate the Illuminance level onto a surface, we simply count up the number of lumens falling onto that surface and divide by the area of the surface.

In the case of a whole room, that surface would likely be the floor, or an imaginary work plane above the floor at task height (often assumed to be 30"). A basic situation where we want to predict lighting effect may look like example 1.

Lumen Method Example 1: Solving for Illuminance Level

Imagine a room that is 10' × 15', with 5 downlights placed evenly around the room. Each downlight emits 1000 lumens. If we imagine that all 1000 lumens from each luminaire end up on the floor of the space, what illuminance level can be expected onto the floor in this room?

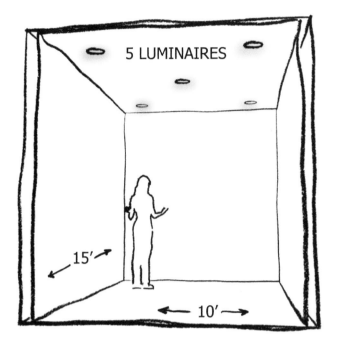

Figure 20.3 A 10' by 15' floor lighted by 5 downlights.

We know that the solution to a problem like this is to simply count up the lumens that make it to the surface in question and divide by the area of the surface.

Using the basic equation

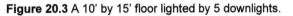

$$\text{Illuminance} = \text{Lumens} \div \text{area}$$

or

$$E = Lms \div A$$

We plug in the values we know.

The area of the floor is

$$A = 10' \times 15' = 150 \text{ square feet.}$$

The total number of lumens that make it to the floor "Lms"

$$1000 \text{ Lumens} \times 5 \text{ downlights} = 5000 \text{ lms.}$$

So the equation

$$E = Lms \div A$$

becomes

$$E = 5000 \text{ Lms} \div 150 \text{ sq.ft.}$$

or

$$E = 33.3 \text{ Lms per sq.ft.}$$

or

$$E = 33.3 \text{ Foot-candles}$$

(Similar to the illuminance level we might picture on the desk of a home office or library).

Lumen Method Example 2: Solving for Lumens or Luminaires Needed

We tend to use the Lumen Method Calculation more frequently for figuring out how to deliver light to provide a desired illuminance level. In these cases, we use this same equation flipped around.

$$\text{Illuminance = Lumens ÷ Area}$$

becomes

$$\text{Lumens = Illuminance × Area}$$

or more specifically

$$\text{Lumens needed = Illuminance level target × Area (in square feet)}$$

A basic situation where we need to solve a lighting challenge may look like this two-part process:

Given the same 10' × 15' room, we would like to light the floor to an average illuminance level of 60 foot-candles. How many lumens need to make it to the floor surface?

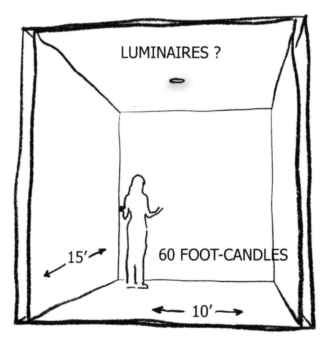

Figure 20.4 How do we deliver the desired illuminance level to a 10' by 15' floor?

We use our basic equation

$$\text{Lumens needed} = \text{Illuminance target} \times \text{Area}$$

or simply

$$\text{Lumens} = \text{Illuminance} \times \text{Area}$$

or

$$Lms = E \times A$$

We plug in the values we know.

Our illuminance target is

$$E = 60 \text{ foot-candles.}$$

Our area is

$$A = 10' \times 15' = 150 \text{ square feet}$$

So the equation

$$Lms = E \times A$$

becomes

$$Lms = 60 \text{ fc} \times 150 \text{ sq.ft.}$$

or

$$Lms = 9000 \text{ Lumens}$$

We need to introduce 9000 functional lumens of light onto the floor to get the average illuminance level we are after.

How do we get those 9000 functional lumens onto the floor? We need to determine what quantity and type of luminaire can accomplish this goal. Hence, the calculation has two parts. In order to answer the question of how many luminaires we need, we need to know the lumen output of those luminaires. For this reason, most luminaire manufacturers provide cut-sheets that provide this information. For this example, we will assume that we have found a luminaire that emits 550 lumens and that all of these lumens will make it to the floor in the space.

If we were to use a luminaire that provides 550 Lumens onto the floor, how many luminaires would we need to evenly place in the space.

This question translates to a simple equation:

$$\text{Luminaires needed} = \text{Lumens needed} \div \text{Lumens per luminaire}$$

We solve this by plugging in what we know

$$\text{Luminaires needed} = 9000 \text{ Lumens needed} \div 550 \text{ Lumens per luminaire}$$

so our answer

$$\text{Luminaires needed} = 16.36$$

gets rounded up to

$$\text{Luminaires needed} = 17$$

So we have determined that 17 of these specific luminaires spaced evenly in the 150 square-foot space will yield us the 60 foot-candles of average Illuminance onto the floor.

Lumen Method Safety Factors

When we perform lumen method calculations for critical situations, it is important to add in two factors that make our calculations much more realistic. The first of these factors is a safety factor called the **Light loss factor, or "LLF."** The second factor is the **Coefficient of Utilization, or "CU."**

The light loss factor is a way to account for the fact that the light performance of our lamps and luminaires will deteriorate over time for a number of reasons. The Light Loss Factor (LLF) accounts for lamps getting dirty and giving off less light over time. It also accounts for loss in performance of ballasts and transformers over the life of the luminaire. There is an articulate method of calculating each of these contributing factors, but it is common to use an **industry standard generic value of 0.85 for a Light Loss Factor.** This means that we perform calculations expecting only 85% of the light from our lighting system to be working in the space as the system ages. This safe assumption says that we are not designing for how we want a system to perform on day one, but rather we are designing for how we want the system to perform 2 or 3 years down the road. Just as an architect over-designs the key structural elements of a building, the lighting designer over designs to make sure that the space will perform as intended well into the future.

The other way to bring the simple lumen method calculation closer to reality is to account for how effectively the luminaires are working with the surfaces of the space to deliver light to the target surface in question. If we are concerned with the light level on a floor plane and we are implementing an indirect lighting system that delivers light upward onto the ceiling where it then is reflected downward, it is safe to say that some of that light will be absorbed and lost before it makes it to the floor. Indeed, it is rare that the majority of the light from a luminaire is directed immediately onto the surface with which we are concerned. It is also important to account for the geometry and reflectances of the room surfaces. Room surface geometry and reflectance will determine how effectively light inter-reflects to reach the surface in question. We accommodate for luminaire orientation, room geometry and surface reflectance by including a factor that takes into account these relationships in each specific situation. We call this factor the *Coefficient of utilization, or CU.* The CU is expressed as a decimal number or a percentage to represent how effectively our lighting system is being utilized. The more directly our luminaires are being utilized and the more favorable the geometry, the higher the CU. In situations where light takes a very indirect path to the surfaces we are calculating, the CU is lower.

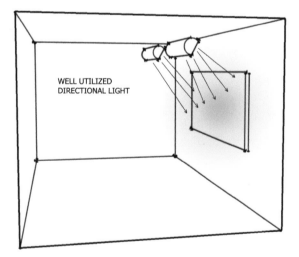
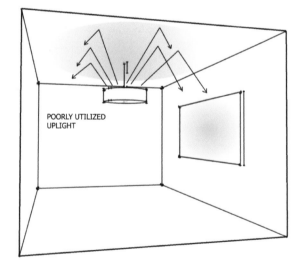

Figure 20.6 Light delivered with a high Coefficient of Utilization (left) and light delivered with a low Coefficient of Utilization (right).

There is a very tedious way to accurately calculate the Coefficient of Utilization that takes into account room geometry, surface reflectances and luminaire placement. For our purposes, we will rely on a few ballpark numbers that will simply add to the usefulness of our lumen method calculations. Like the Light Loss Factor or any other safety factor, we include these numbers in our calculations to make sure that we are over designing and accommodating for non-ideal conditions. The list below shows Coefficient of Utilization values that would be appropriate in a calculation where we are concerned with an illuminance level on the floor or a horizontal work plane. The values also assume that the space in question consists of fairly reflective surfaces:

Direct fixture or downlight:	*CU = 85%*	*(0.85 in an equation);*
Indirect fixture:	*CU = 50%*	*(0.50);*
Spot or accent:	*CU = 95%*	*(0.95);*
Wash or ambient:	*CU = 75%*	*(0.75).*

Lumen Method Calculations with Safety Factors

Both of the factors discussed here simply get added to our equations to convince us to use more light or, conversely, to expect less light from our system.

This creates a more accurate and useful equation for predicting lighting effect. With the addition of the Light Loss Factor and the Coefficient of Utilization, our lumen method calculation goes from:

$$\text{Illuminance} = \text{Lumens} \div \text{Area}$$

to

$$\text{Illuminance} = (\text{Lumens} \times \text{LLF} \times \text{CU}) \div \text{Area}$$

Our formula for determining how much light we need to introduce into a space goes from:

$$\text{Lumens needed} = \text{Illuminance target} \times \text{Area}$$

to:

$$\text{Lumens needed} = (\text{Illuminance target} \times \text{Area}) \div (\text{LLF} \times \text{CU})$$

Oftentimes, when we are after a very basic calculation and we don't want to numerically include these two factors, we refer to the lumens in our equation as "functional lumens," that is, lumens that we know are being utilized to put light onto the task with which we are concerned. In this manner, we can use the basic versions of our equations, without the safety factors, but describe our results in terms of how many "functional lumens" we would need, or how many "functional lumens" we are providing.

Regardless of whether we use the simplified equations, or whether we include the two safety factors, it is important to recognize where lumen method calculations are viable. In order for an "average illuminance level" to be meaningful, the space or surface in question must actually have an "average illuminance level."

So the lumen method calculation is really only valid for large, open areas with even lighting layouts. This means that if we have a space with all of its luminaires placed toward the center of the space, knowing that the average Illuminance level on the floor is 25 foot-Candles tells us very little since we can plainly see that the room is exceptionally bright in the center and very dark toward the perimeter.

Good candidates for lumen method calculations are open office spaces, classrooms, sports arenas, warehouses, public hallways... any rectangular space with an even layout of luminaires and few obstructions.

When we are interested in lighting effects onto objects and specific surfaces, we use the other form of calculation: the point calculation method.

THE POINT CALCULATION METHOD

When we are interested in illuminance levels that exist at a very specific point on an object, we use a simple calculation that takes into account how the delivery of light spreads out as the distance between the light source and the object increases. We generally use this calculation for considering object, accent and task light levels that are a product of a few specifically-placed fixtures that are directing their light immediately onto the surface in question. Because of this, the point calculation method requires that we be able to at least estimate the location of our lighting equipment in reference to the surface and the distance between the two. One of the most common situations to use the point calculation is in accenting artwork or other objects of interest.

The equation we use for the point calculation method is, again, not really an equation at all, but rather an expression based on the unit definition of the candela. Candelas are a measurement of light density exhibited from a specific source in a specific direction. Candle-power (expressed in Candelas) is a very common way to describe the way light leaves directional luminaires.

When we consider a glowing globe, it is fairly obvious that the source distributes light evenly in every direction.

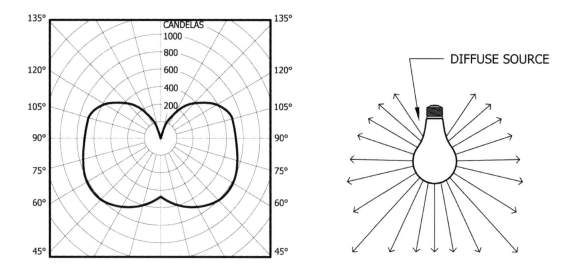

Figure 20.7 A candela distribution diagram (left) for a diffuse source (right).

Architectural luminaires like downlights, accent luminaires and wall-washers have optics and reflectors that drive light in a very specific manner. The Candle-power measurement from a particular fixture is a measure of the light density that a luminaire produces in a specific direction.

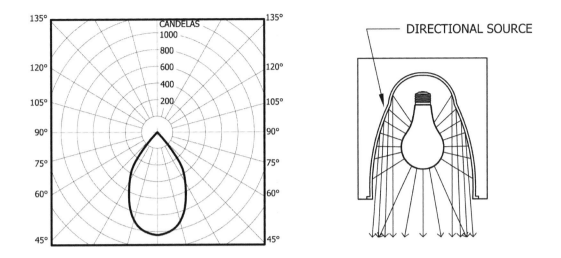

Figure 20.8 A candela distribution diagram (left) for a directional source (right).

There really is no way to estimate the candela values coming from a light source by staring at it, so this information must be given to us by the manufacturer of the lamp or luminaire. Luminaire literature often includes a *candela distribution diagram*. This diagram gives specific candela values at various angles measured from directly beneath the source.

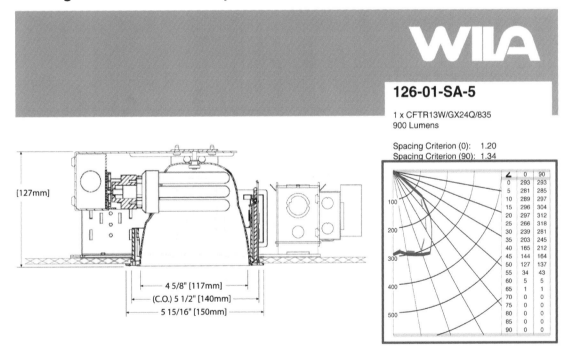

Figure 20.9 Literature for a high-performance luminaire may provide a candela diagram.

Point calculations usually involve very directional fixtures that create pools or spots of light. In these situations, we can usually count on the highest concentration occurring at the center of the pool of light. The candela value from this center point has a special designation: we call it the "Center Beam Candle-Power" or CBCP. Some luminaire and lamp literature will forgo a complex candella distribution diagram and simply publish this CBCP value, assuming that the user is concerned with the brightest area of light.

CENTER BEAM CANDELA VALUE
(CBCP)

Figure 20.10 The highest candela value from a light source is commonly found at the center of the light output.

The point calculation method is based on the principle that light spreads out as it travels away from a source. This spread of light is exemplified by the pool of light created by a directional fixture. As the distance from the source increases, the pool of light gets larger, but also gets less bright. Using this principle, we can determine the illuminance level at a specific point by knowing the Candela value of the source in that direction and the distance from the source to the point. Candelas are an expression of light density or lumens per area where the area is a piece of spherical space. Trying to visualize this is a bit tricky, so we will move forward and simply trust the equation. The most important step in putting the point calculation equation to use is determining the distance value "D" from the source to the point in question. This value must be determined and always expressed in feet before it is squared in the equation.

The equation for a straightforward point calculation looks like this:

$$\text{Illuminance} = \text{Candela value} \div \text{Distance}^2 \text{ (distance in feet squared)}$$

Or

$$E = CD \div D^2$$

The equation is best understood through a simple example.

Point Calculation: Example 1:

Suppose we have an accent fixture recessed into a 10'-0" ceiling directly above a plate that is on a table at 3'-0" above the floor. If that accent fixture has a center beam candle power (CBCP) of 10,000 candelas, what illuminance level can we expect at the brightest point on the plate?

This is best expressed as a diagram as in *Figure 20.11.*

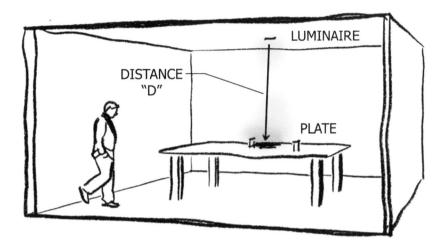

Figure 20.11 Point calculations are commonly used in situations involving one source and one object of interest.

Using our basic Point Calculation equation

$$\text{Illuminance} = \text{Candela value} \div \text{Distance}^2$$

or

$$E = CD \div D^2$$

plug in the values we know:

center-beam candela value of the source

$$CD = 10,000 \text{ Candelas}$$

distance squared: The "Distance" is the distance the light must travel. In this case, it is the mounting height of the luminaire (10 ft.) minus the height of the table (3 ft.)

$$D^2 = 7 \text{ feet squared} = 49 \text{ square feet (the units get squared too)}$$

Our equation becomes

$$\text{Illuminance} = 10,000 \text{ CD} \div 49 \text{ sq.ft.}$$

Or

$$\text{Illuminance} = 204 \text{ Foot-candles.}$$

This is a high illuminance level, but certainly within reason for an object we are trying to accent.

We tend use this calculation more frequently to deduce what type of candela value (and therefore source) we need to accomplish a certain lighting task. An example of such a situation may look like example 2

Point Calculation: Example 2:

Suppose we have an accent fixture recessed into the same 10'-0" ceiling directly above the same plate that is on a table at 3'-0" above the floor. If we want to illuminate that plate to 150 Foot-candles, what kind of center beam candle power value would we need from the luminaire?

The diagram is the same, but we use the flipped version our basic equation

Candela value needed = Illuminance level desired × distance squared

Or

$$CD = E \times D^2$$

We plug in what we know:

illuminance desired

E = 150 Foot-candles

distance squared

$$D^2 = 7 \text{ feet squared} = 49 \text{ sq.ft.}$$

and our solution becomes

CD = 150 FC × 49 sq.ft.

or

Candela value needed = 7350 Candelas.

Of course the second part of this type of situation is figuring out what sort of lamp or luminaire is going to provide this candela value. We may even decide to use two luminaires in which case we need only half of the contribution from each of them. To find a specific luminaire or lamp, we simply look at the various candela values produced by different lighting equipment. In the case of luminaires, the candela values are represented in the form of a distribution diagram.

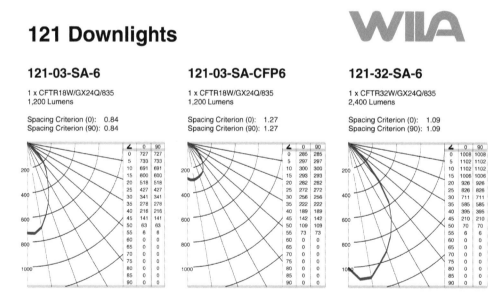

Figure 20.12 Candela distribution diagrams for various versions of a basic downlight.

When we are using one of our many accenting lamps, like an MR-16 or PAR lamp, the candela value will usually be expressed as the center beam candle power (CBCP), tucked in with a host of other information.

CENTER BEAM CANDLE-POWER
VALUE IN CANDELAS

PAR20   PAR30

CAPSYLITE® PAR20
Suitable for use in unshielded fixtures.

Product Number	Symbols & Footnotes	Ordering Abbreviation	Volts	Pkg Qty	Beam Type	Class & Filament	Avg Rated Life(hrs)	Lumens CCT	CBCP	Beam Angle	MOL (in)
14467	★ 🔲🔲 43,118	35PAR20/HAL/NSP10	120	15	NSP	C,CC-8	2500	360 2775	3000	10	3.25
14464	★ 🔲🔲 43,118	35PAR20/HAL/NFL30	120	15	NFL	C,CC-8	2500	360 2775	800	30	3.25
14459	★ 🔲🔲 43,118,137,151	35PAR20/HAL/NFL30	130	15	NFL	C,CC-8	2500	360 2775	800	30	3.25
		@ 120 volts, approximate 31 watts, 275 lumens, 5000 hours									
14506	★ 🔲🔲 43,118	35PAR20/HAL/WFL40	120	15	WFL	C,CC-8	2500	360 2775	500	40	3.25
14461	★ 🔲🔲 43,118,137,151	35PAR20/HAL/WFL40	130	15	WFL	C,CC-8	2500	360 2775	500	40	3.25
		@ 120 volts, approximate 31 watts, 275 lumens, 5000 hours									
14500	★ 🔲🔲 43,118	50PAR20/HAL/NSP10	120	15	NSP	C,CC-8	2500	550 2850	4600	10	3.25
14528	★ 🔲🔲 43,118,137,161	50PAR20/HAL/NSP10	130	15	NSP	C,CC-8	2500	550 2850	4600	10	3.25
		@ 120 volts, approximate 44 watts, 420 lumens, 5000 hours									
14502	★ 🔲🔲 43,118	50PAR20/HAL/NFL30	120	15	NFL	C,CC-8	2500	550 2850	1200	30	3.25
14173	★ 🔲🔲 43,118	50PAR20/HAL/NFL30/RP	120	6	NFL	C,CC-8	2500	550 2850	1200	30	3.25
14529	★ 🔲🔲 43,118,137,161	50PAR20/HAL/NFL30	130	15	NFL	C,CC-8	2500	550 2850	1200	30	3.25
		@ 120 volts, approximate 44 watts, 420 lumens, 5000 hours									
15662	★ 🔲🔲 43,118,137,161	50PAR20/HAL/NFL30/CVP	130	6	NFL	C,CC-8	2500	550 2850	1200	30	3.25
		@ 120 volts, approximate 44 watts, 420 lumens, 5000 hours									
14700	★ 🔲🔲 43,118	50PAR20/HAL/WFL40	120	15	WFL	C,CC-8	2500	550 2850	900	40	3.25

For more complete product information visit www.sylvania.com   Symbols/Footnotes on page 64-68

49

TUNGSTEN HALOGEN

Image courtesy of Sylvania   www.sylvania.com

Figure 20.13 Accent lamp literature commonly describes the Center Beam Candle-power values of a family of lamps.

Point calculations do get a bit more complicated when we consider situations in which the object we are lighting is not perpendicular to the light source. In these situations we include a bit of geometry in our calculation to get a more accurate answer. Basically, if we are aiming the light source to light an object at any angle other than perpendicular to the source, we know our light spreads out and is less effective. This is exemplified by the shape a pool of light takes on. As the aiming angle is increased, the circle becomes a long "scallop" of light.

We modify our point calculation equation to accommodate for how the geometry will spread out the light intensity:

$$\text{Candela value needed} = (\text{Illuminance level desired} \times \text{distance squared}) \div \text{cosine of the angle}$$

The angle in question is the angle created between the aiming line of the luminaire and a line perpendicular to the surface being lighted as displayed in *Figure 20.14*.

or

$$CD = (E \times D^2) \div \text{cosine of angle}.$$

or, if we use the equation to solve for illuminance onto the object, we use this

$$E = (CD \times \text{cosine of angle}) \div D^2$$

An example of this situation might look like example 3

Point Calculation: Example 3:

Suppose we have an accent fixture recessed into a 10'-0" ceiling aimed to light a collectible plate resting on a pedestal 3'-0" from the floor. To accent the plate, the luminaire is aimed at an angle. Aiming the luminaire creates an angle of 30 degrees between the aiming line of the luminaire and the line perpendicular to the plate. If we want to illuminate the plate to 100 foot-candles, what kind of center-beam candela value would we need from the luminaire?

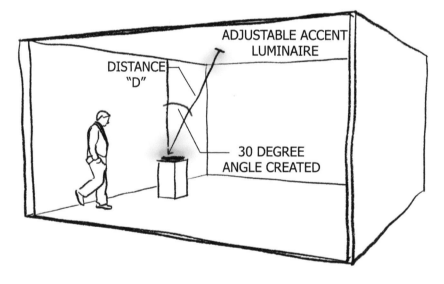

Figure 20.14 A point calculation used to determine how to light an object when an aiming angle is involved.

We use the version of our equation that accounts for lighting at an angle

Candela value needed = (Illuminance level desired × distance squared) ÷ cosine of the angle

or

$$CD = (E \times D^2) \div \text{cosine of angle}$$

We plug in what we know:

illuminance desired

E = 100 Foot-candles

We use simple trigonometry to determine the Distance squared

$$D^2 = 8.1 \text{ feet squared} = 65 \text{ sq.ft.}$$
Cosine of angle = cosine of 30 degrees = 0.87

Our solution becomes

CD = (100 FC x 65 sq.ft) ÷ 0.87

Or

Candela value needed = 7471 Candelas.

Through this example we can see that lighting at an angle reduces the effectiveness of the light source immensely.

It is important to recognize that this chapter presents simple calculations that ignore any inter-reflected light. In these situations, it is assumed that all of the light being measured comes directly from the luminaires in question.

Once a designer gets the hang of the basic principles of these two types of calculations, he/she will begin to gain an instinct for where each can be useful. As mentioned before, it is equally important to recognize where calculations will *not* benefit the design or help to create a good lighting solution. Calculations are merely tools to support and refine the lighting concepts that one draws up as he/she works through the more graphical and imaginative processes that we now associate with lighting design.

All of the tools we have explored through this section are geared towards bringing us to a point where we are ready to prepare drawings that will translate our lighting concepts into a constructible project. The visualizing, the articulating, the sketching, the drawing, the describing, and the calculating are all tools to make the job of selecting the appropriate lighting easier. The next logical step is to use all of the creative and calculative input to create the drawings and details that will allow the project to be built.

Part III
Deliverables

Chapter 21

Deciphering Luminaire Literature and Manufacturers' Cut Sheets

Before we can hope to make intuitive decisions about selecting lighting equipment to solve our lighting challenges, we must dedicate some time to understanding what types of luminaires are available to us. Lighting products, like most specification design products, have a wealth of information published about them to help the designer determine which product is most appropriate. In addition to printed catalogs and websites, most lighting manufacturers employ a local representative to service the needs of the designer. This representative will take the time to explain why a particular piece of lighting equipment may or may not suite ones needs. The manufacturer's rep can also give pricing information and indicate shipping lead times for time sensitive jobs. One of the best things designers can do to position themselves for good lighting knowledge is to contact their local lighting manufacturer's representative agency.

Lighting literature comes in all shapes and sizes and all levels of usefulness. Manufacturers publish what they call "cut sheets" to list the various features, options and capabilities of a lighting product. First and foremost, a product cut sheet should give us an idea of the size, function and overall appearance of a product. Beyond these basics, the level of information provided by various manufacturers varies greatly from very vague to very detailed. Generally, the more technically inclined the luminaire, the more articulate the information. Some of our more exotic decorative luminaires provide very little information. In order to learn to decipher these manufacturers cut sheets, we will look at a few examples and learn how to identify the key pieces of information.

It seems that the complex and cryptic nature of lighting manufacturers' cut sheets is what prevents many designers from taking up lighting as a design tool. If a designer can develop confidence in the ability to gather information from these cut-sheets, he/she will be well armed to make confident luminaire decisions. The ability to decipher manufacturers' cut sheets will determine the ability to build a catalog number to order and receive the specific product needed for a job.

The following is a list of features that the designer should be able to identify from a cut sheet and put together to create a complete luminaire product number. As the designer reads about the pieces of information that he/she is looking for, refer back to the sample cut sheet in *Figure 21.1*.

PHYSICAL BASICS

The first impression of a luminaire should be its size, shape and function. It should be readily apparent how this fixture is mounted (surface, recessed, wall, ceiling, etc.). If the luminaire is recessed into the wall or ceiling, the cut sheet should quickly confirm whether the luminaire will fit into the space available. One should also get an impression of how the luminaire will look in the space.

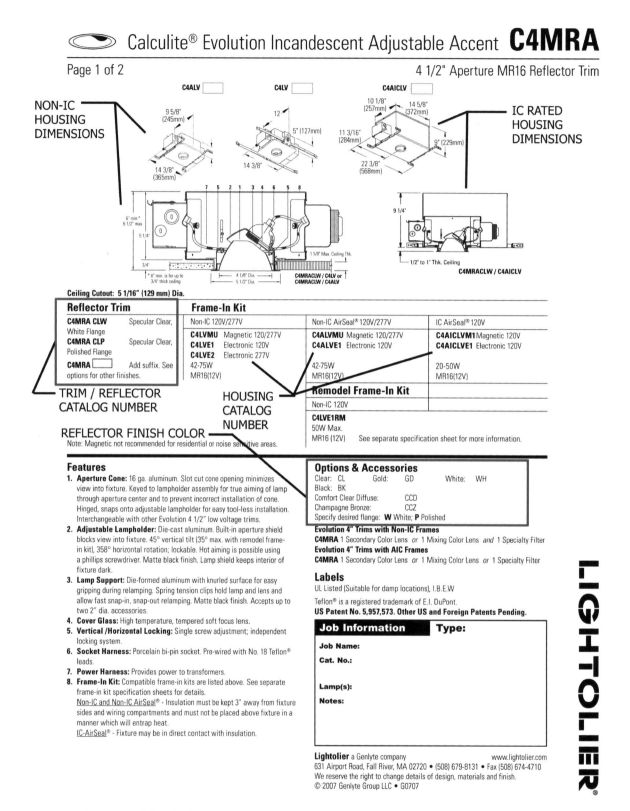

Calculite® Evolution Incandescent Adjustable Accent **C4MRA**

Page 1 of 2   4 1/2" Aperture MR16 Reflector Trim

NON-IC HOUSING DIMENSIONS

IC RATED HOUSING DIMENSIONS

TRIM / REFLECTOR CATALOG NUMBER

HOUSING CATALOG NUMBER

REFLECTOR FINISH COLOR

Note: Magnetic not recommended for residential or noise sensitive areas.

Reflector Trim

C4MRA CLW Specular Clear, White Flange

C4MRA CLP Specular Clear, Polished Flange

C4MRA ☐ Add suffix. See options for other finishes.

Frame-In Kit

Non-IC 120V/277V	Non-IC AirSeal® 120V/277V	IC AirSeal® 120V
C4LVMU Magnetic 120/277V	**C4ALVMU** Magnetic 120/277V	**C4AICLVM1** Magnetic 120V
C4LVE1 Electronic 120V	**C4ALVE1** Electronic 120V	**C4AICLVE1** Electronic 120V
C4LVE2 Electronic 277V		
42-75W MR16(12V)	42-75W MR16(12V)	20-50W MR16(12V)

Remodel Frame-In Kit

Non-IC 120V
C4LVE1RM 50W Max. MR16 (12V) See separate specification sheet for more information.

Ceiling Cutout: 5 1/16" (129 mm) Dia.

Features

1. **Aperture Cone:** 16 ga. aluminum. Slot cut cone opening minimizes view into fixture. Keyed to lampholder assembly for true aiming of lamp through aperture center and to prevent incorrect installation of cone. Hinged, snaps onto adjustable lampholder for easy tool-less installation. Interchangeable with other Evolution 4 1/2" low voltage trims.
2. **Adjustable Lampholder:** Die-cast aluminum. Built-in aperture shield blocks view into fixture. 45° vertical tilt (35° max. with remodel frame-in kit), 358° horizontal rotation; lockable. Hot aiming is possible using a phillips screwdriver. Matte black finish. Lamp shield keeps interior of fixture dark.
3. **Lamp Support:** Die-formed aluminum with knurled surface for easy gripping during relamping. Spring tension clips hold lamp and lens and allow fast snap-in, snap-out relamping. Matte black finish. Accepts up to two 2" dia. accessories.
4. **Cover Glass:** High temperature, tempered soft focus lens.
5. **Vertical /Horizontal Locking:** Single screw adjustment; independent locking system.
6. **Socket Harness:** Porcelain bi-pin socket. Pre-wired with No. 18 Teflon® leads.
7. **Power Harness:** Provides power to transformers.
8. **Frame-In Kit:** Compatible frame-in kits are listed above. See separate frame-in kit specification sheets for details.
   Non-IC and Non-IC AirSeal® - Insulation must be kept 3" away from fixture sides and wiring compartments and must not be placed above fixture in a manner which will entrap heat.
   IC-AirSeal® - Fixture may be in direct contact with insulation.

Options & Accessories

Clear: CL	Gold: GD	White: WH	
Black: BK			
Comfort Clear Diffuse:	CCD		
Champagne Bronze:	CCZ		
Specify desired flange: **W** White; **P** Polished			

Evolution 4" Trims with Non-IC Frames
C4MRA 1 Secondary Color Lens *or* 1 Mixing Color Lens *and* 1 Specialty Filter
Evolution 4" Trims with AIC Frames
C4MRA 1 Secondary Color Lens *or* 1 Mixing Color Lens *or* 1 Specialty Filter

Labels

UL Listed (Suitable for damp locations), I.B.E.W

Teflon® is a registered trademark of E.I. DuPont.
US Patent No. 5,957,573. Other US and Foreign Patents Pending.

Job Information	**Type:**
Job Name:	
Cat. No.:	
Lamp(s):	
Notes:	

Lightolier a Genlyte company   www.lightolier.com
631 Airport Road, Fall River, MA 02720 • (508) 679-8131 • Fax (508) 674-4710
We reserve the right to change details of design, materials and finish.
© 2007 Genlyte Group LLC • G0707

LIGHTOLIER®

Figure 21.1 A typical architectural luminaire cut sheet. In this case, a recessed adjustable accent fixture.

The cut sheet shown for reference in *Figure 21.1* is for the Lightolier C4MRA reflector and the various housings that can accommodate it. This is a recessed adjustable accent luminaire. Upon first glance, it should be obvious that this piece of equipment recesses into the ceiling plane. We should be able to identify the lamp located within the luminaire, and the angle of the lamp should hint that this is an adjustable / aimable luminaire. The other piece of information that should jump out at us is the sheer size of a simple luminaire like this. This recessed accent luminaire is a good example of how large these luminaires can get. If we look at the cut sheet, we see that there are three different sizes of housing available for different uses of this luminaire.

Mounting Style:

Does this fixture recess into the ceiling?

Does this fixture mount to the surface of a wall or ceiling?

Does this fixture mount from a pendant or canopy?

The cut sheet in *Figure 21.1* shows three different housing types for different construction types. Recessed luminaires often have multiple housing options to accommodate insulated (IC) and non-insulated (Non-IC) plenum situations, which we will discuss below.

Fixture Size and Height:

What are the luminaire dimensions?

How will the luminaire dimensions work in our space?

If this is a recessed luminaire, will it fit into our ceiling?

The fixture shown in *Figure 21.1* has an aperture of about 4", which is about as small as recessed adjustable accent fixtures get. There are three housings available for this luminaire, ranging from 8" in height, to 11" in height. All three have a similar footprint of 14" x 10". These physical basics begin to show why it is so important to coordinate recessed luminaire locations when building.

Aesthetics:

What are the colors and finishes available?

What trims, diffusers and accessories are available?

A recessed luminaire like the example in *Fig 21 .1* has relatively little aesthetic impression in the space, but there are decisions to be made nonetheless. For recessed luminaires, we must decide on the color of the reflector cone above the ceiling and the trim ring that rests at ceiling level. The cut sheet in *Figure 21.1* shows that we need to make a color specification for each of these components. Because this luminaire holds an MR-16 lamp, we can also specify any type of colored lens or frosted diffusing lens to soften the light.

Light suitability:

Is the luminaire IC rated (Suitable for insulated ceilings / plenums)?

Is the luminaire listed for damp or wet locations?

Does the luminaire deliver the quality, color, and texture of light that we are after?

Is the luminaire / lamp dimmable?

Is the source instant on / off?

Does the luminaire create excessive glare?

Is the luminaire aimable / adjustable?

The luminaire in *Figure 21.1* is really nothing more than a holder for an MR-16 lamp. As such, the lamp is going to dictate most of the light delivery properties. The MR-16 lamp is a low voltage halogen lamp, so we know that it is instant on and off, is easily dimmable, and is a very directional light.

IC rating is a common issue that comes up with recessed luminaires. IC rating stands for "Insulation Contact." It is a rating that indicates that the luminaire housing is cool enough to be in contact with fiberglass and batt insulation. We encounter this insulation most commonly on residential projects, so when designing for a residence, it is always prudent to determine if the luminaires need to be or are IC rated.

Lamp and Electrical Basics:

Are there multiple lamp / source options?

Does the luminaire require multiple lamps?

What are the fixture voltage options?

What are the fixture wattage limitations (Maximum wattage)?

Does the luminaire require a ballast or transformer?

The luminaire here accepts MR-16 lamps up to 75 watts for the non-IC housing and up to 50 Watts for the IC version. The IC rated housing limits lamp wattage to limit potential heat. Because the MR-16 lamp is a "low voltage" source, we know that the luminaire requires a transformer. In this case, the transformer is integral to the luminaire. Often, a luminaire will not include a transformer, and a remote transformer will be required.

Light Output Performance:

What is the lumen output of the luminaire?

What is the efficacy / efficiency of the luminaire?

What is the distribution shape of the luminaire?

Does the cut sheet provide a distribution diagram?

How would we describe the light distribution shape? Spot, flood, accent, wash, spread, glow, diffuse?

The luminaire in *Figure 21.1* will have the properties of the MR-16 lamp we put into it. MR-16 lamps come in all different beam spreads and candela distributions. Because the lamp defines the light output properties, we can probably learn more about this luminaire's light performance from the lamp manufacturer's literature than we can from the luminaire cut sheet.

Regardless of how thorough or lacking the literature that is available, remember the basics that will get us most of the way towards the right product:

How is this luminaire installed (Recessed, surface, wall mount etc.)?

What type of lamp / source does this luminaire use?

Does this luminaire require a remote transformer or ballast?

What are the dimensions of the luminaire?

If a designer can successfully answer the preceding questions when faced with a luminaire cut sheet, then he/she has a very good chance of selecting appropriate lighting equipment. Just simply knowing that the information is *somewhere* on the cut sheet gives us greater hope and confidence when we are poring over luminaire catalogs and websites.

Chapter 22

Selecting Luminaires: A Basic Family

Every lighting project is entirely unique, and over the course of a design career, one may find oneself becoming more proficient and familiar with certain types of environments. Time and time, again, project situations call for the same styles and types of lighting equipment. For this reason, we will look at a family of the "workhorse" luminaires that commonly appear on luminaire schedules for residential, high-design commercial and hospitality projects. Obviously, lighting design projects span a broad spectrum. There are designers who will never have need for any of the products mentioned here. But these tools seem to be versatile enough that they are useful as a foundation for everyone.

THE BASIC FIXTURE FAMILY

The 4-inch Recessed Downlight

The recessed downlight is, no doubt, one of the darlings of the architectural lighting world. This little device shows up as nothing more than a hole in the ceiling and casts light onto a surface below. The small version of a downlight will usually hold an MR-16 low-voltage lamp or a line-voltage PAR-20 lamp. There are even 4" aperture downlights that hold compact fluorescent lamps. This luminaire may be the first line of defense in placing light in social areas and task areas. This small aperture downlight will generally be useful in ceilings up to 9'-0" high. Be warned, however, that by their very nature, downlights are fairly restrictive. By placing light directly down, this tool often keeps us from being able to place vertical illumination onto the walls or aim light onto specific objects. Some commonly-specified 4" aperture downlights are made by *Lightolier, Prescolite, Leucos, Deltalight, Prima, Capri and Juno*. Below are cut sheets and images of this type of luminaire.

Figure 22.1.1 A 4" aperture downlight from Deltalight.

ERCO LC Downlight
for low-voltage halogen lamps

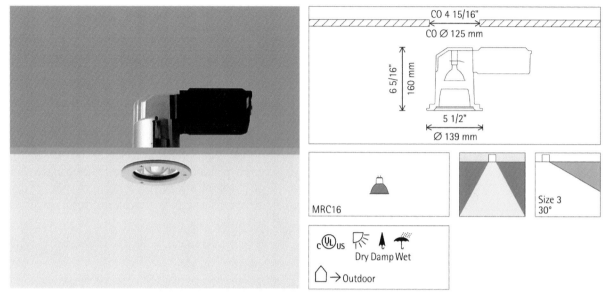

Figure 22.1.2 A 4" aperture downlight from Erco.

Calculite® Evolution Incandescent Open Downlight **C4MRD**

4 1/2" Aperture, MR16 Reflector Trim

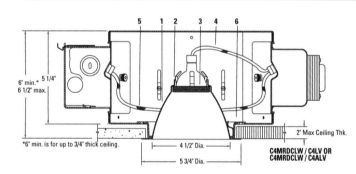

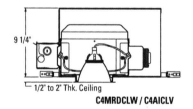

LIGHTOLIER®

Figure 22.1.3 A 4" aperture downlight from Lightolier.

Image courtesy of Deltalight   www.deltalight.us

Figure 22.1.4 An application featuring 4" aperture downlights.

The 6 inch Recessed Downlight

The 6 inch downlight behaves in the same way as its smaller cousin, but it generally contains a larger lamp for more robust effects. It is recommended when using a large aperture downlight to make sure that it can accommodate a PAR38 halogen lamp. These lamps are useful for lighting in ceilings as high as 24 feet. A 6-inch aperture downlight may also house an HID lamp, or high wattage halogen lamp with an ellipsoidal reflector. In all cases, these downlights are a utilitarian way to get light onto the horizontal plane from high ceilings.

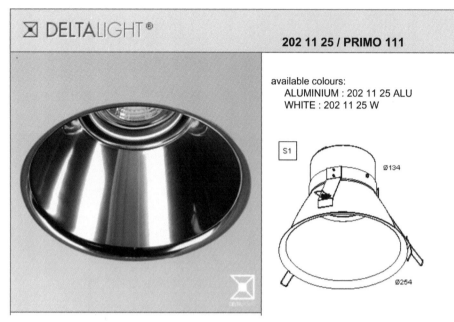

Figure 22.2.1 A 6" aperture downlight from Deltalight.

ERCO

LC Downlight
for low-voltage halogen lamps

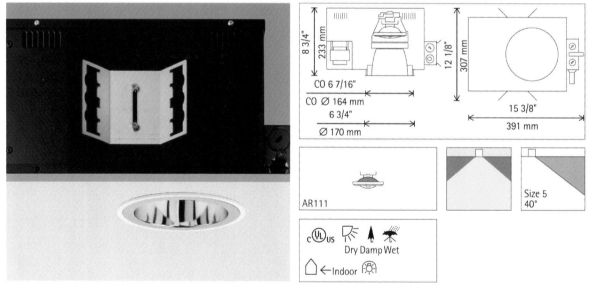

Figure 22.2.2 A 6" aperture downlight from Erco.

Lytecaster® Recessed Downlighting **1176**

6 3/4" Aperture Basic Baffle Reflector Trim

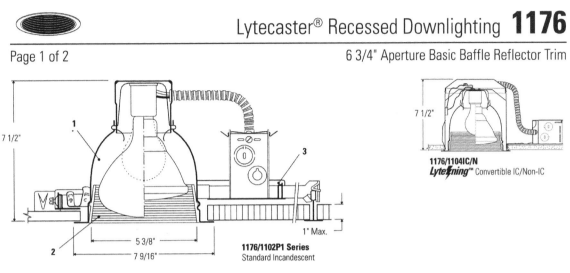

7 1/2"

1176/1104IC/N
Lytening™ Convertible IC/Non-IC

7 1/2"

1" Max.

5 3/8"

7 9/16"

1176/1102P1 Series
Standard Incandescent

Figure 22.2.3 A 6" aperture downlight from Lightolier.

Image courtesy of Deltalight   www.deltalight.us

Figure 22.2.4 An application featuring 6" aperture downlights.

The 4-inch and 6-inch Recessed Adjustable Accent

The recessed adjustable accent is truly the workhorse of the lighting designer. This fixture acts much in the same way as a theatrical lighting device to deliver a defined piece of light onto any surface at which it is aimed. For many applications, the recessed adjustable luminaire can act as a wall-wash, as well as a general downlight. Because this luminaire can be aimed, it can serve many functions. These are the luminaires that we often use to paint pieces of light onto the specific objects and surfaces that we have identified on our light maps. They are versatile enough that many architectural spaces can be lighted entirely with recessed adjustable luminaires. It is worth specifying a luminaire that has the adjusting mechanism recessed above the ceiling plane, rather than the all-too common "eyeball." Some well-known manufacturers of adjustable accents include *Erco, Zumtobel, RSA*, as well as those mentioned under downlights.

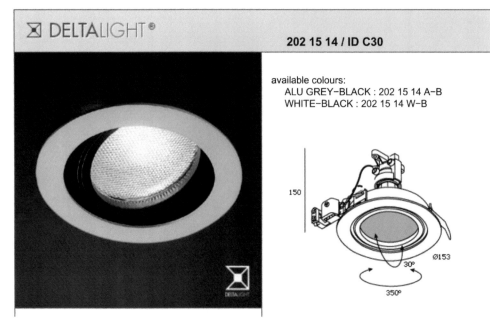

Figure 22.3.1 An adjustable accent luminaire from Deltalight.

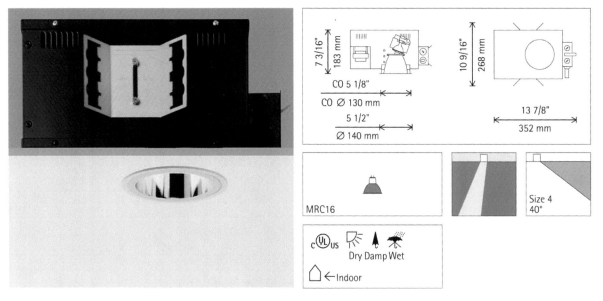

Figure 22.3.2 An adjustable accent luminaire from Erco.

Calculite® Evolution Incandescent Adjustable Accent **C4MRA**

4 1/2" Aperture MR16 Reflector Trim

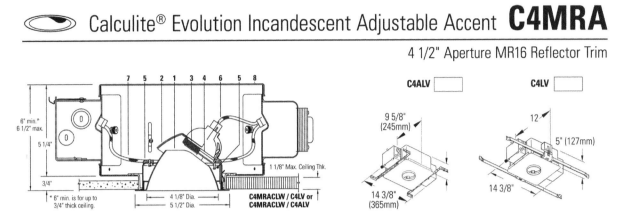

C4ALV

C4LV

9 5/8"
(245mm)

12"

5" (127mm)

14 3/8"
(365mm)

14 3/8"

6" min.*
6 1/2" max.

5 1/4"

3/4"

7 5 2 1 3 4 6 5 8

1 1/8" Max. Ceiling Thk.

* 6" min. is for up to
3/4" thick ceiling.

4 1/8" Dia.
5 1/2" Dia.

C4MRACLW / C4LV or
C4MRACLW / C4ALV

Figure 22.3.3 An adjustable accent luminaire from Lightolier.

Lytecaster® Recessed Downlighting **1129**

6 3/4" Aperture Recessed Adjustable Reflector Trim 30°

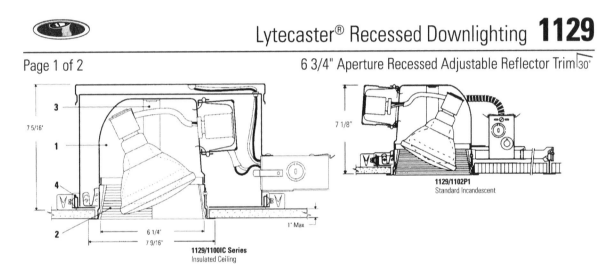

3

7 5/16"

1

4

2

6 1/4"
7 9/16"

1129/1100IC Series
Insulated Ceiling

1" Max

7 1/8"

1129/1102P1
Standard Incandescent

Figure 22.3.4 An adjustable accent luminaire from Lightolier.

Image courtesy of Deltalight   www.deltalight.us

Figure 22.3.5 An application featuring adjustable accent luminaires

The Millwork Downlight

Inevitably, there comes a need for a very small version of an adjustable accent or downlight. As we have seen, the majority of recessed fixtures feature large housings to contain heat. There are, however, recessed products that have reduced housings and are suitable for building into cabinetry, millwork and architectural details. Some commonly used products are available from *Prima lighting, DaSal lighting, and Ardee lighting.*

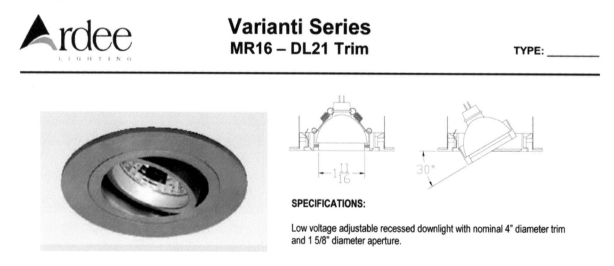

Varianti Series
MR16 – DL21 Trim

TYPE: _____

SPECIFICATIONS:

Low voltage adjustable recessed downlight with nominal 4" diameter trim and 1 5/8" diameter aperture.

Figure 22.4.1 A millwork "puck light" luminaire from Ardee.

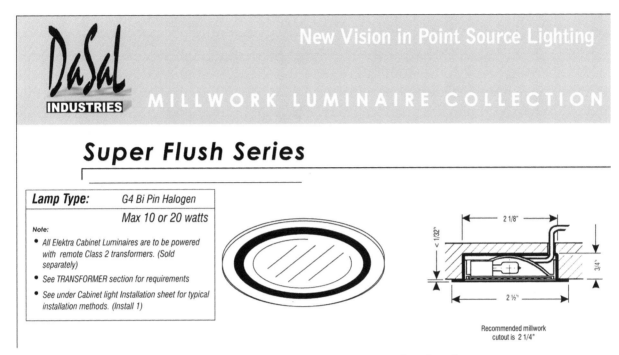

Super Flush Series

Lamp Type: G4 Bi Pin Halogen

Max 10 or 20 watts

Note:

- All Elektra Cabinet Luminaires are to be powered with remote Class 2 transformers. (Sold separately)
- See TRANSFORMER section for requirements
- See under Cabinet light Installation sheet for typical installation methods. (Install 1)

2 1/8"

< 1/32"

3/4"

2 ½"

Recommended millwork
cutout is 2 1/4"

Figure 22.4.2 A millwork "puck light" luminaire from Dasal.

Prima Recessed Architectural - Series 27 Downlight / Accent Trim with Adjustable Gimbal is compatible with Series 84 fixtures. Series 27 may be used with or without Prima Recessed rough-in housings. Compatible with Prima NCH, ICH and RMH rough-in housings.

Adjustable Downlight/Accent for MR16 Lamp - Adjustable Gimbal

Series 84 Adjustable Gimbal for MR16
Adjustable Downlight / Accent light for use with MR16 lamp. Matte Black interior finish. Includes perforated lamp shield.

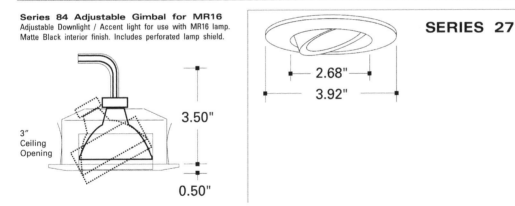

3″ Ceiling Opening

3.50"

0.50"

2.68"

3.92"

SERIES 27

Figure 22.4.3 A millwork "puck light" luminaire from Prima.

Image courtesy of Deltalight   www.deltalight.us

Figure 22.4.4 An application featuring millwork "puck light" luminaires

The Direct-burial or In-grade Floor Luminaire

This family of luminaires mounts directly into the ground or floor of a space and casts light upwards onto walls, columns, and canopies above. It is essentially a robust downlight mounted upside-down. Because it goes in the ground, these fixtures must be durable, water tight and must be considered for the amount of heat they create. Direct burial luminaires are also available in adjustable versions so that their beam of light can be aimed to wash a specific surface. These luminaires are one of the surest ways to introduce a unique light character into a space. Some commonly specified versions of this type of luminaire are from *Lumascape, Lumiere, Hydrel, Kim, and Deltalight.*

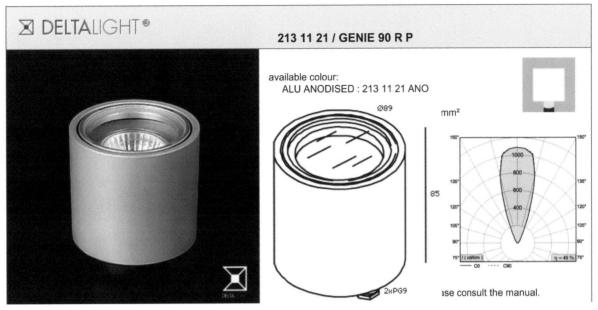

⊠ DELTALIGHT ®

213 11 21 / GENIE 90 R P

available colour:
ALU ANODISED : 213 11 21 ANO

Ø89

mm²

85

2×PG9

...se consult the manual.

Figure 22.5.1 A direct-burial uplight from Deltalight.

ERCO   Nadir Recessed floor luminaire
Directional luminaire for PAR lamps

8 1/2"
Ø 215 mm

8 1/4"
210 mm

CO 7 7/8"
Ø 200 mm

PAR30

c(UL)us   Dry Damp Wet
⌂ → Outdoor

33820.023
PAR30 75W 120V Med. 9°
PAR30 75W 120V Med. 35°

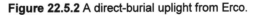

Figure 22.5.2 A direct-burial uplight from Erco.

ERCO **Nadir Recessed floor luminaire**
for compact fluorescent lamps

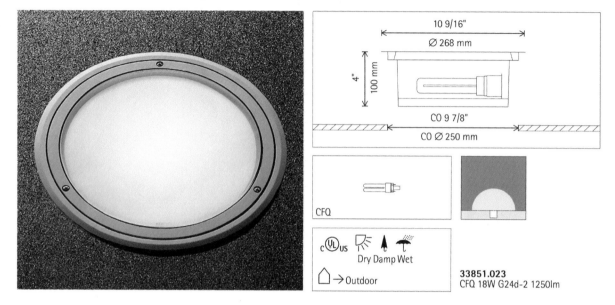

10 9/16"
∅ 268 mm

4"
100 mm

CO 9 7/8"
CO ∅ 250 mm

CFQ

c(UL)us
Dry Damp Wet

△ → Outdoor

33851.023
CFQ 18W G24d-2 1250lm

Figure 22.5.3 A direct-burial uplight from Erco.

Image courtesy of Deltalight   www.deltalight.us

Figure 22.5.4 An application featuring direct-burial uplights.

The Wall Mounted Uplight

Another way to add a unique light character to a space is through the use of luminaires that mount high on the wall and direct their light upwards onto the ceiling or lid above. These luminaires can mount to a wall surface or recess to create a "hole in the wall" effect. These luminaires can come in any architectural style or disappear to have almost no impression at all. These luminaires can deliver an upward glow not possible with lighting mounted in or on the ceiling. Some commonly-specified versions of wall surface mounted uplights are from *Winona, Elliptipar and Insight*. Some wall recessed versions are made by *Belfer, Energie, Eurolite and Deltalight*.

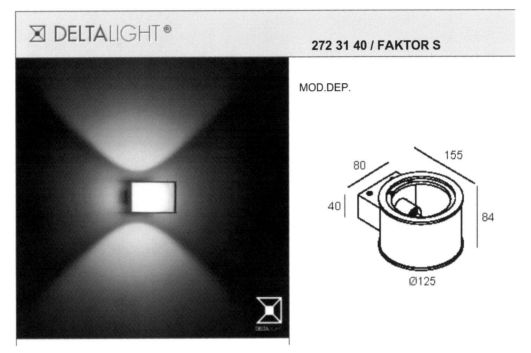

Figure 22.6.1 A wall mounted uplight from Deltalight.

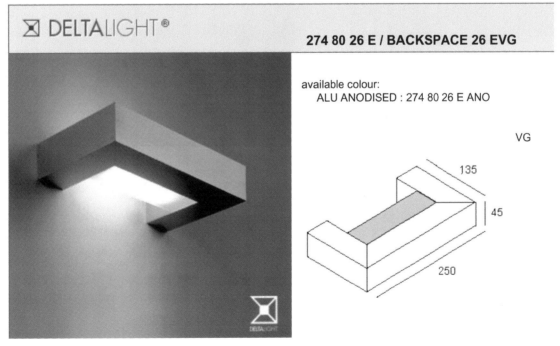

Figure 22.6.2 A wall mounted uplight from Deltalight.

Trion Uplight
for compact fluorescent lamps

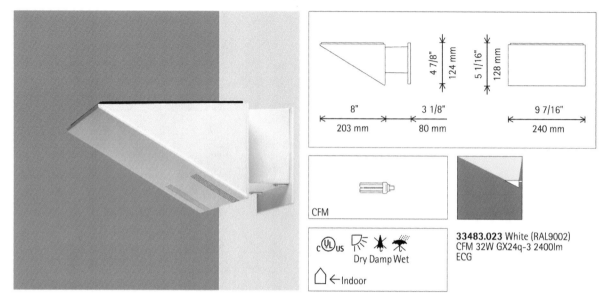

Figure 22.6.3 A wall-mounted uplight from Erco.

ERCO

Atrium Uplight
for compact fluorescent lamps

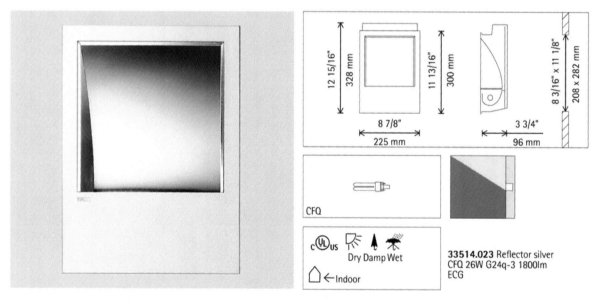

Figure 22.6.4 A wall-mounted "hole in the wall" uplight from Erco.

The Glowing Disc Area Light

Often times an afterthought, some sort of surface mounted area light should be considered for small spaces or utility areas. Too often, these small spaces are left to recessed fixtures that direct most of their lighting effect downward, leaving the space dark and cave-like. A simple dish or slightly decorative disc can provide light onto the ceiling and walls as well as downward. The big manufacturers all make a version of this light. Some commonly-specified versions are from *Tech lighting and Eureka lighting*.

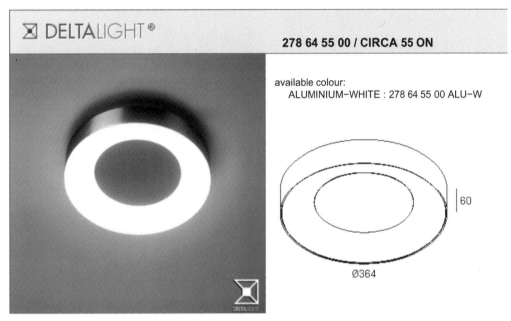

Figure 22.7.1 A glowing surface mounted area light from Deltalight.

TECH LIGHTING®
CEILING COLLECTION

7400 Linder Avenue   T 847.410.4400
Skokie, Illinois 60077   F 847.410.4500

www.techlighting.com

DESCRIPTION
Beautiful round, pressed glass shade with polished surface. Suspended from a die-cast base. Available in two lamp configurations; incandescent and fluorescent.

DIMMING
Incandescent version dimmable with a standard incandescent dimmer (not included).

FINISH
Chrome, satin nickel.

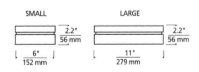

CIRQUE, LARGE
Shown approximately 20% actual size.

CIRQUE

Figure 22.7.2 A glowing, surface-mounted area light from Tech Lighting.

The Compact Fluorescent Downlight

With energy concerns growing, and efficiency and sustainability of design rising on the priority list, fluorescent sources are becoming increasingly popular. This particular fixture is listed because as of this writing, it is not always easy to find an aesthetically-suitable compact fluorescent downlight for residential uses. Plenty of commercial products exist, but residential products that provide an IC rated housing (see chapter 24) are relatively hard to come by. An aesthetic consideration for compact fluorescent downlights is a regressed diffusing lens to conceal the bare lamp. Commonly-specified versions of this luminaire are from *Lightolier, Iris, and Capri*.

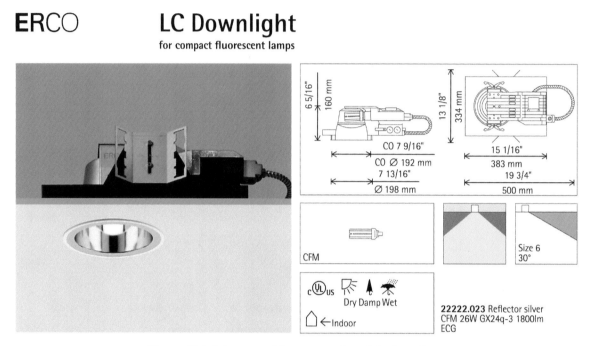

Figure 22.8.1 A compact fluorescent downlight from Erco.

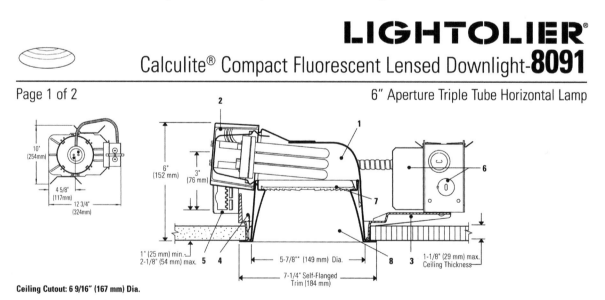

Figure 22.8.2 A compact fluorescent downlight from Lightolier.

The Linear Incandescent or Linear LED Luminaire

Long lines of light are fairly common in contemporary environments. The diminutive linear sources that create these shapes of light are usually smaller than 1" x 1" in profile and are often flexible and can be cut to any length in the field. They are usually low-voltage luminaires that require a remote transformer or "driver". They can serve in coves, slots, niches, and even as under cabinet luminaires. This style of luminaire commonly relies on incandescent or more efficient LED lamps. Some commonly-specified versions of this type of luminaire are from *Tivoli, Solavanti, ColorGlo, and Tokistar*.

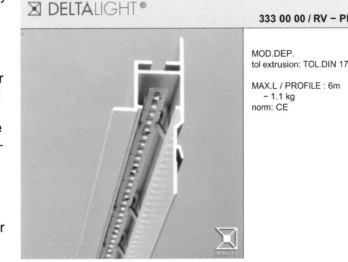

⊠ DELTALIGHT ®

333 00 00 / RV – PROFILE

MOD.DEP.
tol extrusion: TOL.DIN 1748/4 – DIN 17615

MAX.L / PROFILE : 6m
– 1.1 kg
norm: CE

Figure 22.9.1 A linear LED source from Deltalight

LED STRIP OUTDOOR, 100CM, WITH72 SUPERFLUX LED, WARM WHITE	
Article Number:	229812
Product variants	
LED STRIP OUTDOOR, 100CM, WITH72 SUPERFLUX LED, WHITE	229811
LED STRIP OUTDOOR, 100CM, WITH72 SUPERFLUX LED, BLUE	229817
LED STRIP OUTDOOR, 100CM, WITH40X 3IN1 LED, RGB	229813
bulb	72 Super Flux LED's
bulb included	yes
length	39.37 in
voltage	24 Volt
max. load	6 Watt
safety class	IP 55
material	aluminium / plastic
remarks	emitting angle 60°
weight	1.543 lb
Accessories	
POWER UNIT FOR LED STRIPS 12W	470502

solavanti lighting

Figure 22.9.2 A linear LED source from Solavanti Lighting.

179

Image courtesy of Burke Lighting Design   www.burkelighting.com

Figure 22.9.3 An application featuring continuous linear sources to uplight ceiling beams.

Fluorescent Continuous Sources

When we are after a larger quantity of light in a linear fashion, fluorescent sources prove to be a good solution. These luminaires incorporate linear or compact fluorescent lamps mounted end–to-end to create a continuous effect. This can be accomplished with something as simple as a bare lamp, or the luminaire may have a reflector to direct light. These sources are commonly used in commercial and themed environments in coves, slots, and backlight applications. Some commonly-specified versions of this luminaire are from *Belfer, Bartco, Tivoli and Tokistar*.

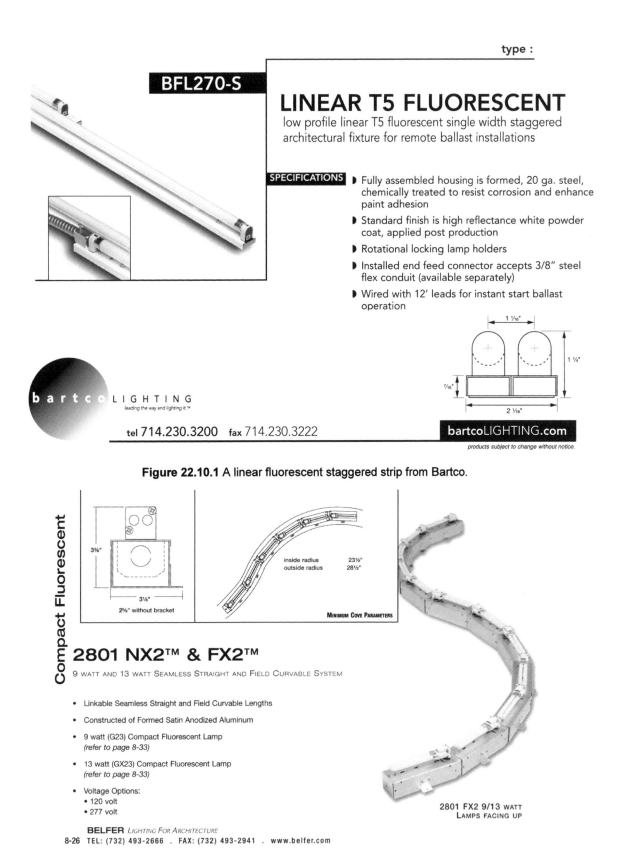

type : _____

BFL270-S

LINEAR T5 FLUORESCENT
low profile linear T5 fluorescent single width staggered architectural fixture for remote ballast installations

SPECIFICATIONS

▶ Fully assembled housing is formed, 20 ga. steel, chemically treated to resist corrosion and enhance paint adhesion

▶ Standard finish is high reflectance white powder coat, applied post production

▶ Rotational locking lamp holders

▶ Installed end feed connector accepts 3/8" steel flex conduit (available separately)

▶ Wired with 12' leads for instant start ballast operation

bartco LIGHTING
leading the way and lighting it.™

tel 714.230.3200   fax 714.230.3222

bartcoLIGHTING.com
products subject to change without notice.

Figure 22.10.1 A linear fluorescent staggered strip from Bartco.

Compact Fluorescent

3⅜"

3⅛"

2⅝" without bracket

inside radius   23½"
outside radius   28½"

MINIMUM COVE PARAMETERS

2801 NX2™ & FX2™
9 WATT AND 13 WATT SEAMLESS STRAIGHT AND FIELD CURVABLE SYSTEM

• Linkable Seamless Straight and Field Curvable Lengths

• Constructed of Formed Satin Anodized Aluminum

• 9 watt (G23) Compact Fluorescent Lamp
  (refer to page 8-33)

• 13 watt (GX23) Compact Fluorescent Lamp
  (refer to page 8-33)

• Voltage Options:
  • 120 volt
  • 277 volt

2801 FX2 9/13 WATT
LAMPS FACING UP

BELFER LIGHTING FOR ARCHITECTURE
8-26 TEL: (732) 493-2666 . FAX: (732) 493-2941 . www.belfer.com

Figure 22.10.2 A continuous compact fluorescent system from Belfer.

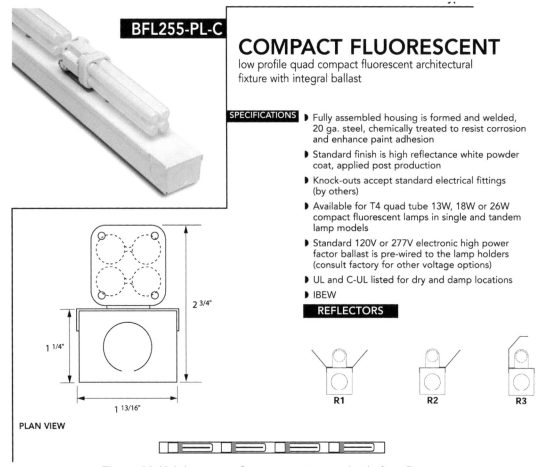

BFL255-PL-C

COMPACT FLUORESCENT
low profile quad compact fluorescent architectural
fixture with integral ballast

SPECIFICATIONS

▶ Fully assembled housing is formed and welded,
20 ga. steel, chemically treated to resist corrosion
and enhance paint adhesion

▶ Standard finish is high reflectance white powder
coat, applied post production

▶ Knock-outs accept standard electrical fittings
(by others)

▶ Available for T4 quad tube 13W, 18W or 26W
compact fluorescent lamps in single and tandem
lamp models

▶ Standard 120V or 277V electronic high power
factor ballast is pre-wired to the lamp holders
(consult factory for other voltage options)

▶ UL and C-UL listed for dry and damp locations

▶ IBEW

REFLECTORS

R1   R2   R3

2 3/4"

1 1/4"

1 13/16"

PLAN VIEW

Figure 22.10.3 A compact fluorescent staggered strip from Bartco.

LIGHTOLIER® SN SERIES **SN STRIP**

Page 1 of 2   NARROW WIDTH CHANNEL
2 1/2" WIDE x 1 13/16" DEEP x 18", 24", 36", 48", 72", 96" LENGTHS, ONE LAMP, T8 OR T12

Features
• Fixtures suitable for individual, row, surface, or
  suspension mounting.
• Efficiency 94% (T8).
• Quarter turn latch secures channel cover for easy
  wireway access.
• Heavy duty channel of code gauge die formed
  steel.
• Only 2-1/2" wide.
• Fully enclosed wiring.
• U.L. Listed snap-on end caps.
• Combination end cap for continuous row mounting.
• Green grounding screw installed in channel.
• UL listed for direct mounting on low density
  ceilings and damp locations.

2-1/2"
(66mm)

3-13/16"
(94mm)

Figure 22.10.4 A linear fluorescent strip from Lightolier.

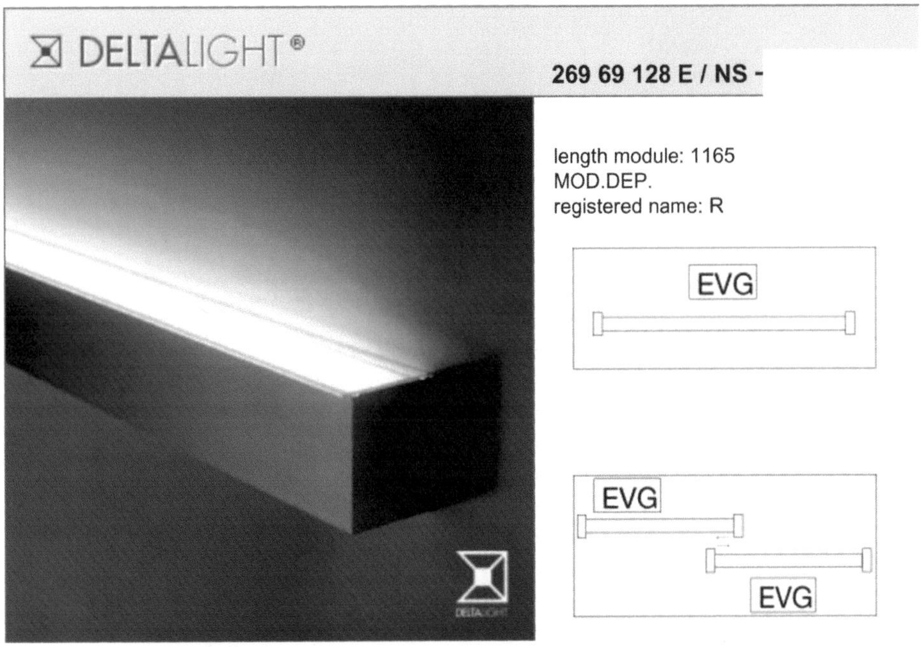

Figure 22.10.5 A modular linear fluorescent system from Deltalight.

Image courtesy of Deltalight   www.deltalight.us

Figure 22.10.6 An application featuring continuous linear fluorescent sources.

Low-Level Steplight

The low-level area light or "steplight" is a superb tool for delivering light directly to a ground plane. Too often, when a design calls for light onto the floor, luminaires are placed up high, and, consequently, light is wasted. Steplights can deliver focused lighting for safety on pathways and stairs. Steplights succeed in delivering a controlled pool of light that does little to disturb the existing lighted environment. Larger versions of this low-level area light are used in larger settings for illuminating seating areas or exterior areas bound by low walls.

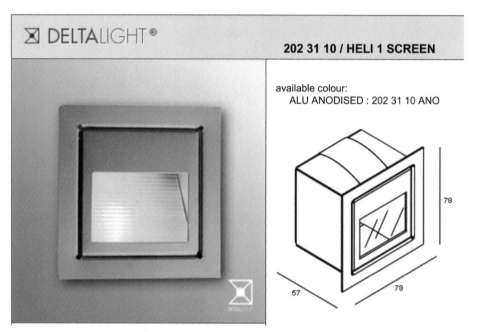

Figure 22.11.1 A small aperture halogen steplight light from Deltalight.

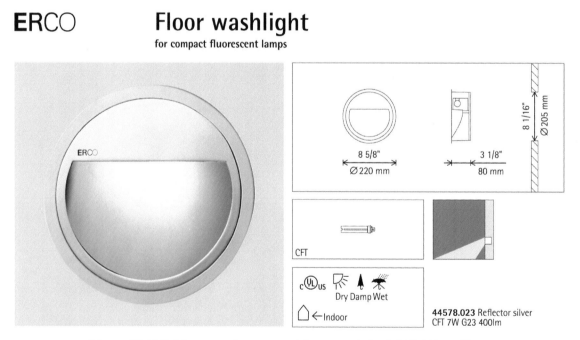

Figure 22.11.2 A large aperture compact fluorescent steplight light from Erco.

184

Image courtesy of Erco   www.erco.com

Figure 22.11.3 An application of typical steplights.

This small family of fixtures gives a glimpse of just how many ways there are to deliver light into our designs. There are many more, but at the core of design, we are still simply dealing with shapes of light, color of light, texture of light, and the other controllable aspects. It is important to remember that luminaires are often nothing more than lamp holders. A designer should be able to recognize when the lamp is doing most of the work and when the luminaire is actually integral to the delivery of light. Hopefully, this representation of some more common lighting tactics will broaden horizons as the designer moves on to actually lay out and specify lighting equipment for his/her design.

Chapter 23

Switching, Dimming and Control Systems

An integral part of completing the lighting design thought process is to consider how the lighting elements in a space will be controlled. There is a significant chasm between simple, wall-mounted switches and dimmers and the whole-building, computer-based control systems that allow tremendous flexibility. The key to making use of these technologies is to make decisions about the specific functionality the project needs. Design of the control systems should be treated similarly to designing the light itself. The effects of dimming, mixing, fading and timing functions are the components that complete a lighting application. Lighting control systems should be chosen with a consideration for how they can *simplify* the project. When lighting controls are added as a means to provide more options and infinite flexibility, unwieldy chaos can be the result.

TYPICAL SWITCHED CIRCUITS

To make sense of the benefits and features of the various level of control system, it is most helpful to understand how basic in-line "light switches" work to control the delivery of power to luminaires.

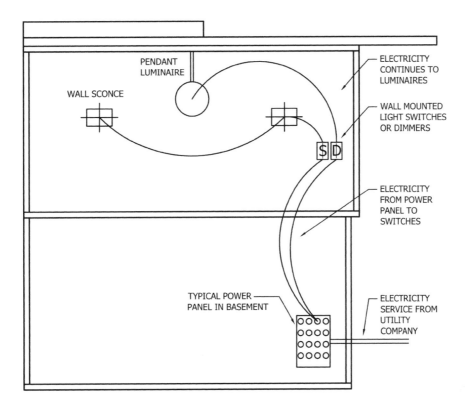

Figure 23.1 Elevation diagram of typical electrical delivery for lighting.

In a typical electrical set-up like the basic residence in *Figure 23.1*, electrical service from the utility is connected to distribution panels tucked away in the structure. From these distribution panels, the electricity is split into branch circuits that run out to the receptacles (plugs) and the various hardwired luminaires on the project. The only way to interrupt power to the receptacles is to engage a circuit breaker that physically opens the electrical connection back at the panel. To control power to luminaires, simple wall "switches" are employed. The light switch is either on (closed) and passes electricity to the lighting device, or the switch is off (open) and electricity is not delivered. The important thing to visualize is the flow of electricity from the panel, to the switch, and then onto the luminaire.

WALL MOUNTED CONTROL DEVICES

There are also a number of wall mounted devices that can add helpful levels of functionality to a lighting design without the expense and complexity of a complete computer-based lighting control system.

Dimmers

Dimmers are devices that control lighting intensity. Common incandescent dimmers simply limit the current of electricity. Low voltage sources and fluorescent sources often require a dedicated dimmer matched to the source type. Dimmers are commonly available and serve in place of a typical "light switch."

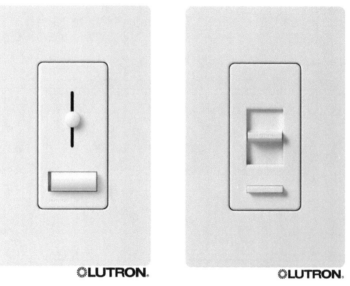

Figure 23.2 Two versions of typical wall mounted dimmers from Lutron.

Timer Switches

A timer is a simple light switch that holds the lighting load on for a set amount of time, and then automatically shuts it off. Many timers offer the ability to modify or program the timer function.

Time Clocks

A time clock is a device with mechanical or electronic means of keeping time. The time clock allows lighting functions to automatically occur at specific times throughout the day. Sophisticated time clocks may also know the time of sunrise and sunset through the seasons as well as daylight savings changes. Controlling lighting through a time clock allows lighting functions to be programmed to reliably activate at certain times of day throughout the year.

Occupancy Sensors

Occupancy sensors are light switches with built-in sensors to detect people and activity through heat, motion, sound or obstruction. These control devices can often be programmed to come on and turn off manually or automatically when they detect a presence. Many lighting efficiency codes require that these devices be used to automatically switch lights off if occupancy is not detected.

All of these devices are intended to add to the functionality of a lighting design. Without the consideration of these technologies, one is living in a world of light switches on the wall that must be manually turned on and manually turned off. Each time a lighting addition is implemented, consider how it will be controlled and whether these systems might simplify the interaction of the space and the user. Lighting control manufacturers employ local representatives who can assist the designer in specifying components for these systems.

Figure 23.3 An example of a typical wall mounted occupancy sensor

INTELLIGENT CONTROL SYSTEMS

Most of our more sophisticated lighting control systems deviate from this simple model in an important manner. When an intelligent control system is employed, power is delivered from the distribution panel to a nearby intelligent lighting control panel (we will call it the "lighting panel"). Electricity then flows directly from the "lighting panel" to the luminaires. This means that the only control of electricity flowing to a luminaire is the intelligent lighting panel itself. In the set-up shown in *Figure 23.5*, individual control devices like multi-button keypads send a signal to the lighting panel telling it to deliver electricity to the luminaire or not to. The biggest benefit of this type of design is that control devices can send a signal to the lighting panel to tell it to operate any luminaire that is connected to the lighting panel. A button on a keypad in the kitchen can tell the lighting panel to activate the lights in the laundry room. More practically, a keypad next to the bed can tell the lighting panel to turn on every luminaire in the house. The system then becomes a system made up of three types of devices:

Figure 23.4 A typical Scene Controller or "Keypad"

1. *The intelligent lighting control panel (usually only one per project);*

2. *The control devices like multi-button keypads that replace common light switches;*

3. *The groups of luminaires that we want to control together (called "lighting loads" or "lighting zones").*

The function and design of the system branches out from this basic concept. The lighting loads get specific names (or more likely address numbers), and we program the lighting panel to recognize these names or addresses. We then program the individual control devices to send the appropriate signal to the lighting panel.

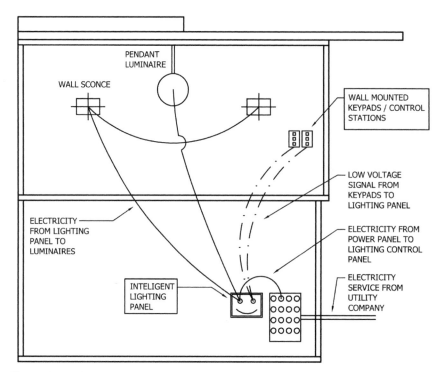

Figure 23.5 Elevation diagram of electrical delivery for an intelligent "whole-project" lighting control system.

In a set-up like *Figure 23.5*, we would program the top button of a keypad to send a signal to the lighting panel to send power to a load in the room. In this fashion, we can program the buttons on a keypad to control different lighting loads to different intensities to create "Scenes." When this type of control synchronization is distributed throughout an entire project, we call it a "whole building" lighting control system.

Some well-known manufacturers of intelligent lighting control systems include the following:

Lutron,

Litetouch,

Vantage, and

Crestron.

Localized Control Panels

Lighting control intelligence does not have to be remotely located as in *Figure 23.5*. Smaller control systems can be located to incorporate only the luminaires in a single room as in *Figure 23.7*. These smaller, local control systems usually control up to six lighting loads and can be connected to control devices anywhere in the room. A typical situation may be an auditorium or a home theater where numerous lighting loads need to be controlled from numerous locations. The local control system can reduce the number of traditional wall-mounted light switches used and can add dimming and scene creating abilities. The normal "switched" lighting layout for a space may look like *Figure 23.6*. In this case, the wall sconces, wall-wash luminaires, steplights, and pendants are each controlled by a light switch. A local control system would be installed in place of the light switches. The groups of luminaires would now be considered "lighting loads," and each would be connected back to the local control system.

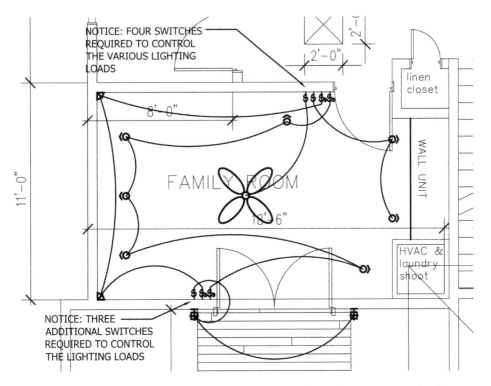

Figure 23.6 Using standard light switches to control complex spaces can lead to an over-abundance of light switches.

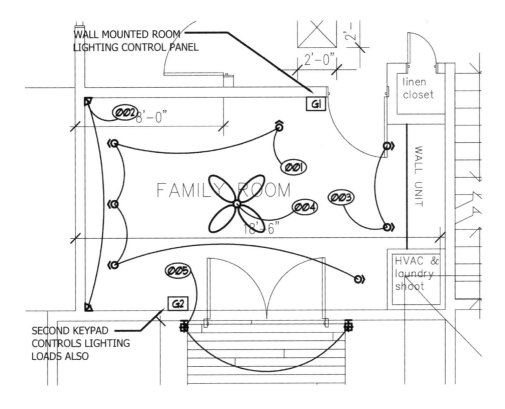

Figure 23.7 A localized "whole room" control system can reduce clutter and confusion.

The local control system would have a set of visible buttons that would be programmed to turn on the various lighting loads. We can keep the programming simple and program each button to control one lighting load, or we can program each button to activate a scene of multiple lighting loads at varying light levels. We can also install other control devices capable of telling the local lighting control system to activate the same scenes. *Figure 23.7* shows how a space might look when such a system is implemented. These local systems can often be retrofit into existing lighting situations. A common candidate is a room that has four or five wall switches in a row. Rather than fuss with each switch, the local control system replaces all of the switches and opens up the possibility of programming scenes and dimming levels.

Some common manufacturers of small, localized lighting control systems include the following:

Watt stopper,

Lutron "Grafik Eye", and

Crestron.

These types of local lighting control systems can also be located far from the lighting loads that they control. In many commercial projects, a simple local lighting panel is used only for its built-in time-clock and all-on and all-off functions.

The various levels of control capability are the crowning touch on the lighting design in a space. A careful consideration of cost, complexity, control and convenience will dictate the appropriate lighting control system for each design.

Chapter 24

The Preliminary Lighting Layout "Redline"

Now that we have been introduced to a vocabulary of luminaire types, applications, and control methods, we are ready to move forward in our design. The intermediate step between lighting concepts and lighting construction drawings is an evolving layout of lighting fixture locations that gives the designer the opportunity to ponder and select lighting equipment and fine-tune the locations and applications of these luminaires. This preliminary layout is often referred to as a "redline layout" because it is often done in red pencil and undergoes numerous changes and tweaks before it is finalized. The redline layout is where our graphics, descriptions and calculations are translated to individual symbols that represent specific pieces of lighting equipment. If one lays a sheet of trace or velum over the graphic light map, he/she will have a roadmap of lighting events to refine and translate into fixture locations and types.

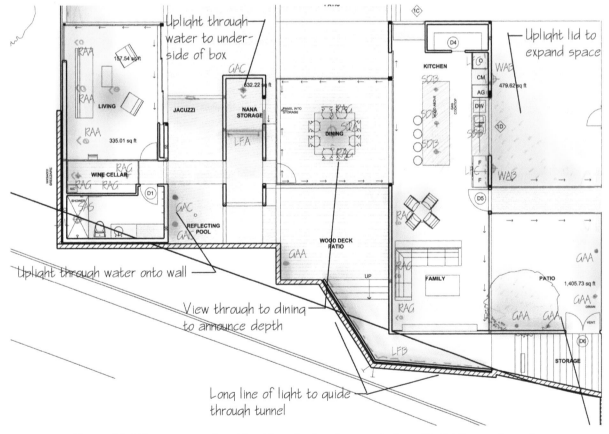

Figure 24.1 The process of marking ideas for the placement of specific lighting equipment.

The two significant tasks that are accomplished through this redline layout are the locating and selecting of luminaires. Once we have made decisions about how we will deliver our lighting design ideas, we turn this information into our Lighting Plan, Luminaire Schedule and Luminaire Cut Sheets.

There are very few rules for laying out preliminary lighting symbols. The goal is simply to clarify the locations and types of luminaires to be used in the design. If symbols alone cannot successfully translate ideas, additional notes and comments can be used to provide more information. Luminaire mounting dimensions and mounting heights are also a useful addition.

THE PRELIMINARY LUMINAIRE SCHEDULE

As a designer goes through the redline layout, they will ponder over the types of luminaires that will solve the particular lighting challenges they have mapped out. While they are creating this preliminary layout, they should be simultaneously creating the rough draft of their luminaire schedule. As fixture symbols are placed to represent lighting equipment, they should be given luminaire "type" labels that will serve as the coordination between the lighting drawing and the luminaire schedule. The preliminary luminaire schedule should be a running list of luminaires to be used. The list should indicate at least a "type" label and a description for each luminaire. This simple step will keep a designer from repeating luminaire types and will streamline their selection process.

The luminaire type labels can be whatever a designer chooses, but they should be unique to each luminaire that end up being used on the job.

As the designer goes through and solves lighting challenges indicated on the redline layout, he/she should give the luminaires a home on the preliminary luminaire schedule as soon as he/she has even an inkling of what type of luminaire may be used for a particular application.

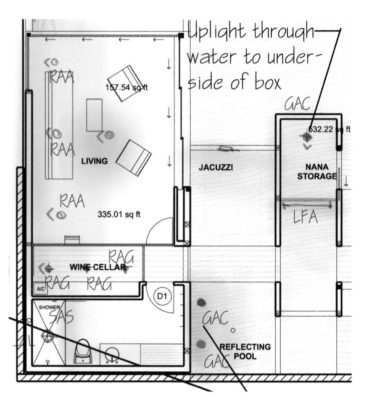

Figure 24.2 Identify each unique luminaire with a "type" label as soon as it is drawn into the space.

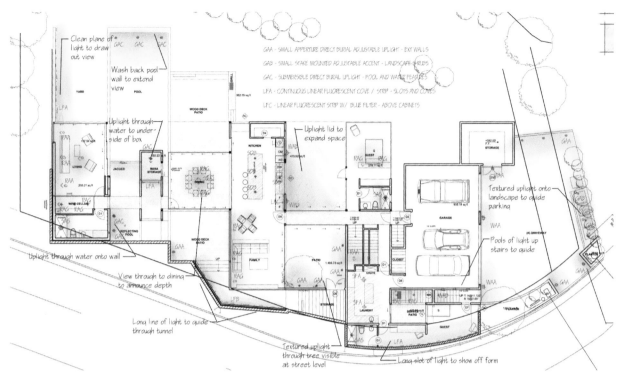

Figure 24.3 A completed "red line" layout shows ideas for all luminaire locations. Each lighting application is based on the light map.

The "redline layout" should act as a link from the graphics and descriptions of the light map to the precision and clarity of the drafted lighting plan from which the project will be built. The redline layout gives the designer the opportunity to move luminaires and experiment with different solutions.

Chapter 25

Luminaire Schedules and Cut Sheets

The most important support documents that accompany a lighting plan are the luminaire schedule and cutsheets that illustrate exactly what lighting equipment is required to bring the lighting plan to life. All of the deliverable documents must be accurate and error free, but this holds especially true for the schedule and cut sheets. On complex projects, architects and engineers create specification documents that articulate the specific nuances of every product and material that is necessary for the construction of the project. The luminaire schedule and cut sheets are the closest a lighting designer gets to true specification. As such, they are the documents that must list products accurately and completely. The luminaire schedule is the document that the electrical contractor will use to price, order and install the lighting equipment. This means that a slight error in catalog number can affect the budgeting, delivery and installation of every instance of a particular fixture type. The two secrets to a thorough luminaire schedule are to get started early (as discussed in Chapter 24), and to check and re-check the schedule and cut sheets for errors. By now, readers have seen enough manufacturers' literature to know that the catalog numbers for lighting products can become rather lengthy and complex. A simple typo can cause a product to be delivered in the wrong size, the wrong color, or not at all.

THE LUMINAIRE SCHEDULE

The sample luminaire schedule shown in *Figure 25.1* includes most of the pertinent information one would need to provide for a project. Each category has critical information that must be presented in a manner that makes things clear and obvious. The contents of the various categories of information are discussed here.

Heading

The first piece of information that should go on a luminaire schedule is the name of the project and the date the schedule was created. With so many projects going on at once, and so many changes being made to luminaire selections, this labeling ensures that those involved with the project are referring to the right document. The heading should also include the name of the firm or individual preparing the document so that contractors know whom to contact with questions.

Luminaire Type Labels

Luminaire type labels will connect all of the luminaire symbols on the lighting plan to the specific pieces of equipment that they represent as defined by the luminaire schedule. Designers can use whatever "type" logic makes sense for the project. Often a two or three digit or alphanumeric code is employed. To keep luminaire selections clear, it is advisable to give a unique type to every variation of every piece of lighting equipment. Even if the variation is simply a lens, lamp type, or finish color, it should warrant a unique luminaire type.

Luminaire Manufacturer

This indicates who the product is made by and where specific questions regarding mounting, installation and electrification should be directed. Be sure to list the true manufacturer of the product, not a third party middleman who is supplying the luminaire.

The Light Studio
1335 Vista Rd, Suite 100
La Jolla, CA 92037
tel: (858) 555.6436
fax: (858) 555.7703
www.saqerussell.com

Parker Headquarters
Luminaire Schedule
11-Aug-08

Type	Manufacturer	Description/ Catalog Number	Lamp	Volts	Mounting	Notes
F1	PANASONIC OR EQUAL	**FV-11VQL3 (or equal by E.C.)** Recessed compact fluorescent exhaust fan / light combo. Provide with whisper quiet fan motor, integral electronic ballast, white finish	(2) 13 Watt CFL lamps provided with fixture	120	Recessed	Mount at bathrooms
G1	LIGHTOLIER	**C4MRD C4AICLV Low voltage recessed downlight. Provide with 4" apperture, IC rated housing, specular black trim, integral transformer**	(1) SYLVANIA 50MR16/IR/NFL25 /C	120/12	Recessed	Mount at downlight locations
G3	DA-SAL LIGHTING	**520-229-38 (elektra super-flush)** Low voltage millwork recessed accent fixture. Provide with stainless steel finish, clear lens, 20 watt lamp, remote transformer.	(1) 20 Watt halogen lamp provided with fixture	12	Recessed	Mount at undercabinet locations Remote transformer required
G4	LEUCOS	**"DROP" trim IC housing** Low voltage recessed decorative downlight. Provide with integral transformer, clear glass decorative glass trim, IC housing	(1) SYLVANIA 50MR16/IR/NFL25 /C	120	Recessed	Mount at general downlighting and accenting locations
L7	LIGHTOLIER	**1184CD trim 1104 ICX housing** Incandescent recessed gasketed shower light. Provide with self sealing gasket, frosted glass trim ring, IC housing	(1) SYLVANIA 80PAR38/CAP/IR /FL25	120	Recessed	Mount at showers and tubs

Figure 25.1 The luminaire schedule lists the information a contractor needs to price and order all of the luminaires.

Catalog Number

The most important piece of information to accurately list is the product code that will be used to price and order the equipment. The catalog number is usually full of letters and numbers that indicate specific finishes, colors, mounting styles, and other options. Any small errors in catalog number will come back to cause larger problems during construction.

Lamp Specification

The schedule should include information on the quantity and type of lamp required for the luminaire. Sometimes it will be necessary to list a specific lamp product. Other times it will suffice to list the desired wattage and source type. It is always good practice to make sure that the lamp specification provides information about color-rendering index (CRI) and color temperature (CCT) to ensure that a suitable product is used.

Voltage

There are many service voltages that power various lighting projects. 120 volts is common line voltage for residences in the US, but it cannot be assumed. Larger commercial projects and projects that house heavy machinery often use 277 Volts as the primary voltage. The luminaires specified for a project must be designed to operate at the voltage that will be present on the job. This is one of the first pieces of information that should be confirmed with the electrical engineer or contractor on the job. Luminaires that use low-voltage lamps typically require electricity delivered at 12 or 24 volts. These low-voltages require that a transformer be integral to the luminaire or located nearby.

Mounting style

This piece of information will help an electrical contractor prepare the site for the luminaire well before it arrives. It can also head off any major conflicts with building conditions and space constraints.

Locations

This simple description of where the luminaire is actually used on the project will save hours of looking for luminaire symbols on the lighting plan later.

Notes

This area is where any additional information for clarity goes. The most common notes that show up on a luminaire schedule are related to ballasts and transformers that need to be provided, IC housing requirements, and wet-listing designations. This is the place to put information that is essential to the successful use of the luminaire.

Remember that all of this information will serve the designer *and* the electrical contractor on the job. The electrical contractor is one of the best friends one can have on a lighting design job, so anything you can be done to make their job easier and clearer will benefit the design as a whole.

LUMINAIRE CUT SHEETS

To take the job of providing clear information a step further, a lighting designer includes job specific cut sheets to accompany the other construction documents. These sheets are usually some form of the manufacturers' luminaire literature put into a format that will benefit the particular lighting design project. Many manufacturers include blank spaces on their literature so that designers can turn them into job specific cut sheets very easily.

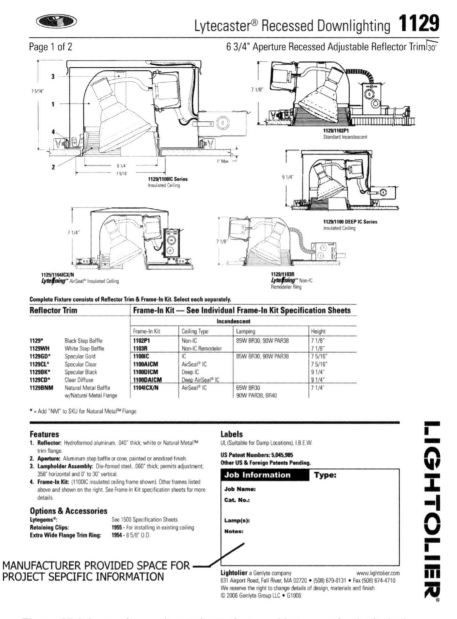

Lytecaster® Recessed Downlighting **1129**

Page 1 of 2

6 3/4" Aperture Recessed Adjustable Reflector Trim 30°

1129/1100IC Series
Insulated Ceiling

1129/1102P1
Standard Incandescent

1129/1100 DEEP IC Series
Insulated Ceiling

1129/1104ICX/N
Lytefning™ AirSeal® Insulated Ceiling

1129/1103R
Lytefning™ Non-IC
Remodeler Ring

Complete Fixture consists of Reflector Trim & Frame-In Kit. Select each separately.

Reflector Trim		Frame-In Kit — See Individual Frame-In Kit Specification Sheets			
		Incandescent			
		Frame-In Kit	Ceiling Type	Lamping	Height
1129*	Black Step Baffle	1102P1	Non-IC	85W BR30, 90W PAR38	7 1/8"
1129WH	White Step Baffle	1103R	Non-IC Remodeler		7 1/8"
1129GD*	Specular Gold	1100IC	IC	85W BR30, 90W PAR38	7 5/16"
1129CL*	Specular Clear	1100AICM	AirSeal® IC		7 5/16"
1129BK*	Specular Black	1100DICM	Deep IC		9 1/4"
1129CD*	Clear Diffuse	1100DAICM	Deep AirSeal® IC		9 1/4"
1129BNM	Natural Metal Baffle w/Natural Metal Flange	1104ICX/N	AirSeal® IC	65W BR30 90W PAR38, BR40	7 1/4"

* = Add "NM" to SKU for Natural Metal™ Flange

Features
1. **Reflector:** Hydroformed aluminum, .040" thick; white or Natural Metal™ trim flange.
2. **Aperture:** Aluminum step baffle or cone, painted or anodized finish.
3. **Lampholder Assembly:** Die-formed steel, .060" thick; permits adjustment; 358° horizontal and 0° to 30° vertical.
4. **Frame-In Kit:** (1100IC insulated ceiling frame shown). Other frames listed above and shown on the right. See Frame-In Kit specification sheets for more details.

Options & Accessories
Lytegems®:   See 1500 Specification Sheets.
Retaining Clips: 1955 - For installing in existing ceiling
Extra Wide Flange Trim Ring: 1954 - 8 5/8" O.D.

Labels
UL (Suitable for Damp Locations), I.B.E.W.

US Patent Numbers: 5,045,985
Other US & Foreign Patents Pending.

Job Information   **Type:**

Job Name:

Cat. No.:

Lamp(s):

Notes:

MANUFACTURER PROVIDED SPACE FOR PROJECT SEPCIFIC INFORMATION

Lightolier a Genlyte company   www.lightolier.com
631 Airport Road, Fall River, MA 02720 • (508) 679-8131 • Fax (508) 674-4710
We reserve the right to change details of design, materials and finish.
© 2006 Genlyte Group LLC • G1006

LIGHTOLIER®

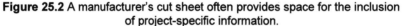

Figure 25.2 A manufacturer's cut sheet often provides space for the inclusion of project-specific information.

Like the schedule, cut sheets are a direct link between the symbols and "type" labels on the lighting plan and a specific piece of lighting equipment. A good cut sheet helps a contractor be certain that the luminaire that is about to be installed does, indeed, belong. It is a good idea to include on the cut sheet information directly from the luminaire schedule, such as catalog number and lamp information. Some manufacturers' literature will show multiple luminaires or options on the same page. In these cases, is it very helpful for the designer to highlight or draw attention to the specific piece of equipment being specified. *Figure 25.3* is a customized cut sheet made for a specific job. The manufacturer's information was simply downloaded from a website and inserted into the blank cut sheet. It is certainly worth a designer's time to develop a blank template that serves this purpose while providing project and designer information.

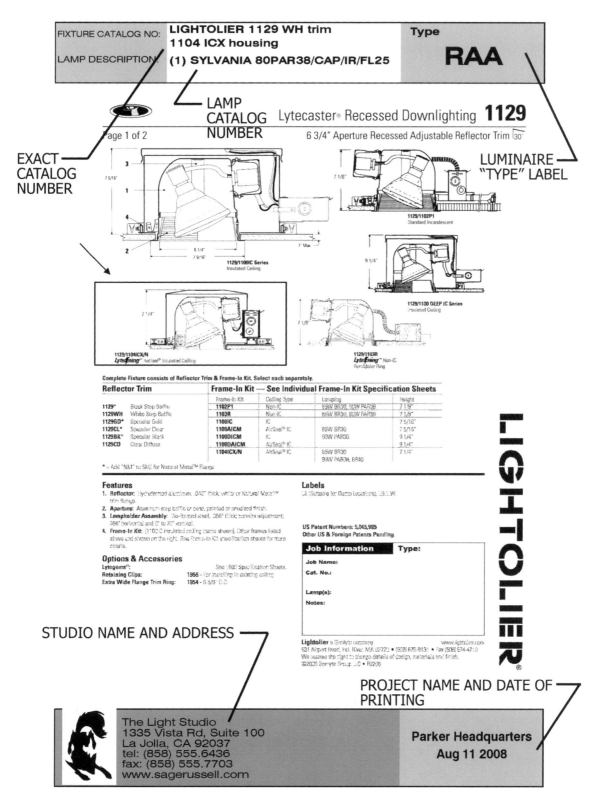

| FIXTURE CATALOG NO: | **LIGHTOLIER 1129 WH trim** **1104 ICX housing** | **Type** |
| LAMP DESCRIPTION: | **(1) SYLVANIA 80PAR38/CAP/IR/FL25** | **RAA** |

LAMP CATALOG NUMBER

EXACT CATALOG NUMBER

Lytecaster® Recessed Downlighting **1129**
Page 1 of 2
6 3/4" Aperture Recessed Adjustable Reflector Trim |30°|

LUMINAIRE "TYPE" LABEL

Complete Fixture consists of Reflector Trim & Frame-In Kit. Select each separately.

Reflector Trim		Frame-In Kit — See Individual Frame-In Kit Specification Sheets			
		Frame-In Kit	Ceiling Type	Lamping	Height
1129*	Black Step Baffle	1102P1	Non-IC	65W BR30, 90W PAR38	7 1/8"
1129WH	White Step Baffle	1103R	Non-IC	65W BR30, 90W PAR38	7 1/8"
1129GD*	Specular Gold	1108IC	IC		7 5/16"
1129CL*	Specular Clear	1100AICM	AirSeal® IC	65W BR30	7 5/16"
1129BK*	Specular Black	1100DICM	IC	90W PAR38	9 1/4"
1129CD	Clear Diffuse	1100DAICM	AirSeal® IC		9 1/4"
		1104ICX/N	AirSeal® IC	65W BR30 90W PAR38, BR40	7 1/4"

* = Add "NM" to SKU for Natural Metal™ flange

Features
1. **Reflector:** Hydroformed aluminum, .040" thick, white or Natural Metal™ trim flange.
2. **Aperture:** Aluminum step baffle or cone, painted or anodized finish.
3. **Lampholder Assembly:** Die-formed steel, .060" thick; permits adjustment; 358° horizontal and 0° to 30° vertical.
4. **Frame-In Kit:** (1102 C insulated ceiling frame shown). Other frames listed above and shown on the right. See Frame-In Kit specification sheets for more details.

Options & Accessories
Lytegems®: See 1600 Specification Sheets.
Retaining Clips: 1955 - For installing in existing ceiling
Extra Wide Flange Trim Ring: 1954 - 8 5/8" O.D.

Labels
UL (Suitable for Damp Locations), I.B.E.W.

US Patent Numbers: 5,045,985
Other US & Foreign Patents Pending.

Job Information	Type:
Job Name:	
Cat. No.:	
Lamp(s):	
Notes:	

Lightolier a Genlyte company
631 Airport Road, Fall River, MA 02722 • (508) 675-8131 • Fax (508) 674-4710
We reserve the right to change details of design, materials and finish.
©2006 Genlyte Group LLC • F0206

LIGHTOLIER®

STUDIO NAME AND ADDRESS

The Light Studio
1335 Vista Rd, Suite 100
La Jolla, CA 92037
tel: (858) 555.6436
fax: (858) 555.7703
www.sagerussell.com

PROJECT NAME AND DATE OF PRINTING

Parker Headquarters
Aug 11 2008

Figure 25.3 A custom luminaire cut sheet created by the designer for a specific project

Chapter 26

The Lighting Plan

The final construction document that must be prepared in order to build the design is the finalized lighting plan itself. The lighting plan is a formally-drafted construction document that must provide specific information clearly enough to allow a contractor to actually build the design. A lighting plan will ideally show all of the lighting equipment on a job: lighting installed in the ceiling, lighting in the walls, lighting in floors, millwork and niches. If a device creates light, it should show up on the lighting plan. It is recommend to *not* use a reflected ceiling plan as the basis for a lighting plan. The preference for most jobs is to start out with a furniture plan and add pertinent ceiling information to it. Lighting equipment typically has much more relationship to floor and furniture conditions than to ceiling conditions. In theory, the designer is not relying on the lighting plan to aid in design as he/she is already totally immersed in a spatial understanding of the project. A proper lighting plan is a tool for construction. It is not a tool for design. At this point a designer is merely translating information from a highly-evolved light map and redlined preliminary lighting layout. The drafted version is simply a finalized drawing that clarifies everything. There are only a few ingredients that absolutely must be on every lighting plan. There is plenty of room to tweak the formula and add or subtract to make the lighting plan work for each individual. Some of the basic ingredients are listed in the following paragraphs.

Luminaire Symbols

These can be of your any design. They can relate literally or loosely to the shape of the luminaire. It is encouraged, however, to draft these symbols to represent the actual size of the luminaire if one is drafting a plan at ¼"=1'-0" or ⅛" = 1'-0" scale. If one is drafting a plan at a very small scale, it is advisable to size the symbols so that they are clearly visible. *Figure 26.1* presents a list of commonly-used luminaire symbols.

Fixture Type Labels

There is plenty of room to invent convenient and helpful ways to tag luminaires on the lighting plan. The safest and simplest is to put the fixture type next to every single occurrence of every luminaire on the lighting plan. More technically oriented lighting plans may include information like wattage and source type, but for a basic lighting plan, clarity of luminaire "type" and the ability to reference a luminaire symbol back to the luminaire schedule is paramount.

COMMON LUMINAIRE SYMBOLS

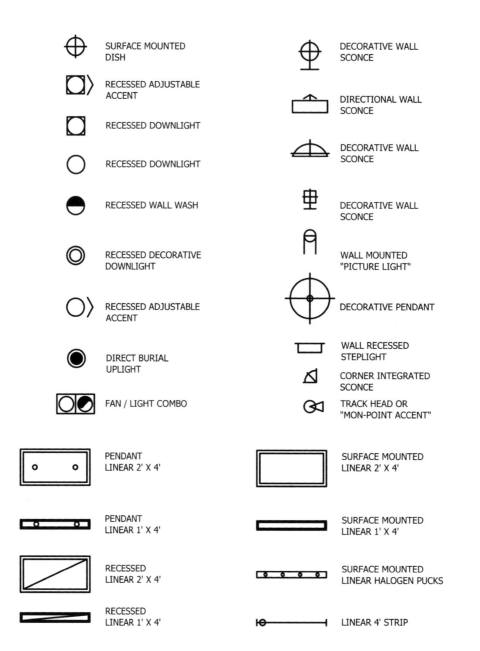

⊕	SURFACE MOUNTED DISH
⬓〉	RECESSED ADJUSTABLE ACCENT
⬓	RECESSED DOWNLIGHT
○	RECESSED DOWNLIGHT
◒	RECESSED WALL WASH
◎	RECESSED DECORATIVE DOWNLIGHT
○〉	RECESSED ADJUSTABLE ACCENT
●	DIRECT BURIAL UPLIGHT
◻◻	FAN / LIGHT COMBO

	DECORATIVE WALL SCONCE
	DIRECTIONAL WALL SCONCE
	DECORATIVE WALL SCONCE
	DECORATIVE WALL SCONCE
	WALL MOUNTED "PICTURE LIGHT"
	DECORATIVE PENDANT
	WALL RECESSED STEPLIGHT
	CORNER INTEGRATED SCONCE
	TRACK HEAD OR "MON-POINT ACCENT"

	PENDANT LINEAR 2' X 4'
	PENDANT LINEAR 1' X 4'
	RECESSED LINEAR 2' X 4'
	RECESSED LINEAR 1' X 4'

	SURFACE MOUNTED LINEAR 2' X 4'
	SURFACE MOUNTED LINEAR 1' X 4'
	SURFACE MOUNTED LINEAR HALOGEN PUCKS
	LINEAR 4' STRIP

Figure 26.1 Common luminaire symbols used on drafted lighting plans

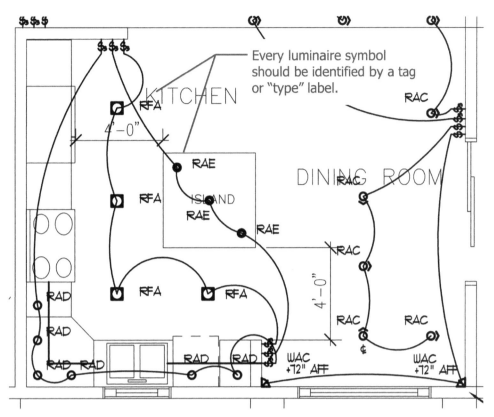

Figure 26.2 "Type" labels or tags are crucial for referencing a drafted symbol to a specific luminaire on the luminaire schedule.

Notes

Don't be stingy with the application of lighting related notes on the plan. If there is any ambiguity, clarify it with a note in plain English. When we rely on a single plan to show luminaires in ceilings, walls, and millwork, notes are imperative for clarifying where a piece of equipment actually belongs and what it is doing there. A simple note at the end of a leader can save numerous phone calls and coordination headaches.

Dimensions

Placement of lighting equipment is a relatively exact science, so it is preferable to note exact locations of luminaires with dimensions. Luminaires for accenting, wall washing, linear slots and coves all may warrant the addition of dimensions that refer back to nearby architectural elements.

Control Intent

The lighting designer is also responsible for translating which luminaires are controlled together (turned on, turned off and dimmed) and where that control takes place. Most lighting control intent takes the form of arcs connecting luminaires to wall switch devices or numbers and letters keyed to wall-switch devices. Control intent can get a little more complex when we integrate intelligent control systems and scene control devices as covered in Chapter 23.

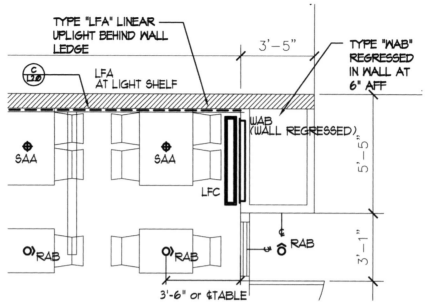

Figure 26.3 Notes and leaders clarify any ambiguities.

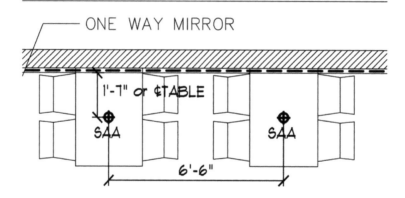

Figure 26.4 Dimensions ensure that luminaires are implemented properly.

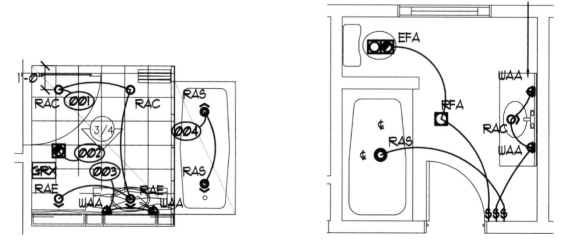

Figure 26.5 Numbered lighting control zones and keypads (left) take the place of traditional switching symbols (right) when a control system is implemented.

Luminaire Schedule or Legend

If one has the means, it is helpful to include the entire luminaire schedule as a drawing sheet that gets submitted along with the lighting plan. This clarity will ensure that the right information is always available.

In addition to the luminaire schedule, a basic legend like the one shown in *Figure 26.6* can be helpful to explain some of the other symbols used on a lighting plan. It is common practice to create a legend that clarifies not only luminaire symbols, but controls dimensions and details.

Detail Call-outs.

Many lighting applications are simply too cumbersome to be understood in plan. When this is the case, we develop lighting details that show specific construction situations and dimension in a very precise manner. These details will usually accompany the plan on their own sheet. Numerous examples of typical lighting details appear in Chapter 29

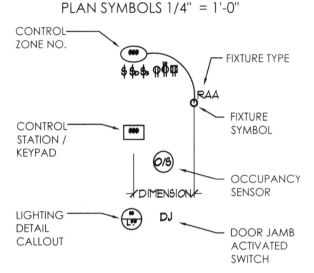

Figure 26.6 A simple legend can help clarify various lighting related symbols.

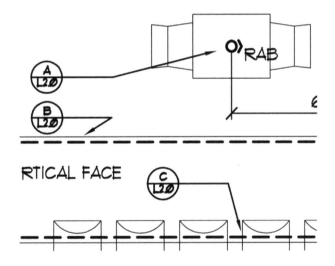

Figure 26.7 (example of detail callout)

As with any other construction drawing, proper formatting will add the finishing touches that will get the lighting plan the respect it deserves. The construction documents that come out of the studio are the only product that much of the design team gets to see. All of the development materials, sketches, renderings and light maps can lead to great design, but it is all for naught if the construction documents are not complete, correct and easy to use. In the end it really does boil down to these few black and white drawings and how easy they are to translate to the built environment.

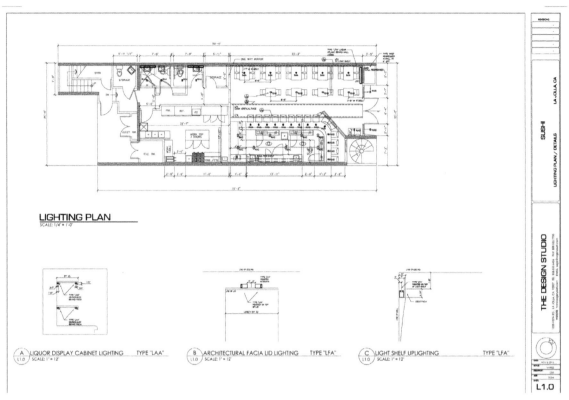

Figure 26.8 A completed drawing sheet of a lighting plan for a commercial project, including lighting details and title block.

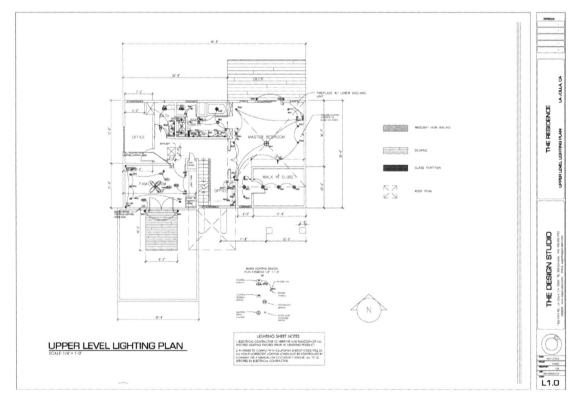

Figure 26.9 A completed lighting sheet for a residential project, including legend and notes.

Chapter 27
Lighting Layouts for Residential Spaces

The following chapter includes lighting tactics commonly found in typical residential spaces. The point of typical layouts is really just to lend some familiarity and a jumping-off point. Every project has unique programming criteria that must be thoroughly understood. It is good practice to dissect any and all lighting layouts that one comes across to gain a familiarity with the various techniques available. The lighting layouts in this chapter are annotated to describe what lighting principles are at work. Take such "typical" layouts with a grain of salt. Regardless of how many times the same space is lighted in the same manner, it always behooves the designer to investigate all of the available lighting options.

Layout 1

Lighting a Residential Dining Room

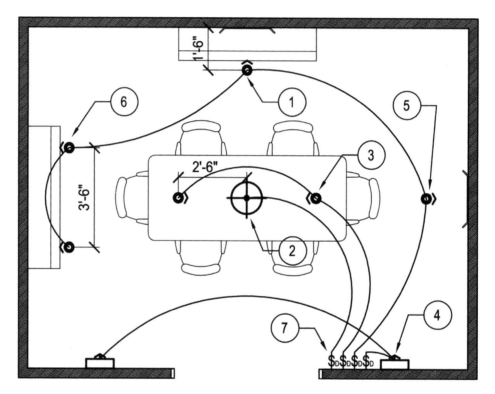

A residential dining room is a good opportunity to make use of different textures and intensities of light. A formal dining room has very few critical tasks, so lighting decisions can focus on environmental effect. Like many rooms, the fundamental light elements of a dining room are the vertical surfaces that will define the brightness of the space and the accented objects that will create visual interest and add a unique character. Softness, warmth, and intimacy are usually the desired qualities. These can be accomplished through uncommon tactics, such as up-lighting from the floor or walls, as well as more traditional pendants and recessed luminaires. Even in its simplest form, dining room lighting should be more than a single decorative pendant. At the very least, luminaires should be dedicated to painting light onto the table and vertical surfaces to allow a balancing act between task and ambient light levels

Addressing Layers

Choreography: The decorative pendant serves to anchor the space and create a clear draw and area for gathering. The lighted character of the back wall will serve as the visual goal compelling a visitor to move towards the space.

Mood and Ambience: Multiple textures can be created by implementing various diffusing sources. Wall-mounted uplights lend a softness, and the decorative pendant contributes to the mood and atmosphere

Accenting: Crisp pieces of accent light cast onto art or furniture objects provide visual logic and interest through contrast. A brilliant pool of light onto the surface of the table itself will serve to accent the objects on the table and create a bright plane in the space.

Revealing Architecture: Wall mounted uplights add volume contribute to an all-encompassing glow that expands the space. The central pendant can also cast light upward to illuminate the ceiling above.

Task Lighting: Dedicated recessed adjustable luminaires paint pools of light onto the surface of the table as well as the buffet or any other task-related furniture. The recessed luminaires and pendant at the dining table also serve to illuminate the faces of the diners.

Common Features

1. Recessed adjustable halogen luminaires cast light onto the objects that adorn the back wall.

2. An incandescent or fluorescent decorative pendant can serve as the main focal element in a dining area. It serves as a glowing object to draw attention and ultimately congregate around. Decorative elements are at their best when they are free to be dimmed to an appropriate level for ambience and mood.

3. Recessed adjustable halogen luminaires (ideally with diffusing lenses) at the table provide light for eating and rendering the faces of the diners. Implementing these luminaires frees up the decorative pendant to serve only as ambience and décor.

4. Incandescent or compact fluorescent, Wall-mounted decorative sconces or, better yet, wall-mounted uplights add a layer of diffuse light.

5 and 6. Additional adjustable halogen luminaires paint pools of light onto the other important objects in the room and create more visual interest through contrast.

7. Wall dimmers or a localized lighting control system can be used to control any loads that can be dimmed. The flexibility that dimming adds to a space will facilitate the creation of different environments for different moods and uses.

Layout

Lighting a Residential Kitchen

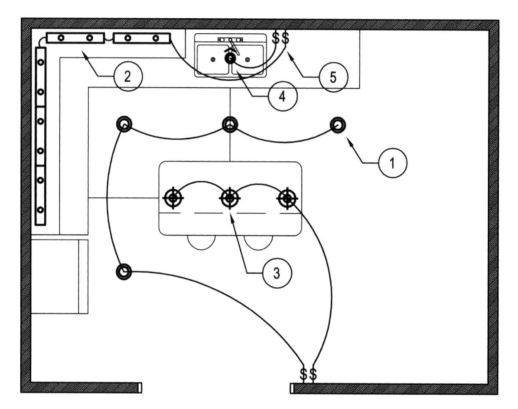

The residential kitchen is a place not only for food preparation, but socializing and gathering. The kitchen island often becomes a multi purpose task surface used for studying and quick dining. The program for such a space is certainly not purely task driven. Ingredients should be added to draw people to the space and contribute to the mood and scale.

Addressing Layers

Choreography: Decorative pendants over the island can serve as a focal point and a point of gathering to draw people into the space. Lighting the vertical surfaces of the back walls can also help create an inviting atmosphere.

Mood and Ambience: The glow or sparkle of the decorative pendants can serve to reduce the scale of the space and create a more intimate area. Sources should also be warm in color temperature to contribute to an inviting feeling.

Accenting: Light washed down the face of cabinetry can create visual interest and hierarchy. A distinct pool of light onto the island surface can also serve as the bright centerpiece of the space.

Revealing Architecture: The pendants over the island serve to reduce the scale and break up the volume of the space. The under cabinet luminaires can create a band of light that breaks up the surfaces of the back wall.

Task Lighting: Under-cabinet luminaires serve to put light directly on the task surface where it is needed. Small pendants cast task lighting onto the task surface of the island. These two applications eliminate the need to create task level lighting throughout the space.

Common Features

1. 6" aperture recessed downlights help to create an above average illuminance level throughout the space so that tasks can be accomplished anywhere. These could be incandescent, halogen, or carefully-selected compact fluorescent luminaires.

2. Under-cabinet luminaires provide localized task lighting on counter tops. These could be linear incandescent, linear halogen, linear fluorescent or individual puck lights.

3. Incandescent or compact fluorescent decorative pendants direct light onto the island task surface. They should direct light downward in addition to simply glowing.

4. A small aperture recessed adjustable halogen luminaire or fluorescent downlight can augment light levels over the sink area.

5. Switches to activate task specific lighting can be located near the area they serve.

Layout 3

Lighting a Residential Bathroom

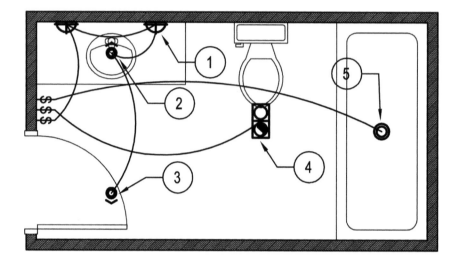

Even a simple bathroom should be treated with care to create a space that serves all of the functional needs while creating an environment for long-term comfort. Lighting the vertical surfaces will dramatically improve the perception of brightness, and a few, well-placed accents can add some sparkle and elegance to the space.

Addressing Layers

Choreography: Even a simple bathroom should have areas of brightness to determine a visual order. Self-Luminous sconces and a pool of accent light at the vanity serve as the bright core.

Mood and Ambience: Diffuse decorative sconces at the vanity serve to define a soft mood. Light onto the back wall and at the toilet create a heightened light level to make the space more inviting.

Accenting: Recessed accent luminaires can create pools of light to show off the vanity hardware, art on the walls, and even the toilet itself.

Revealing Architecture: Glowing wall sconces help to volumize the space. Even the recessed luminaire in the shower can add to the perceived depth of the space

Task Lighting: The vanity is a critical task area, where light sources should be chosen for texture and color rendering. Lighting at the vanity must provide soft, diffuse light from above and below with excellent color-rendering capability for revealing faces. The even qualities of vanity lighting can also be enhanced by using light-colored surfaces to reflect light. The shower should also get a dedicated light source to aid in all of the important tasks related to keeping clean.

Common Features

1. Diffuse decorative sconces at the vanity are the first line of defense for making the space functional and inviting. Even with today's energy concerns, it is worth working to find a way to stick with incandescent or halogen sources to ensure good color rendering and pleasing color temperature.
2. A small aperture recessed halogen luminaire can serve as additional vanity lighting to accent the area and provide additional task light

3. Additional recessed adjustable halogen or fluorescent wall wash luminaires can paint light onto artwork or simply illuminate vertical surfaces. Light across from the vanity can reduce contrast by creating a luminous background for looking at one's self in the mirror.

4. A fan and light combination unit is a reasonable way to dedicate light to the toilet area.

5. The shower or tub should have its own dedicated source of light. This incandescent or fluorescent luminaire must be suitable for use in wet areas.

Layout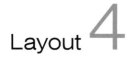

Lighting a Residential Bedroom

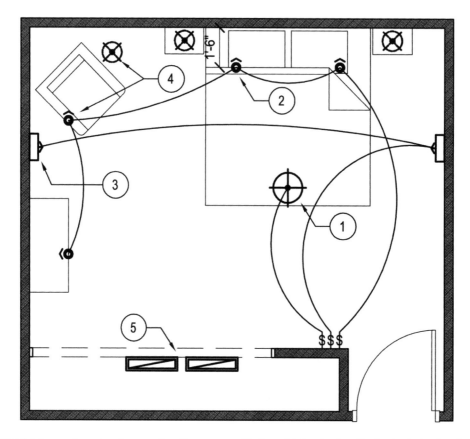

The residential bedroom is a good example of a space with few driving task criteria, but plenty of need for versatility. The lighting system in a bedroom needs to be able to cast light effectively onto tasks, like dressing and reading. All of the lighting ingredients need to contribute to the generally inviting and comfortable feeling. The bedroom can survive with a few lighted vertical surfaces and a few accented objects. Additions of decorative light or uplight can be implemented to add volume and warmth to the space. The various lighting loads should be independently controlled so that different moods can be created for different times of day and different uses.

Addressing Layers

Choreography: Washing light onto art and the back surfaces of the room helps to draw in the eye. Accenting the reading nook creates an inviting area of respite. The glowing table lamps and floor lamp also create objects that draw attention and create hierarchy.

Mood and Ambience: Wall-mounted uplights brighten the ceiling and create an open, inviting space. The glowing lamps and the center glowing dish contribute to the intimate feeling. The warmth of incandescent sources or carefully-selected fluorescent sources will create a desired mood.

Accenting: Recessed accent luminaires cast pools of light onto artwork, reading areas and the various furniture elements in the space. Each serves to add visual interest and contrast to the space. The decorative lamps also add a bit of sparkle.

Revealing Architecture: Accent luminaires paint light onto the back walls to give a perception of depth, while the wall-mounted uplights and center glowing dish wash light on to the ceiling surface to expand the space and reduce the feeling of confinement.

Task Lighting: Reading in bed is accommodated through recessed adjustable luminaires or typical bedside table lamps. The vanity desk or dresser also receives dedicated task light from above. Closets benefit from dedicated luminaires so that they do not depend on the ambient light from the bedroom itself.

Common Features

1. A surface-mounted glowing dish serves to cast a quantity of diffuse light to all reaches of the space. This luminaire is a good place to integrate fluorescent lamps.

2. Recessed adjustable halogen luminaires paint light onto artwork and the vertical surfaces of the space as well as areas for dressing or the head of the bed for reading.

3. Wall mounted halogen or fluorescent uplights cast light onto the ceiling to expand the space. These luminaires are a good place to integrate fluorescent lamps.

4. A dedicated incandescent or compact fluorescent floor lamp or recessed luminaire provides ample lighting for reading and creates an attractive nook for relaxing.

5. Linear fluorescent luminaires mounted to the backside of the closet header can be activated by a door jamb switch to turn on whenever the closet is opened. The luminaires are out of sight and lend a nice glow for navigating the contents of the closet.

Layout 5

Lighting a Residential Living Room

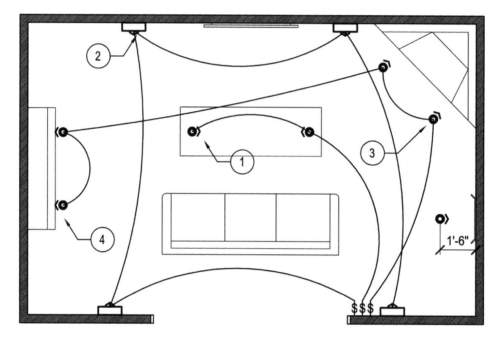

The residential living room sees frequent use and accommodates a number of different activities. The primary program is a space that is inviting and comfortable for long spells of socializing. The lighting ingredients should donate multiple textures of light; directional accents to create visual interest and obvious areas of activity, as well as diffuse light that lends soft ambience for long term visual comfort. The living room should also be capable of providing low-level ambient lighting for television viewing. The various lighting loads should all be independently controlled so that the space can serve the various functions.

Addressing Layers

Choreography: Light cast onto the fireplace acts as a focal element to draw attention. Pools of light onto the coffee table create an attractive area for gathering and socializing.

Mood and Ambience: Wall-mounted uplights cast soft, warm light onto the ceiling to create an enveloping comfortable space. Distinct pools of accent light onto wall objects and furniture serve to brighten up areas and create a "lived-in" feeling.

Accenting: Recessed adjustable luminaires paint light onto the fireplace, art and furniture to create visual interest and hierarchy.

Revealing Architecture: Accented vertical surfaces serve to expand the perimeter of the space, while upward directed light adds volume and an evenly-lighted ambient atmosphere. Light painted onto the coffee table and fireplace keep the attention down at a human level.

Task Lighting: Recessed luminaires push light down onto the central area for reading and rendering faces for socializing.

Common Features

1. Recessed adjustable halogen luminaires balance light between the surface of the coffee table and the social seating area.
2. Wall-mounted halogen or fluorescent uplights create volume and inviting softness. The luminaires provide a low level of ambient light without casting light directly onto the television.
3. Small-aperture recessed adjustable halogen luminaires accent the hearth of the fireplace to create visual interest and a choreographic goal.
4. Recessed halogen luminaires paint light onto the various furniture and secondary task areas in the space.

Chapter 28

Lighting Layouts for Light Commercial Spaces

Light commercial spaces tend to be areas where visual tasks take priority. This does not, however, preclude their need for thoughtful application of light for the sake of emotional state. It is increasingly common to find work spaces that recognize the impact that environmental comfort has on productivity. Work environments also commonly support multiple uses, serving workers as they move from computer tasks to physical layout tasks, filing, reading and writing. The most successful work environments are those that keep a space fresh by accommodating different lighting feelings throughout a workday. Task-focused lighting too often means the uniform texture of downward directed light. The addition of lighting ingredients that alter mood in a space and reveal the architecture can greatly improve upon an otherwise drab and lifeless environment. Remember that the layouts here are just some common tactics. A successful lighting design is a thoughtful lighting design where the program of the space is considered, along with all available lighting options.

Layout 1

Lighting Open Office Space

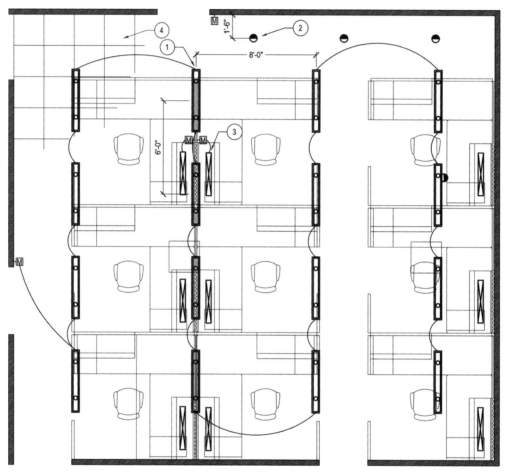

Open office spaces often suffer under the uniform treatment of task light directed downward. The monotony of the single light texture can cause eye strain and mental fatigue. The inclusion of multiple light textures can improve the long-term comfort of such spaces. Lighting the perimeter of open office spaces also works wonders to create a space that feels bright and lively. Office lighting systems must also be designed to minimize visible lamps and glare that can interfere with computer screens and sensitive tasks. Work spaces that are computer-focused may even benefit from a lower overall ambient light level to avoid a hazy reflection in the screens. Spaces that are more concerned with diversity of tasks and interaction with documents and graphic materials benefit from changeable lighting effects and emphasis on the color-rendering capabilities of the light sources. Integrating daylight harvesting adds an additional level of complexity to the situation.

Addressing Layers

Choreography: Long lines of linear fluorescent luminaires create a pattern that directs an already symmetric space. A row of recessed wall wash luminaires creates an additional bright vertical surface to draw attention through the space.

Mood and Ambience: Individual work stations have the benefit of more directional, color rendering, localized task lighting to punch through the diffuse lighting created by pendant-mounted indirect luminaires. Fluorescent lamps with good color rendering indices (80+) provide reasonably accurate color rendition. Color temperature is selected to complement the color palette of the materials and finishes.

Accenting: Wall wash luminaires provide a punch of light onto the vertical wall surfaces. Local task lighting provides directional light at each work station.

Revealing Architecture: Long lines of indirect linear fluorescent luminaries complement the linear nature of the lay-in ceiling tiles and the arrangement of the workstations. Luminaires are mounted perpendicular to the long axis of the room to avoid an overly-long, bowling alley effect.

Task Lighting: Linear fluorescent, direct-indirect pendants create a combination of diffuse and downward-directed light for long-term visual comfort. Localized task lighting at each work station accommodates critical tasks and provides improved color rendering.

Common Features

1. Linear fluorescent pendants distribute light up onto the ceiling and downward. The combination of textures avoids an overly diffuse experience and eliminates visibility of bare lamps. The luminaires are mounted 18" to 24" from the ceiling to allow light to spread evenly over the ceiling plane.

2. Recessed fluorescent wall wash luminaires mounted 18" to 24" from the wall create a bright vertical surface to enhance the perception of brightness in the space and define the perimeter

3. Localized fluorescent or halogen under cabinet task luminaires at each work station provide a directional source to punch thought the haze of the general office-wide light. The task light can also be selected to provide improved color rendering. These luminaires are independently controlled by each workspace occupant.

4. 2'x2' or 2'x4' acoustical ceiling tiles are a common finish in commercial spaces. These tiles often restrict the layout or types of luminaires that can be used in the space. An indirect lighting system must consider the reflectance of these ceiling tiles.

Layout 2

Lighting a Private Office

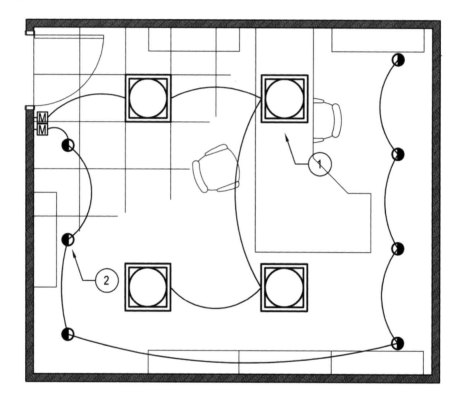

A private office serves as an area of industry and an area of respite. It must play the part of a work station while also serving as a meeting room and thinking environment. The lighting systems must be versatile to create varying environmental effects. A business executive may spend more time in a private office than any other space. Different light texture, bright vertical surface and control over individual lighting zones help to serve all of these functions.

Addressing Layers

Choreography: A wash of light on the back wall directs attention through the space. Heightened light levels on the desk surface and other furnishings provide visual interest and hierarchy.

Mood and Ambience: Multiple textures are achieved through the combination of more direct wall wash luminaires and diffuse linear fluorescent troffers. The 2'x2' troffers in this space create a downward directed light component that has directional and diffuse qualities.

Accenting: Wall wash luminaires can serve to accent art on the walls. The directional component of the troffers casts a crisp light onto the desk surface below, creating a lighted centerpiece to the room.

Revealing Architecture: The wall wash luminaires help to expand the perimeter of the space by brightening the vertical surfaces.

Task Lighting: Diffuse and direction light textures combine over the desk area to provide comfortable lighting for visual tasks, as well as conversing with colleagues.

Common Features

1. Well-designed 2'x2' fluorescent troffers provide a directional downlight component and a diffuse spread of area light. Recessed indirect 2'x2' luminaires might also provide a desirable light texture.
2. Compact fluorescent wall wash luminaires around the perimeter define the space and add to the perceived brightness.

Layout 3

Lighting a Conference Room

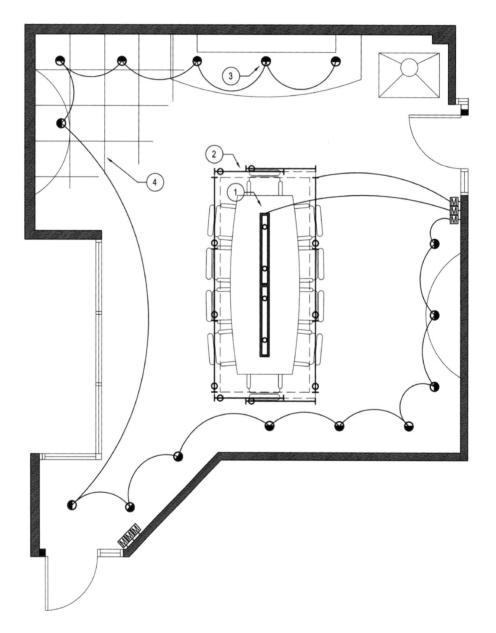

Corporate conference rooms serve as areas of congregation that bring colleagues together to discuss business and build camaraderie. These spaces also act as the calling card that defines the image of the business to outsiders. Conference rooms serve a multitude of uses from business dealings to presentations, luncheons and video conferencing. The lighting systems in a conference room should be dynamic and easy to control to create different lighting environments. The luminaires in a conference room also tend to have an aesthetic appeal, fitting of the image that the company wants to convey.

Addressing Layers

Choreography: The conference table is, appropriately, the obvious organizing element of the space. Linear fluorescent pendants overhead serve as bright objects to draw attention, as well as to light the conference table. A ceiling cove system creates a bright halo above this gathering area.

Mood and Ambience: The multiple textures of light create areas of distinct gathering importance. The soft uplight of the cove and the brightness of the pendants and the lighted table create a sense of severity and importance. Perimeter lighting helps to lighten the mood when necessary.

Accenting: The pendants and the table surface are the notable elements of visual interest and organization. The wall wash luminaires can also serve to accent art work or graphics on the wall.

Revealing Architecture: Wall wash luminaires serve to define the perimeter of the space while the central cove creates height and a focal element to anchor the space.

Task Lighting: Various textures are at work to provide different types of light at the conference table for reading tasks, as well as rendering occupants. Conference rooms intended for video conferencing need additional layers of controllable light to render occupants, as well as balance out the brightness of the background.

Common Features

1. A decorative, direct / indirect pendant casts light up into the coffer volume and down onto the conference table and the faces of the occupants.

2. Staggered linear fluorescent strips serve as an uplighting cove to fill the coffer with light that inter-reflects to cast diffuse light into the core of the space.

3. Compact fluorescent, recessed wall-wash luminaires add the necessary perimeter brightness to soften the space and increase the perception of brightness.

4. Acoustic ceiling tiles may dictate the layout of some luminaires and must be considered for how they will reflect light back into the space.

Layout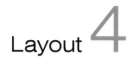

Lighting a Reception Area

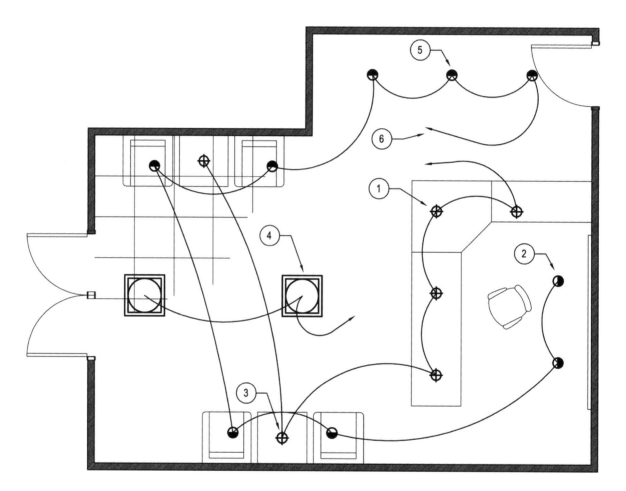

A reception area is often the first point of contact for an outsider and defines much of the identity of a facility and a company. These spaces must be, at once, welcoming and comfortable, not to mention impressive and intriguing. Defining distinct zones of use within the reception area helps to organize the space by creating points of specific interaction. Seating areas, display areas, and task areas all deserve unique lighting characters and their own physical space. Decorative elements and attention to corporate signage work wonders to enhance the appeal of reception areas. Light sources should also be chosen with concern for color rendering and color temperatures that are complementary to the color palette and materials involved in the décor.

Addressing Layers

Choreography: A pattern of recessed luminaires creates brightness onto the floor that surrounds an occupant in brightness upon entry. Light painted onto the back wall serves as the visual goal and draws visitors through the space or into the space if the entry has glass doors or walls. A row of decorative pendants can also create a visual curtain that stops progress at the point of interaction with the receptionist. Wall wash luminaires and pendants also draw attention to the seating areas on the periphery.

Mood and Ambience: Multiple light textures liven-up the space and create a welcoming experience. Light painted onto the walls increases the perception of brightness. Pendants add a human scale and a touch of sparkle and a comfortable diffuse quality of light at the entry point.

Accenting: Recessed wall wash luminaires place light onto the art and graphics on the vertical surfaces. Decorative pendants catch the eye and push light down onto furniture and horizontal surfaces as points of visual interest.

Revealing Architecture: Light onto the back wall defines the length of the space while lighted vertical surfaces expand the perimeter. Decorative pendants drop specific areas down to a human scale.

Task Lighting: Accented signage on the back wall lends corporate identity. Pendants draw light onto the receptions desk and the seating area tables.

Common Features

1. Incandescent or fluorescent decorative pendants add sparkle, reduce scale and put light onto the task surface below them.

2. Compact fluorescent, recessed wall wash luminaires paint light onto the back wall and any signage that may be there.

3. Incandescent or fluorescent, decorative pendants draw visitors to the seating area, creating visual interest and reducing the scale of the space. A little bit of decorative character goes a long way to create a welcome environment.

4. Recessed, fluorescent troffers can create a volume of diffuse lighting necessary to enliven the transition from outside to inside. Recessed, indirect luminaires can be specified to provide a combination of diffuse light without the sterile, corporate feeling of traditional parabolic troffers.

Chapter 29
Common Lighting Details

To create lighting ideas that really come together, a fair amount of time and effort must be put forth in refining the construction details of each lighting application. Many lighting effects are the result of precision and subtlety. Without the proper considerations, unusual lighting applications can become sources of glare or simply wasted electricity. To understand what is possible with light, it is important that a designer have a fair understanding of typical construction methods. Every project has unique conditions which will accommodate certain types of lighting integration better than others. Knowledge of issues such as plenum space, framing type and wall thickness will determine lighting options. As one references these details, remember that every project is unique, and the details presented here are for reference only. Be sure to coordinate with the design team to develop lighting applications that will work for the specific project

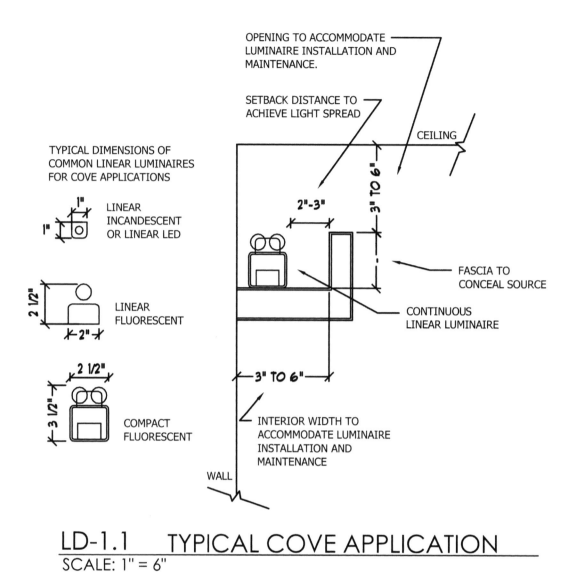

LD-1.1 TYPICAL COVE APPLICATION
SCALE: 1" = 6"

A wall or ceiling-integrated cove is a great way to volumize a space by casting light up onto the ceiling plane above. This kind of clean shape of light harmonizes well with the geometry of the space and lends a soft, enveloping light. Coves can be implemented with a variety of linear sources, including linear fluorescent, linear incandescent and linear LED sources.

Keys to Success:

- Socket shadow that occurs where luminaires butt against one another is a common problem. Consider whether the light has room to spread out, or whether the luminaires should be staggered to overlap and eliminate these dark areas.
- Geometry of the cove should create an opening large enough for light to leave, as well as for maintenance of the luminaires.
- Cove-specific luminaires which incorporate reflectors and optics that drive light out of a cove in a very efficient manner exist.
- Cove geometry should be designed to eliminate the possibility of lamp visibility.

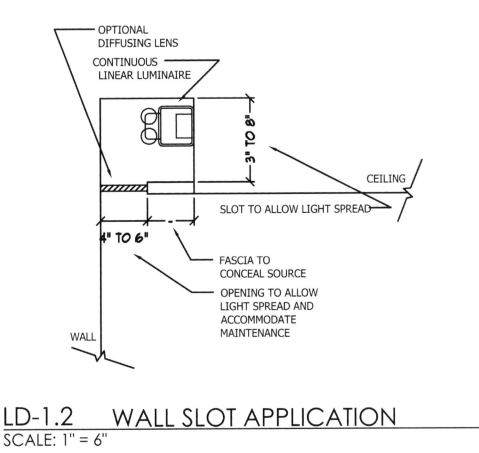

OPTIONAL DIFFUSING LENS

CONTINUOUS LINEAR LUMINAIRE

3" TO 8"

CEILING

SLOT TO ALLOW LIGHT SPREAD

4" TO 6"

FASCIA TO CONCEAL SOURCE

OPENING TO ALLOW LIGHT SPREAD AND ACCOMMODATE MAINTENANCE

WALL

LD-1.2   WALL SLOT APPLICATION
SCALE: 1" = 6"

Wall slots integrate continuous linear sources concealed and directed downward to create a wash of brightness on the vertical surfaces of a space. These bands and planes of light can break up a space and add to the perception of lightness by disconnecting the walls from the ceiling.

Keys to Success:
- Socket shadow that occurs where luminaires butt against one another is a common problem. Consider whether the light has room to spread out or whether the luminaires should be staggered to overlap and eliminate these dark areas.
- Geometry of the slot should create an opening large enough for light to leave as well as for maintenance of the luminaires.
- Slot-specific luminaires which incorporate reflectors and optics that drive light out of a slot in a very efficient manner exist.
- Slot geometry should be designed to eliminate the possibility of lamp visibility
- Consider the materials and craftsmanship of the wall being lighted. Because of their grazing nature, wall slots tend to show off imperfections. Beware of specular or shiny wall surfaces as they tend to reflect images of the lamp.

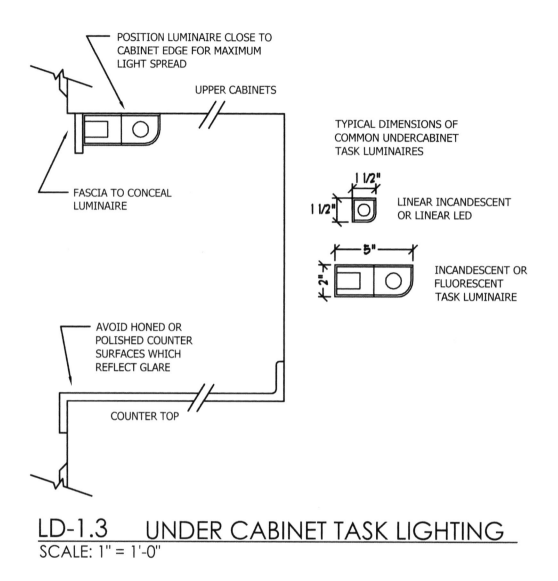

POSITION LUMINAIRE CLOSE TO CABINET EDGE FOR MAXIMUM LIGHT SPREAD

UPPER CABINETS

TYPICAL DIMENSIONS OF COMMON UNDERCABINET TASK LUMINAIRES

FASCIA TO CONCEAL LUMINAIRE

1 1/2"

1 1/2"

LINEAR INCANDESCENT OR LINEAR LED

AVOID HONED OR POLISHED COUNTER SURFACES WHICH REFLECT GLARE

5"

2"

INCANDESCENT OR FLUORESCENT TASK LUMINAIRE

COUNTER TOP

LD-1.3   UNDER CABINET TASK LIGHTING
SCALE: 1" = 1'-0"

Under cabinet lighting is a good way to localize task light. This can be accomplished with a variety of source types, but color rendering and color temperature should always be a priority.

Keys to Success:
- Under cabinet lighting should be accomplished with a solid front luminaire or include a fascia or proper geometry to eliminate the possibility of lamp visibility.
- Under cabinet systems can include local switching at the task location or may be controlled from typical wall switch locations.
- Under cabinet systems can utilize luminaires as small as 1" x 1" linear incandescent or more robust puck lights and linear fluorescent sources.
- If linear fluorescent lamps are used for under cabinet light, they should be specified with good color rendering and color temperature in mind.
- Consider the location for the transformer that is required for the low voltage sources commonly used.

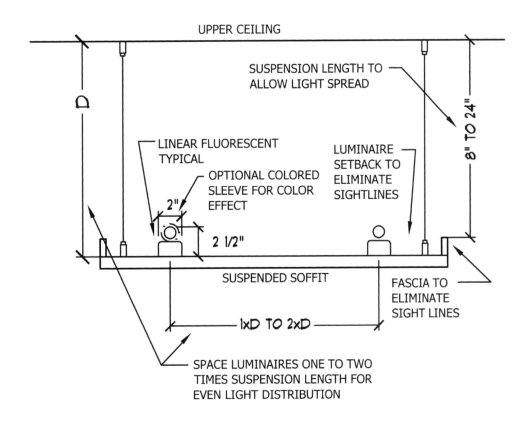

UPPER CEILING

SUSPENSION LENGTH TO
ALLOW LIGHT SPREAD

LINEAR FLUORESCENT
TYPICAL

OPTIONAL COLORED
SLEEVE FOR COLOR
EFFECT

LUMINAIRE
SETBACK TO
ELIMINATE
SIGHTLINES

8" TO 24"

2"

2 1/2"

SUSPENDED SOFFIT

FASCIA TO
ELIMINATE
SIGHT LINES

lxD TO 2xD

SPACE LUMINAIRES ONE TO TWO
TIMES SUSPENSION LENGTH FOR
EVEN LIGHT DISTRIBUTION

LD-1.4   SUSPENDED SOFFIT UPLIGHTING
SCALE: 1" = 1'-0"

Suspended soffit panels and floating lids are good ways to reduce the scale of space and cast a volumizing light upward. Such systems can be very simple structurally and can make use of common sources like linear fluorescent strips. With the addition of inexpensive color filters, a dropped lid can transform the mood and spatial effect of a space very thoroughly. Dropped soffits can serve as the anchor for seating areas, office work stations and retail displays.

Keys to Success:
- Consider the geometry and location of the luminaires to eliminate the possibility of lamp visibility.
- Consider the material above the soffit. It should be reflective enough to spread the light back into the room. Specular (shiny) surfaces should be avoided as they will reflect the image of the lamps or luminaires.
- The suspension distance should be considered to ensure that light has room to inter-reflect within the space.
- Luminaire placement should be studied to ensure even lighting without apparent stripes or hot spots.

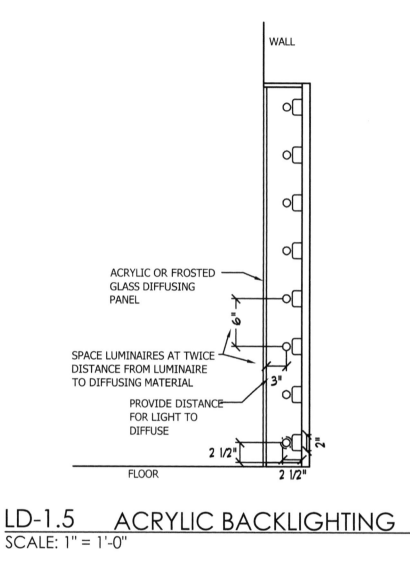

LD-1.5   ACRYLIC BACKLIGHTING
SCALE: 1" = 1'-0"

Backlit walls and large glowing panels add a lightness that transcends typically constructed spaces. The challenge with large scale applications is achieving an even plane of light that truly appears to be self-luminous.

Keys to Success:
- Ample space behind the backlit panel must be available for light to diffuse evenly.
- Maintenance and access must be designed into the panel system.
- The diffusing properties of the panel material will dictate the geometry and luminaire layout. Be sure to mock-up the application with the specific material that will be used.

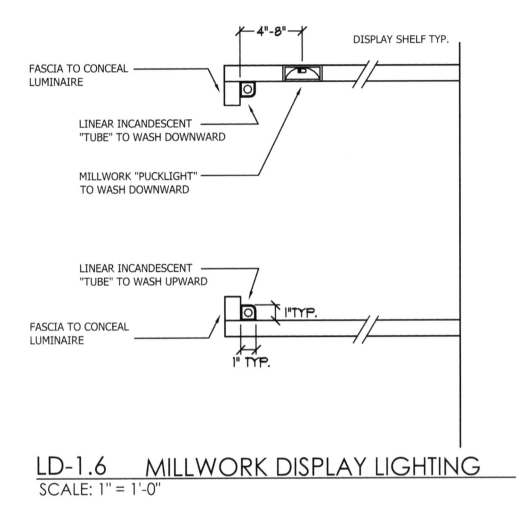

LD-1.6 MILLWORK DISPLAY LIGHTING
SCALE: 1" = 1'-0"

Millwork integrated lighting creates a very distinct and attention drawing display element. This type of feature is commonly used for retail display and food and beverage display.

Keys to Success:
- Consider the heat output of the light source and how it will affect the object being lighted.
- Subtle changes in source location will affect the light quality and should be studied and mocked-up.
- Display lighting can be accomplished with a single line of light; both top and bottom light, individual puck lights or a combination of treatments as shown here.
- Consider the location for the transformer that is required for the low-voltage sources commonly used.

Chapter 30
Daylight and Electric Light Integration Details

Some of the best lighting details are those that combine the effects of daylight and electric light sources. The human affinity for the quality, color and texture of daylight crosses over to electric light applications that can mimic these same traits. Well thought-out details that manage to fuse the two together can create remarkable lighting effects that can define a space. These details have a dynamic character that will change through the course of a day while maintaining a desirable effect.

If the electric light component can be put on a dimmer, a photo-sensor that detects variation in light levels can be implemented to control the exact quantity of electric light being contributed to augment the daylight. Such systems ensure that the electric light is not wasted.

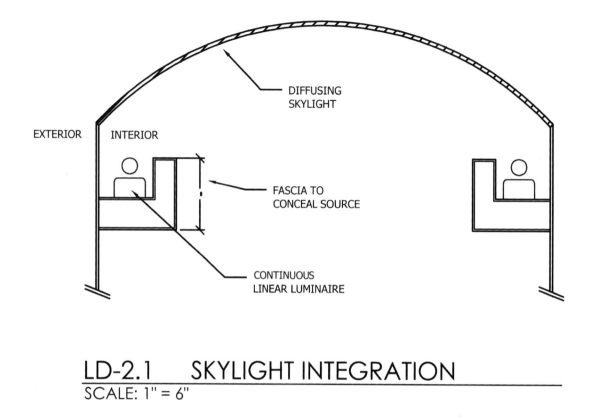

LD-2.1 SKYLIGHT INTEGRATION
SCALE: 1" = 6"

Typical skylights can be augmented with the addition of upward-directed light sources. The electric light system can be as complex as a shelf or cove system or as simple as surface mounted luminaires that cast light upward. Under daylight conditions, sunlight will diffuse through the skylight material. When activated, the electric light will wash up, filling the volume of the skylight and reflecting back into the space.

Keys to Success:
- Consider the diffusing material of the skylight as it may reflect an image of the electric luminaires.
- Consider the geometry and location of the luminaires to eliminate the possibility of lamp visibility.
- Consider accessibility and maintenance of the electric light system.
- Consider switching or dimming options and photo sensors to regulate the contribution of the electric light system.

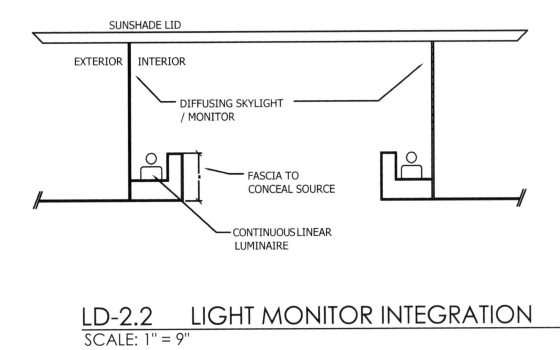

LD-2.2   LIGHT MONITOR INTEGRATION
SCALE: 1" = 9"

A light monitor is a perfect candidate for electric light integration. A shelf or cove system can be integrated to cast light upward onto the ceiling surface of the monitor. The electric light will wash up, filling the volume of the monitor and reflecting back into the space.

Keys to Success:
- Consider the diffusing material of the monitor as it may reflect an image of the electric luminaires.
- Consider the geometry and location of the luminaires to eliminate the possibility of lamp visibility.
- Consider accessibility and maintenance of the electric light system.
- Consider switching or dimming options and photo sensors to regulate the contribution of the electric light system.

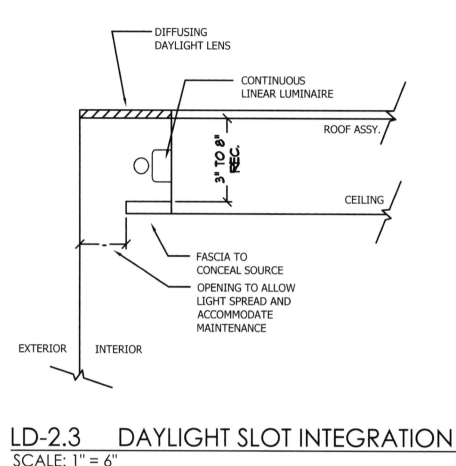

LD-2.3   DAYLIGHT SLOT INTEGRATION
SCALE: 1" = 6"

A ceiling slot is a great way to harvest daylight and is the perfect candidate for electric light integration. The clean plane of light created by the daylight can be seamlessly complemented by the same shape and texture of electric light. A simple fascia to conceal the electric source is all that is needed.

Keys to Success:
- Consider the diffusing material of the daylight slot as it may reflect an image of the electric luminaires.
- Consider the geometry and location of the luminaires to eliminate the possibility of lamp visibility.
- Consider accessibility and maintenance of the electric light system.
- Consider switching or dimming options and photo sensors to regulate the contribution of the electric light system.

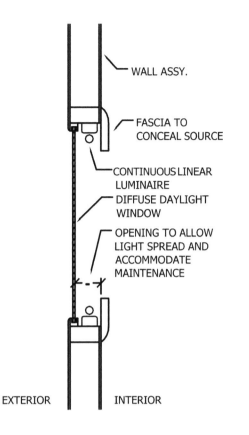

WALL ASSY.

FASCIA TO
CONCEAL SOURCE

CONTINUOUS LINEAR
LUMINAIRE

DIFFUSE DAYLIGHT
WINDOW

OPENING TO ALLOW
LIGHT SPREAD AND
ACCOMMODATE
MAINTENANCE

EXTERIOR   INTERIOR

LD-2.4   WINDOW INTEGRATION
SCALE: 1" = 1'-0"

Even simple windows can be used to harvest daylight when they are fitted with a diffusing material to control the light contribution. During daylight conditions, a clean, diffuse light filters in. During electric light operation, light washes the interior surface of the diffusing window and reflects a soft glow back into the space.

Keys to Success:
- Consider the diffusing material of the diffusing window as it may reflect an image of the electric luminaires.
- Consider the geometry and location of the luminaires to eliminate the possibility of lamp visibility.
- Consider accessibility and maintenance of the electric light system.
- Consider switching or dimming options and photo sensors to regulate the contribution of the electric light system.

Part IV
Final Thoughts on Design

The Fundamental Lighting Design Process

LIGHTING DESIGN IN A NUTSHELL

The following shortcuts will serve to jog your memory and act as a checklist for the thought processes and production processes that yield good design and implementation.

The Design Development Process

Brainstorm and develop concepts

The Controllable Aspects of Light (Ch. 5)

    Intensity of light

    Color of light

    Texture of light

    Shape of light

    Origin of light

Lighting techniques (Ch. 9, 10, 11, 14)

Graphic development

Light Map choreography goals (Ch. 17)

Light Map remaining design goals (Ch. 17)

Identify and label Illuminance level criteria (Ch. 19)

The Specification and Refinement Process

Concept refinement

Redline Lighting Layout (Ch. 24)

Select luminaire types (Ch. 21, 22)

    Downlights

    Adjustable accent luminaire

    Floor uplights

    Wall-mounted uplights

    Linear sources

    Low-level steplights

The Final Construction Documents

    Luminaire schedule (Ch. 25)

    Luminaire cut sheets (Ch. 25)

    Drafted lighting plan (Ch. 26)

Green Design and Sustainability

There is no shortage of interest in the sustainable aspects and energy-saving potential that can result from lighting design. In the United States, roughly 33% of the electricity we consume is for electric lighting. This is a huge percentage, and means that even small improvements in the application of light can mean large reductions in our consumption of non-renewable resources. You may live in a municipality where energy conservation codes are written into building codes and certain criteria must be met in order to get a building permit. I encourage all designers to research and investigate the organizations that are taking the initiative to suggest and mandate methods for consuming less electricity to create light in our designed environments.

California State Energy Code Title 24	*www.energy.ca.gov/title24*
ASHRAE 90.1	*www.ashrae.org*
USGBC including LEED Program	*www.usgbc.org*
Savings by Design	*www.savingsbydesign.com*
International Dark Sky Association	*www.darksky.org*
Energy Star	*www.energystar.gov*

Some conservation recommendations take the form of very clinical methods for reducing the use of electric light in design. Many programs are based on a "lighting power density", watts-per-square-foot prescription that categorizes the use type of the project spaces. Remember that your intuition of where light belongs in a space and your understanding of how to accomplish more with less light are the foundation of your ability to create impacting design with minimal light waste. The more you rely on brightness through contrast and visual interest, the more you will find yourself using less light through good design without having to "reduce" or eliminate design ideas.

Put light where it belongs, decide what lighted surfaces will contribute best to your lighting goals, and you will be well on your way to conservative design through conscious placement of light.

Designing with New Eyes

Remember that as designers, we are ultimately responsible for how people feel and, therefore, interact with the built environment around them. There are numerous lessons to be learned from classical design, as well as the natural world all around us. Look at the world with designer's eyes. Always be on the hunt for tools and techniques that you can use in your design to impart a specific feeling or function. Light has immense power. It is safe to say that architectural projects are rarely recognized as great without having consideration for the integration of light. Many good projects use light as an afterthought, but every great project has light integral. There is no right lighting just as there is no right design. There is only design and designed light that is thought-through and that which is not. If you know your space, you know more than enough to get to work placing light onto the surfaces and objects that will enhance your design. The tools presented here are simply ways to get you to better visualize and draw light. If you can conceive of ideas and communicate them to others, you are eighty percent of the way to great design. Hopefully, the more technical aspects of implanting these ideas will serve you as you solve your own lighting challenges.

Design is a state of mind. A true designer can design anything. It is the processes that you put your mind through that will give you confidence in the form of a bottomless well of great ideas that jump from your mind onto paper. Let those ideas out. Write them down, sketch them up. Do whatever it takes to empty your head of concepts to create room for new ones. There is no need to self-censor your creative ideas. There is a whole world out there that will help you weed through your thoughts and filter out the best of them.

Good luck in designing and never stop observing and learning from the environment around you.

Sage

Appendix A

Glossary of Lighting Terms

A

Accommodation: The function of the dynamic components of the eye to focus on objects at different distances.

Adaptation: The function of the eye and brain working together to operate under varying amounts of light.

Adjustable (Luminaire): Describes a luminaire that includes mechanical means to aim light output in a specific direction.

Ambient light: A description of the light quality that defines the overall experience of a space.

Aperture: An opening cut into a form or surface. Often describes the opening a recessed luminaire creates in the ceiling

B

Backlighting: The tactic of placing a light source behind an object or translucent surface. This creates an effect of silhouetting solid objects or creating a luminous plane from a translucent material.

Baffle: a visual control device that mounts to the face of a light source to control the angles at which the light source is directly visible.

Ballast: An electronic or magnetic device used to control electricity to start and operate fluorescent and HID light sources.

C

Candela (CD): a unit measurement of light density from a light source or reflective object. 1 Candela is the equivalent one lumen of light emitted evenly from a portion of spherical surface area called a steradian.

Candlepower: an expression of luminous intensity from a light source expressed in Candelas.

Candlepower Distribution curve: A graphical representation of the light intensity leaving a light source in specific directions.

Center Beam Candlepower (CBCP): A commonly-used expression of luminous intensity from the centermost area of a light source. (This is typically the most luminous area of a light source)

Choreography: the direction of movement and path of experience of an individual in the designed environment.

Chromaticity: The level of saturation evident in a colored material or colored light source.

Coefficient of Utilization (CU): A factor used in lumen method calculations to express how effectively light is being delivered from a luminaire to the surface in question

Color Rendering Index (CRI): An expression of the completeness of the spectral output of a light source. Indicates how accurately a light source will reveal colors in the lighted environment. Expressed on a scale from 1 to 100: the higher the number, the more complete the spectral output and the more accurate the color rendition.

Color temperature: A manner of describing the apparent color of a light source. Commonly used to express the cool or warm color of a source that deviates from neutral. Expressed in degrees Kelvin or Kelvins (K)

D

Daylight: A general reference to the quality of light received from the sun as it diffuses through the atmosphere of the earth, including both direct sunlight and diffused skylight.

Diffuse Light: Light which is scattered in all directions in relation to its source

Diffuser: Lens material used to scatter the light output of a source in all directions

Dimmer: A lighting control device that varies the electricity delivered to a luminaire to control the output of light.

Directional Light: Light that leaves a source in a single direction through means of reflectors or optical control.

Direct Burial (Luminaire): A luminaire that resides primarily in the ground or floor structure of a space and casts light upward.

E

Efficacy: Used in lighting as an expression of how well a light source converts electricity into radiant light energy. Expressed as Lumens of light per Watt of electricity for Lumens per Watt (L / W)

Exitance: An expression of the light quantity leaving a reflective surface in all directions.

F

Flood (Light): describes light cast in a confided manned over a broad area as a result of interaction with optics and reflectors.

Fluorescent Lamp: A light source technology that relies on the excitement of phosphors to convert a limited spectrum of radiation into a more complete spectrum of visible light

Foot-Candle (FC): The (English) unit of expressing and measuring light flux onto an object, where 1 Foot-candle is the equivalent of one lumen of light arriving evenly onto a surface area of 1 square foot.

G

Glare: Excessive brightness created by an un-shielded light source. Also describes the reflection of bright objects visible in a specular surface

Grazing: The tactic of lighting a surface at a severe angle from a nearby light source. Tends to spread light over a great distance and reveal texture

H

Halogen lamp: A light source technology that relies on an incandescing filament within a pressurized environment of halogen gas.

High Intensity Discharge (HID) Lamp: A light source technology that relies on an arc of electricity passed between electrodes to excite an environment of vaporized metal. Includes sources such as Mercury Vapor, High Pressure Sodium and Metal Halide.

I

Illuminance: An expression of light quantity incident onto a surface. Expressed and measured in Foot-candles (FC) (English unit) or Lux (LX) (SI unit).

In-grade (Luminaire): (See direct burial)

Incandescent lamp: A light source technology that relies on radiant energy emitted from a metal filament resisting a flow of electricity.

Indirect Light: light distributed after it reflects or interacts with a shielding surface

Inter-reflection: The product of light interacting with the objects and surfaces of a space.

L

Lamp: The generic term for an engineered light source

Lamp Life: An expression of the expected operating life of a light source expressed in hours.

Light: Electro-magnetic radiation that stimulates the visual system of a typical human.

Light Emitting Diode (LED): A Light source technology that relies on electricity passed through a solid state electrical device that emits a single wavelength of radiation.

Light Loss Factor (LLF): A safety factor used in lighting calculations that accommodates for the loss of light production of a luminaire over time due to dirt, ballast depreciation and lumen output depreciation

Light Map: The author's term for a visual document that expresses lighting intent through colored graphics on an architectural furniture or floor plan.

Louver: A bladed shielding device implemented in a luminaire to reduce the visibility of a bare lamp

Lumen: an expression of radiant energy flux as it impacts the human visual system.

Luminaire: A device that controls the delivery of light through the management of electricity and the inclusion of ballasts, transformers, optical elements, reflectors and architectural mounting mechanisms.

Luminous Flux: The total quantity of visible radiant energy that leaves a light source in all directions. Expressed in Lumens.

Lux (LX): The SI unit of expressing light flux incident onto a surface (illuminance)

O

Occupancy sensor: Device that implements heat, sound and motion detection to determine whether a space is in use.

P

PAR Lamp: Lamp shape that utilizes a parabolic aluminized reflector to deliver controlled directional light. Commonly associated with Halogen and Metal Halide sources

Photometry: The science of measuring light output distribution, patterns and effects from light sources.

R

Recessed Luminaire: A luminaire that resides primarily in the plenum above the ceiling line of a space.

Reflectance: An expression of the percentage of light incident onto a surface that in turn leaves the surface.

Reflected Ceiling Plan (RCP): An architectural plan that shows the contents and details of an architectural ceiling system as it would appear if viewed from within a space.

Re-strike Time: An expression of the time required for a light source to cool off before it can be re-ignited after an interruption of power. Commonly used in reference to HID sources.

S

Sconce: A wall-mounted lighting device commonly associated with a decorative character.

Seasonal Affective Disorder (SAD): A human physiological condition associated with inadequate exposure to various wavelengths of light contained in daylight.

Soffit: An architectural feature of geometry added to a space through built-up construction

Solar Geometry: The predictable movement of the sun in the local sky, due to the earth's rotation, revolution and declination.

Specular: Description of a material's ability to directly reflect light images. Commonly expressed as "shiny".

Spot (Light): Describes directional light delivered in a confined beam as a result of interaction with optics and reflectors.

Step Light: A luminaire that typically recesses into the lower portion of a wall for the purpose of illuminating stairs.

Steradian: A unit of spherical area such that any size sphere consists of 2π Steradians. Used in measuring luminous intensity (see Candela).

T

Transformer: an electromagnetic device that alters the voltage of electricity delivered to a light source.

Translucent: The descriptive property of a material that allows light to pass through but alters the direction of the light, resulting in diffusion.

Transmission (of light): The passage of light through various materials.

Transparent: The descriptive property of a material that allows light to pass though it with minimal refraction or change of direction.

Troffer: Description of luminaires, commonly of a rectangular nature, that utilize linear fluorescent lamps to deliver a uniform light texture.

W

Warm-up Time: Reference to the time required for a lamp to come to full light output. Commonly used in reference to HID light sources.

Wash: Describes light delivered in an even fashion across a large surface.

Watt: Unit of expressing and measuring electrical work potential in a circuit as a product of potential voltage and amperage.

Appendix B

Professional Organizations and Agencies

Professional and Educational Organizations

American Institute of Architects
www.aia.org

American Lighting Association
www.americanlightingassoc.com

American Optometric Association
www.aoanet.org

American Society of Heating, Refrigeration and Air-Conditioning Engineers
www.ashrae.org

American Society of Interior Designers
www.asid.org

American Society of Landscape Architects
www.asla.org

American Solar Energy Society
www.ases.org

Illuminating Engineering Society of North America
www.iesna.org

International Association of Lighting Designers
www.iald.org

International Commission on Illumination
www.cie-usnc.org

International Dark-Sky Association
www.darksky.org

International Interior Design Association
www.iida.org

National Council for Interior Design Qualification
www.ncidq.org

National Council on Qualifications for the Lighting Professions
www.ncqlp.org

National Lighting Bureau
www.nlb.org

Publications

Architectural Lighting Magazine
www.archlighting.com

Lighting Design + Application Magazine
www.iesna.org/lda/iesnalda.cfm

Metropolis Magazine
www.metropolismag.com

Mondo Arc Magazine
www.mondoarc.com

Professional Lighting Design Magazine
www.via-verlag.com

Search Tools

Elumit (Lighting search and specification tool)
www.elumit.com

Design guide.com
www.designguide.com

Lightsearch.com (Lighting product search tool)
www.lightsearch.com

Conferences

Lightfair International
www.lightfair.com

Professional Lighting Design Convention
www.pld-c.org

The Arc Show
www.thearcshow.com

Appendix C

Descriptive Words for Lighting

Bold
Brilliant
Confined
Contrasty
Crisp
Dramatic
Dreamy
Diffuse
Direct
Effervescent

Even
Expansive
Gleaming
Harsh
Liquid
Muddy
Murky
Radiant
Restrained
Sharp

Smooth
Soft
Sparkling
Sprawling
Subtle
Theatrical
Understated
Vivid

Appendix D

Directory of Contributors and Other Manufacturers

Special Thanks to the following manufacturers who were gracious enough to furnish reproductions of literature, technical data and images. Without this material, the pages of this text would not be nearly as colorful.

Ardee Lighting
888.442.7333
www.ardeelighting.com

Bartco
714.230.3200
www.bartcolighting.com

Belfer
732.493.2666
www.belfergroup.com

DaSal
604.464.5644
www.dasalindustries.com

Deltalight
954.677.9800
www.deltalight.us

Erco
732.225.8856
www.erco.com

GE Lumination
216.606.6555
www.led.com

Lightolier
508.679.8131
www.lightolier.com

Lutron Electronics
610.282.3800
www.lutron.com

Osram Sylvania
978-777-1900
www.sylvania.com

Tech Lighting
847 410 4400
www.techlighting.com

Wila Lighting
714-259-0990
www.wila.net

The following represent a small cross section of manufacturers of lighting equipment.

Lamps

GE Lighting
www.gelighting.com

Osram Sylvania
www.sylvania.com

Philips Lighting
www.lighting.philips.com

Ushio
www.ushio.com

Venture Lighting
www.venturelighting.com

Luminaires

Artemide
www.artemide.us

Bega US
www.bega-us.com

Bruck Lighting Systems
www.brucklighting.com

Color Kinetics
www.colorkinetics.com

Columbia Lighting
www.columbia-ltg.com

Cooper Lighting
www.coooperlighting.com

Flos
www.flos.com

Juno Lighting
www.junolighting.com

Lightolier
www.lightolier.com

Louis Poulsen Lighting
www.louispoulsen.com

Lithonia
www.lithonia.com

Index of Contents

CPSIA information can be obtained
at www.ICGtesting.com
Printed in the USA
264125LV00001B